The Ringing Grooves of Change

The Ringing Grooves *of* Change

Brunel and the Coming of the Railway to Bath

WITH

The Story of Box Tunnel
&
A Brunel Trail from Keynsham to Box

ANDREW SWIFT

Published by
AKEMAN PRESS
www.akemanpress.com

© Andrew Swift 2006

Thanks to Colin Johnston and Lucy Powell of Bath Record Office; Margaret Bailey and Stephanie Round, Local Studies Librarians, Bath Central Library; Stuart Burroughs of the Museum of Bath at Work; Audie Baker of Kidderminster Railway Museum; Hannah Lowery and Michael Richardson of the Brunel Archive, Bristol University; staff at the Somerset Record Office, the National Newspaper Library, Bristol Reference Library, the Public Record Office; and Kirsten Elliott, for her encouragement and support, and help with the manuscript.

Typeset in *Caslon* by Ambrose Blimfield.
Printed by *Short Run Press*, Exeter.

PICTURE CREDITS:
Bath Central Library, *79, 110, 134, 139, 153, 154, 156, 197 (top), 222, 237*;
Bath Record Office, *8, 13, 29, 37, 40, 84, 92, 94, 96, 101, 103, 116, 141, 148, 155 (2), 163, 207, 265, 266 (bottom), 277, 281*;
Brunel Collection, Bristol University: *95, 151, 286;*
Kidderminster Railway Museum, *184, 202, 217, 248.*

ISBN 0-9546138-5-6

ALL RIGHTS RESERVED. NO PART OF THIS PUBLICATION MAY BE REPRODUCED, STORED IN A RETRIEVAL SYSTEM, OR TRANSMITTED, IN ANY FORM OR BY ANY MEANS, ELECTRONIC, MECHANICAL, PHOTOCOPYING, RECORDING OR OTHERWISE, WITHOUT THE PRIOR PERMISSION OF AKEMAN PRESS.

A NOTE ON THE TITLE:

The title comes from the poem *Locksley Hall*, by Alfred Lord Tennyson, published in 1842:

> *Not in vain the distance beacons. Forward, forward let us range,*
> *Let the great world spin for ever down the ringing grooves of change.*

The lines are often taken – out of context – as evidence of Tennyson's whole-hearted endorsement of the Victorian ideal of progress. In fact, the poem is deeply ambivalent about the prospect of change. That, however, is not why it was chosen to provide the title for this book.

Many years after it was written, Tennyson was asked how he had come up with one of his most memorable phrases. This was his reply:

> *When I went by the first train from Liverpool to Manchester (1830), I thought that the wheels ran in a groove. It was a black night and there was such a vast crowd round the train at the station that we could not see the wheels. Then I made this line.*

So there you have it. One of the most stirring lines in English literature was based on a fundamental misconception: "We could not see the wheels."

What follows is an impressionistic account, put together from Brunel's words and those of his contemporaries, of how the railway came to Bath. By going to original sources wherever possible, I have attempted to sift fact from fiction, always aware that, if Tennyson could get it so badly wrong when he was actually there, the chances of someone almost two centuries down the line avoiding similar pitfalls are slim.

But with that proviso, this – or something very much like it – is what happened …

Contents

THE RINGING GROOVES OF CHANGE

The White Lion, with William Lane's name above the door. The northern extension of the Guildhall now covers the site.

ONE

Before the Railway

As William Lane, the landlord of Bath's White Lion Inn, completed his Census return on the evening of 7 June 1841, one of the names must have given him pause. The coaching business, which had fuelled the inn's – and the city's – prosperity for over 150 years, had less than three weeks left to run. The man responsible for its demise was on Lane's list. Isambard Kingdom Brunel, Chief Engineer of the Great Western Railway, in town to oversee the completion of the line from London, was staying at the inn.

The first regular stagecoach from London had rolled into the yard of the White Lion one evening in 1667. It had taken three days for the journey: London was just over a hundred miles away. Many stretches of road were little better than quagmires. In wet weather, coaches were often axle-deep in mud; when the mud baked hard, they stood the chance of having their axles broken as they bounced over the deep rutted ways. There was a constant danger of highwaymen. The worst spots were just out of London, at Hounslow Heath and Maidenhead Thicket, but any point where coaches had to slow down to negotiate a hill – at Sandy Lane or Cherhill or King's Down, for example – was likely to attract a gentleman of the road. It was customary for travellers, when they set out on a long journey, to make their wills and bid solemn farewells to their friends and relations. It is difficult for us, with no major world city more than a day's journey away, to imagine what it must have been like to travel from London to Bath in 1667.

It is also difficult to imagine what the city those intrepid travellers arrived in, after three harrowing days being shaken half to death on the road, was like. Bath was still a walled city, with many vestiges of its medieval past still standing. By the time mailcoaches were introduced, just over a century later, not only had roads – and stagecoaches – improved so markedly that the journey could be

In this advertisement from 1837, William Lane describes his inn as a family hotel.

undertaken in one day; Bath had been transformed, spreading out beyond the confines of its walls in a efflorescence of squares, crescents and terraces. Much of the old city – the walls included – had been demolished to make way for Europe's first pleasure resort.

The first mailcoach arrived in Bath in 1784, hauled by a pair of horses, changed every six or eight miles, and carrying only four passengers. It took 13 hours. By 1835, after further road improvements, a regular stagecoach had not only cut half an hour off the time; it stopped at Thatcham for passengers to take dinner. This was, in the words of Thomas Burke, the "golden age, the high noon of coaching; and it never declined from noon to sunset. When it ended, it was still at its meridian. It was the age of fast coaches whose names have passed into history … coaches which seemed to have a being and a pace of their own … There was a passion and a precision about the whole business of coaching; something that stirred men's minds … and moved them to rhapsody."

William Lane had taken over the White Lion in 1836. From tentative beginnings in the mid-seventeenth century, the inn had grown until now it was one of the city's top inns, with stabling for 115 horses. Brunel and his assistant engineers, along with the directors of the Great Western Railway, had adopted it as their unofficial headquarters in the city. Meetings to drum up support for the railway, to enquire into its merits, expound its virtues, or settle compensation for those dispossessed by it, had become regular events at the inn over the previous eight years. The business had been very welcome, but there was no doubt that, once the railway was open, trade would collapse.

When the railway opened, the journey time to London would be cut to less than four hours. Some coach proprietors had expressed their intention to keep going, claiming that people did not trust the railway or would soon tire of it, but, on any objective assessment, it was clear the coaching age was effectively over.

As the railway had crept nearer, first to Maidenhead, then to Twyford, to Reading, to Steventon, to Faringdon Road, to Wootton Bassett Road, and finally to Chippenham, a mere 13 miles away, coaches had run from Bath to each successive railhead. Now the great tunnel through Box Hill was nearly complete; the rails to bring the trains on into Bath were already being laid.

The city had seen its first railway over a century earlier, when John Padmore constructed a tramway from Ralph Allen's quarries at Combe Down, down what is now Prior Park Road to a wharf at Widcombe. It was one of the wonders of eighteenth-century Bath, but, when Ralph Allen died in 1764, the quarries were sold and the line was dismantled. Later, when the Kennet & Avon Canal was being built, inclined planes were laid down steep hillsides, carrying stone for bridges, wharves and aqueducts – at Conkwell in 1801, Murhill in 1803, and Bathampton in 1808. As on Ralph Allen's tramway, the loaded trucks relied on gravity, their descent controlled by a brakeman; once unloaded, horses hauled them back up. There were hundreds, if not thousands, of similar lines all over the country, all relying on gravity or horsepower, and all built to carry stone, coal, or other minerals. Then came the oft-retold saga of experiments with steam, and, within a few years, people were thinking about railways not as a way of carrying heavy goods short distances, but as a means of getting from one end of the country to the other at speeds never before deemed possible.

The first proposal for a railway from Bath to Bristol came in 1824. The prospectus spoke of the "advantages of the locomotive steam engine, for the conveyance of passengers and merchandise on a railroad. By means of this power, a company will be enabled to transport the heaviest goods with certainty and security, by day and night, at all times of the year – in periods of frost or of drought, at the rate of at least eight miles an hour, and passengers at a rate of twelve."

The directors of the Kennet & Avon Canal Company were in favour of the line; they even sent their engineer, Mr Blackwell, to the north of England to inspect railways there. Their idea was that a line should run from Bath to Bristol, and another from London to Reading, with the Kennet & Avon linking them. The idea that the railway could be a serious threat to the canal does not even seem to have occurred to them.

Nothing came of this scheme, nor of the next one, in 1829. In the intervening years, significant advances in technology had been made. Instead of twelve miles an hour, the prospectus now held out to passengers the prospect of travelling at twenty. "I think it is clearly proved," said one of the promoters, "that the journey to Bath may be effected with perfect safety in an hour; so that the parties of pleasure in Bath may pay their morning visits to Clifton with little or no fatigue, and without abridging their usual arrangements at home."

On 4 January 1830, a meeting was called at the Assembly Rooms in Bath to drum up support for the railway. Thomas Pycroft of Bath and John Harford of Bristol headed the committee. The engineer was William Brunton, a 52-year-old Scots engineer whose chief claim to fame was as the inventor of a steam engine with a pair of mechanical feet which helped it climb gradients. Although initial tests proved promising, the design was abandoned after the prototype exploded at a public demonstration, killing 13 people. Brunton told the audience at the Assembly Rooms that, "the railway, when completed, will be most perfect; and by the judicious selection of the line, and the arrangement made to form the necessary embankments with arches of stone masonry, the road will be nearly level throughout, except in one place, and there the rise and fall will only be as 1 in 800."

A few weeks later, with interest in the line growing, Thomas Pycroft and John Harford inspected the site of the proposed terminus in Bath near Queen Square, and sent their proposals to the Town Clerk. The line was to run to the north of the Upper Bristol Road, before crossing Charlotte Street to terminate on Stable Lane, directly

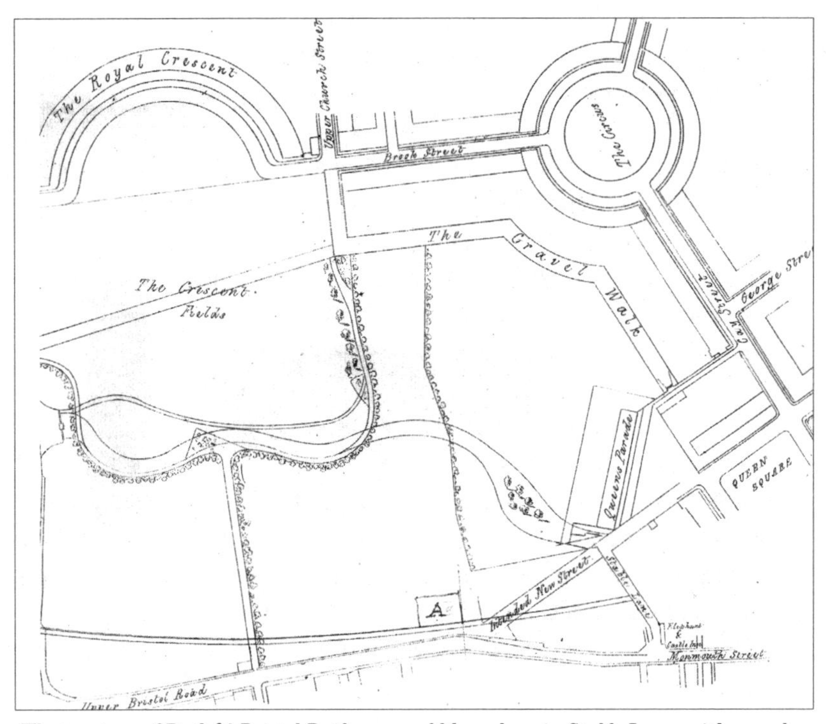

The terminus of Bath & Bristol Railway would have been in Stable Lane, with a goods depot (marked A) *at the bottom of the newly-built Charlotte Street.*

behind the New Inn in Monmouth Place. The goods depot would be 100 yards to the west, at the bottom of Charlotte Street. They also sought to put the Town Clerk's mind at rest over the effect of the line on what was soon to become Royal Victoria Park, adding that, "we also viewed the line through the Common Field and do not think the rail road will at all interfere with the intended improvements. The ground north of the rail road may be planted and thereby the rail road hid from the rides and walks."

The railway soon ran up against some formidable opposition. On 1 February 1830, John Hurle, a prominent citizen, took the chair at "a numerous and respectable meeting of landowners" in the Lamb Inn at Keynsham. They passed – unanimously – the following two resolutions:

> That it appears to this meeting that the contemplated railway if executed, will be productive of serious injury to the land, houses and

> property generally through and near its line without any adequate benefit to the landholders and occupiers whose interests it will so prejudicially affect.
>
> That in the opinion of this meeting the land and water communications now existing between the cities of Bristol and Bath are fully sufficient for all purposes of conveyance and that the proposed railway is uncalled for upon public grounds which would alone justify the inroad it will make upon private property and the rights and comforts of individuals.

And that, for the moment at least, was that.

A few miles to the north, however, a railway – the grandly-titled Bristol & Gloucestershire Railway – had got off the ground, gaining parliamentary approval on 17 June 1828. Despite its name, this was a horse-drawn tramway, built to carry coal. The main shareholder was the Kennet & Avon Canal Company. Brunel eventually converted part of it to a broad-gauge steam-hauled line, when it was incorporated into the Bristol & Gloucester Railway. For now, it will suffice to record that it was responsible for the first railway fatality in the Bath area, when a man left the pub at Willsbridge late one night in July 1830, "and fell into the hollow, through which the railway is made, a height of 36 feet."

While Messrs Pycroft and Harford were trying to win support for a railway from Bath to Bristol, other promoters, with far bigger ambitions, were canvassing support for a line from London to Bristol. This was not a railway line, however: it was a canal, a ship canal capable of carrying "vessels of upwards of 400 tons burthen." It was linked with a similar proposal for a ship canal to Portsmouth, which would bear ships "of 700 tons burthen." It would cost a staggering £8,000,000; annual revenue was calculated at £500,000. At the dawn of the railway age, there were many who saw no reason why trains should be the transport of the future. Why not canals, bigger and better than ever before, fed, where necessary, by enterprises like the Bristol & Gloucestershire Railway? It was, as we now know, a vision of the future that was never to be realized. Like it or not, railway mania was about to sweep everything before it.

TWO

Brunel Comes to Bath

It is probably fair to say that no single individual had a greater impact on Bath than Isambard Kingdom Brunel. If the Great Western Railway had not engaged him as Chief Engineer, if the Great Western's bid to build a line from Bristol to London had succumbed, as it very nearly did, to a rival scheme, then somebody else would have brought the railway to Bath. Nobody else, though, would have brought it through in such dramatic style.

However great was Brunel's impact on Bath, his impact on Bristol was greater still. Almost a century and a half after his death, his creations – the Clifton Suspension Bridge, Temple Meads station, the *SS Great Britain* – remain among the most potent symbols of the city's identity. Brunel stamped his personality on Bristol in a way nobody else has done before or since. Yet his association with the city came about – literally – by accident.

On 12 January 1828, he was at work in a tunnel beneath the Thames at Rotherhithe, designed by his father, and one of the most audacious and difficult engineering projects of its time. The works had flooded eight months earlier; it taken almost six months to plug the breach with clay and clear the works of silt. Now work had started again. When the water burst through again on 12 January, the results were even more devastating. Two of the men working with Brunel were killed, and he was only saved by sheer luck. His legs were badly crushed and he was knocked unconscious, but the wave that swept into the tunnel did not drown him, but bore him along towards a shaft where his assistant was on hand to haul him out of the rising waters.

Despite his injuries, he struggled to continue with the project for a couple of days, before he was persuaded to take a holiday. He chose Brighton, but, on his return to London, it was clear he had not returned to health. With the tunnel sealed off and all work suspended, Brunel took up the offer of a stay in Clifton. The story of

Brunel's stay in Clifton, of how he learnt of the competition to design a bridge over the Avon Gorge, and eventually won it, are well known. His early association with Bath is somewhat less so. It first surfaces in some fragmentary, enigmatic – and extremely badly-written – entries in his diary:

4th July 1830: Started by coach for Bath, taking with me drawings of [...?] Detail of Castle and model of Do and drawing of Mr Harford's Gothic Gateway.

5th July 1830: Arrived at Bath at twenty to seven. [...] went to Mr Frere – saw him. Fixed tomorrow at eleven to meet him at Bristol.

6th July 1830: Breakfasted at Acraman's – showing my drawing and model of Norman Gateway. Went with Mr A to John Haythorne. He appeared still favourable to me and my plans. Called on Cookson – went to Mr Isaacs, told him my suspicions about [Bates?] intended new place. Showed him my drawing and model, expressed himself much pleased – he improves every time. Went to Guppy, thence to Mr Frere – to Mr Garrard – Mr Burgess there, Mr G as usual very confident about my success

9th September 1830: Went to Harford's at bank according to appointment – he asked me to bring my models to show Mr Miles – brought them all – Mr M appeared pleased. Mr Harford as friendly as ever

16th September 1830: Went to Harford's. Got an order for Miles' paintings and to take my drawings to Mr Miles. Went with Burgess in a chair to Leigh Court – a splendid collection of paintings – Lunched with Mr M who appeared pleased (as much I supposed as he could be) with my plans. Returned. [...?] went to Blaise Castle – beautiful grounds, fine paintings, and most hospitable reception.

17th September 1830: After breakfast went to Acraman's and all started for Bath. Called on English's – went to Beckford – well

Beckford's Tower as Brunel would have known it.

> *received – an agreeable gentlemanly well informed man – talking a great deal, evidently very warm and always in motion – his house a pattern of elegance – splendour rendered agreeable and unostentatious by purity of taste – and well studied luxury of the highest degree – paintings, gems and articles of vertu crowded in costly cabinets and on beautiful tables. He entered warmly into the bridge affair, admiring much the Giant's Hole plan and praising strongly the architecture I had adopted – approving of Egyptian but condemning in strong terms all the others – on the whole I was highly delighted and only regretted that Benyon was not with us.*

Much of this, even after diligent enquiry, is incomprehensible; it also throws up more questions than it answers. Some of the names here – especially Harford and Guppy – we will encounter again, as promoters and directors of the Great Western Railway. Frere was to become the resident engineer on the Bristol section of the line. Over two years before plans for a railway to London were being discussed – at least in public – Brunel was already on good terms not only with the people who would engage him to build the railway, but also with his future assistant on that project.

The Clifton Suspension Bridge as designed by Thomas Telford.

The diary extracts also show another side to Brunel – the connoisseur, making sketches and admiring works of art. The reference to William Beckford, the wealthy dilettante who had built Lansdown Tower, is the most intriguing of all. Beckford was interested not only in works of art; he was also passionately interested in developments in architecture and engineering. He would almost certainly have been captivated by the young Brunel and his ideas for the Clifton Bridge. Brunel for his part would have been fascinated not only by the objects of vertu, but by the tower Beckford had built on Lansdown, and tales of the Abbey at Fonthill. But the intriguing possibility is that this was more than just a social visit. Beckford, despite the reversal in his fortunes that had led him to sell Fonthill and move to Bath, was still fabulously wealthy. How else could he have afforded to build his tower and continue to amass works of art? He was a patron of projects and individuals, but an extremely secretive one. He was, for example, one of the principal subscribers to the Royal Victoria Park, but always appeared, when the list of subscriptions was published, as "a Gentleman of Lansdown Crescent."

It is not known whether Beckford subscribed to the Clifton Bridge project, but it was the kind of thing he would have been inspired by. His interest in Brunel's designs – indeed the reason for Brunel's audience with the great man – could have been due to involvement with the bridge project. There is another, albeit somewhat tentative, reason to suppose that Beckford was more deeply involved with the bridge project than anyone has guessed. When Thomas Telford was called in to judge the entries for the bridge competition and rejected them all – including Brunel's – he was asked to come up with his own design. Bearing in mind that Telford was one of the greatest engineers of all time, and that, a few years earlier, he had designed a suspension bridge across the Menai Strait, one of the most ground-breaking and aesthetically perfect bridges ever built, the design he came up with for Clifton was a monstrosity – Gothic towers linked by suspension cables, a hideous mélange of old and new. The question has to be – why? Was it perhaps to impress Beckford, the creator of the biggest Gothic folly of all? It is impossible to say, but one thing is certain – Beckford made it quite clear that he hated it. The difference in style between Fonthill and Lansdown was ample demonstration that he had moved on from his Gothic phase. Even if he had not, it is unlikely that he would have responded favourably to what amounted to a clumsy pastiche. Nevertheless, when Telford unveiled his design, it was greeted rapturously – such was the respect due to a great man like Telford. However, once the initial euphoria had died down, Telford's plan was quietly shelved, and Brunel was invited to submit another design, which was eventually accepted. It was while this final design was under consideration that he made his visit to Beckford. Was he summoned to Bath to present his case? Was it perhaps on Beckford's nod that the decision to award the contract to him was finally made? Who can say? The evidence, such as it is, is highly circumstantial, but with a character as congenitally secretive as Beckford this would be hardly surprising.

Brunel's next recorded visit to Bath was in June, after he had been awarded the contract, when he visited Bath Races on Lansdown and "met a number of Bristol people – did a little bridge business." On 11 July, he rode to Murhill Quarry to inspect stone, presumably for the bridge, which he found "excellent … very hard and very durable but too white." A ceremony to mark the commencement of work on the bridge had taken place the previous month, but little or nothing had been done. Indeed, Brunel's visit to Murhill, if it was with a view to using it for the bridge, was more than a little premature, for the bridge committee, despite all the publicity surrounding the contest, did not yet have the money to build it.

The riots in Queen Square, Bristol.

The summer of 1831 was one of extreme discontent. Reform was in the air, and nowhere was the discontent more keenly felt than in Bristol, whose corporation had hung on to age-old, time-worn privileges more blatantly and more indefensibly than almost anywhere else in the kingdom. The proposed parliamentary reforms, by today's standards, seem very conservative. The franchise would be extended to middle-class men; the working classes, along with women, would still be excluded. But, while it sought to improve the lot of the middle-classes, the reform movement was fuelled from below, by those who, although they stood to gain nothing directly, believed that the middle classes would give them a better deal than those determined to stop them having a vote. And, as always, there were those who had nothing to lose, for whom the prospect of unrest and civil disobedience was reason enough in itself.

The Bristol Riots of October 1831 were among the worst this country has ever experienced. Their causes and consequences, and the reasons they took the course they did, have been discussed and argued over many times. For now, it will suffice to say two things about that sorry episode: first, Brunel enlisted as a special constable and acquitted himself honourably, thereby increasing the esteem in which he was held by the city's chief citizens; second, the riots had a devastating effect on a city that was already teetering on the brink of a sharp economic downturn. In this it was not following a national trend; this was Bristol's problem alone. For centuries, it had been Britain's second city, and the most important port on the western seaboard. The abolition of the slave trade and the loss of the American colonies had had a major impact on its trade. To these were added the boom in the Lancashire textile industry, resulting from mechanization, which had decimated the textile industry of the West Country. Lancashire's mills sent their products out through Liverpool; the West Country used Bristol. Ships sailing into Bristol had to negotiate a winding, tidal gorge and contend with an antiquated harbour; ships sailing into Liverpool had no such problem. Finally, and most tellingly, Liverpool had a railway, linking it with Manchester; other railways, linking Liverpool to the powerhouses of the industrial revolution, were planned. It is hardly surprising that, in the aftermath of the Bristol Riots, business confidence in Bristol dropped to an all-time low. Hardly surprising, too, that work on the bridge at Clifton, which had hardly started, was suspended indefinitely.

Bristol's lack of a railway had already exercised minds other than those of the future directors of the Great Western. A few months before the riots, the Southampton, London & Branch Railway & Dock Company had been formed. The branch in its title was to run – like the ship canal proposed the previous year – from Basingstoke to Bristol. In July 1832, no doubt influenced by the continued downturn in Bristol's fortunes, the company announced it would concentrate on building the main line from London to Southampton before seeking authorization for the branch. This was the spur that prompted four Bristolians – Thomas Guppy, William Tothill, George Jones and John Harford – to produce their own plans for a railway to London. In January 1833, the committee of what they referred to as the London and Bristol Railway first met.

A few weeks later, in February 1833, Brunel, who was back in Bristol to superintend dredging and construction work in the Cumberland Basin, was summoned by the committee who told him they wanted a survey of the line. Funding had come from a number of influential bodies, including the Bristol Corporation, the Society of Merchant Venturers, the Bristol Dock Company, the Bristol Chamber of Commerce, and the Bristol & Gloucestershire Railway. Three names had already been put forward for the job of surveyor – WH Townsend, who had surveyed the line of the Bristol & Gloucestershire

Railway, William Brunton, who had surveyed the Bristol & Bath Railway in 1830, and Henry Price, who, with Brunton, had tried unsuccessfully to drum up support for a Bristol to London Railway, following the course of the Kennet & Avon Canal, in 1832.

Brunel was invited to apply for the post, and two weeks later, on 7 March 1833, was appointed Chief Engineer to the London & Bristol Railway. To Brunel's dismay, Townsend was appointed his deputy. "How the devil I am to get on with him tied to my neck I know not," he commented in exasperation.

Townsend was a local land surveyor and valuer, with little experience of engineering. While his skills were more than adequate for laying out a mineral line such as the Bristol & Gloucestershire Railway, he had neither the expertise nor the imagination to comprehend the scope of Brunel's majestic vision for a "*ligne à grande vitesse*" linking Bristol to London. So it was that, two days after the appointments had been confirmed, Townsend offered to show Brunel the route he believed the railway should take between Bristol and Bath. It lay north-westward, following the course of the Bristol & Gloucestershire Railway as far as Mangotsfield, before turning south-eastward through Wick and running down the Lambridge Valley to Bath. Admittedly, Robert Stephenson was to choose almost exactly the same route when he surveyed a line for the Midland Railway 13 years later, but, from Brunel's point of view it was wholly impracticable. Stephenson's line, which was never built, not only involved a 1518 yard-long tunnel under Tog Hill, but a long climb at 1 in 95 on either side of it. Such gradients still posed operating difficulties in 1846, when more powerful locomotives were available, but in 1833 they were major obstacles.*

Brunel wasted no time in telling Townsend what he thought of his plan, informing him that the only logical course for the line to take was along the Avon valley. It was a route he had taken many times, on horseback, in his trips between the two cities; when he rode down to Bath two days later, it was not to see if the route was practicable, but to establish the exact course the line would take.

* *Although the line Brunel built between Bristol and London contained two sections of 1 in 100 – at Box and Wootton Bassett, these were unavoidable, and many trains needed banking up them in the early years. The prospect of all trains between Bath and Bristol having to be banked was simply not acceptable, when an alternative route was available.*

The new Warminster Road near Bathampton, with the Kennet & Avon Canal on the left.

There was another reason for his journey. He had been asked to act as one of the mediators in a dispute between the Kennet & Avon Canal Company and the Black Dog Turnpike Trust. The turnpike trust was building what is now the A36 along the Limpley Stoke Valley. It was a major undertaking, the most impressive structure being the viaduct at the bottom of Brassknocker Hill, built by David Aust and completed in October 1834. Much of the route lay along the side of a steep and somewhat unstable hill. Many people believed it would fall down the hillside; among them was the Kennet & Avon Company, whose canal lay directly below it. Naturally they were worried and called in two eminent engineers from Bristol – Brunel and Brunton – to assess the stability of the road. Brunel recorded the visit in his diary:

> *Started at six thirty on horseback to Bath. Had a fall at starting. Arrived at Mr McAdams at a quarter past nine. After waiting a little for Brunton, breakfasted. Brunton came, proceeded with him and Mc & Son on foot to Claverton. The proposed road runs for a short distance parallel to the canal. The side of the hill is a rotten description oolite laying on clay.*
> *Many slips have occurred owing no doubt to the washing of the clay by the rain and considerably assisted by the bad management of the canal. Blackwell, the canal engineer, a bigotted, obstinate,*

practical man, says the road will make the hill slip – but couldn't tell us why. Cotterell, a quaker [?] surveyor attending on the part of Vivian the landowner, also opposing, could not or would not either say how or why. Merriman, the canal solicitor, appeared to think his advisers rather unsupported by reason. After a useless discussion during which Merriman twice said that Mr B would not of course be convinced and did not come to be convinced (Mr M the last time tried to say this as a joke tho' perfectly true) we parted. Mr Tring, our solicitor, took my card and promised to let me know in good time when they went into committee. Brunton and I then returned to McAdams, wrote our opinions separately and sealed mine and I returned to Bristol.

Despite Brunel's dismissal of the canal company's fears, the Warminster Road did slip, and has gone on slipping, intermittently, ever since. There are still plans to build a bridge across Bathampton Meadows, linking the A36 to the A46 and A4, sending even more heavy traffic along it. A road that was hardly adequate for coaching traffic, which should be, at best, be a weight-restricted byway along one of the most picturesque valleys in the country, is, against all common sense it seems, to be pressed into service as a superhighway.

In August 1833, with the survey of the line well advanced, the Great Western Committee in Bristol met for the first time with a committee established to drum up support in London. The cost of the line, they were told, would be nearly £3 million; projected annual revenue would be three-quarters of a million.* They also decided to change the name of the projected railway from the London & Bristol to the Great Western. There are two theories as to why this happened: the first is that Brunel, inspired by dreams of future glory, sold the idea to the directors in a speech of impassioned oratory; the other is that the members of the London committee, aware that many people thought Bristol was in terminal decline, felt that having Bristol in the title would put potential investors off. If it was sold to them as a line giving access to South Wales, Ireland and America, with Bristol just a transfer point, they would be more likely to invest in it. It is worth

* *The line eventually cost £6,500,000. In the first full year of operation, the Great Western recorded receipts of £551,099.*

mentioning, however, that the name was not new; as early as 1825, a meeting had been held at Taunton to promote a Great Western Railroad between Bristol and Exeter.

Brunel's diary for the latter part of 1833 contains several references to him surveying the line between Bristol and Bath:

24th September 1833:
Bath: [...] urged again the necessity of opening a communication with Bath ...
Mr Harford brought up the subject of entrance into Bristol and particularly Queen's Square. I was directed to devote as much time to this as I could and report at next meeting upon it.
Frere and his brother dined with me. [...] to meet me at Bath tomorrow.
Mr Osborne called – we are to meet at the York House tomorrow.

24th September 1833:
Arrived at Bath [after an overnight trip from London].
Met Townsend. Breakfasted and started in his phaeton.
Went as far as Keynsham; got out and walked over line.
Arrived at the valley at Brislington, found the staffs up – all to double the curve agreed on. Could not make [Townsend] understand the theory or rationale.

25th September 1833:
Went over to Bath in a gig – arrived there, called at several places with TSO, but everybody out, at last I went to Goodridge's.

22nd October 1833:
Started from York House with [...] in a chaise to Saltford where we met Townsend, breakfasted together and walked over the ground from there to the point where we proposed crossing the road – gave him directions upon this part and returned to Bath.
Gave Bell directions how to proceed and gave him a letter to Goodridge.
Returned to Bristol. Arrived in time for the committee, received positive instructions not even to include Queen's Square in the notice, but to stop at Temple Meads. Suggested to them the

possibility of stopping at the Angel at Bath to save crossing the river upon this point. Lake read [?] positive instructions to cross into Lord Manvers' Garden Ground.

These cryptic jottings raise some interesting points. Relations with Townsend had clearly not improved; Queen Square (much of which had been destroyed in the Bristol Riots two years earlier) was initially under consideration as the site of the Bristol terminus, perhaps as part of a more ambitious scheme to regenerate the area; and Brunel floated the idea of building Bath station at the bottom of Holloway ("at the Angel") to save the expense of a double crossing of the River Avon in Bath.*

The most intriguing name here, however, is that of Goodridge. The architect, Henry Edmund Goodridge, was a protégé of William Beckford, and had designed the tower on Lansdown for him in 1825. Evidence recently discovered suggests that Beckford not only commissioned Goodridge to build the tower, but was closely involved in Goodridge's subsequent commissions, such as Cleveland Place. Deeds of properties in this development were witnessed by Beckford's servants at his house in Lansdown Crescent. Goodridge appears in Brunel's diary because he had been appointed surveyor to the Great Western Railway in Bath. Is it perhaps fanciful to see Beckford's influence once again at work here? The building of a railway through Bath is the sort of project he would have been deeply interested in. Once built, he would have had a grandstand view of the line west of Bath from his tower. He had already had a long meeting with Brunel and doubtless listened with interest to his schemes and dreams. Was his way of keeping abreast of – and possibly influencing – developments ensuring that his protégé was appointed local surveyor? With his influence and connections, it would not have been difficult.

* *The idea of extending the line from Temple Meads to Queen Square resurfaced in 1861, when there were discussions about building a joint station with the Bristol & Exeter and Midland Railways. The joint station was eventually built adjacent to the original terminus at Temple Meads.*

THREE

A Practicable Object

By the autumn of 1833, the Great Western was running into problems. The project had not attracted the anticipated level of support. Already the terminus of the line had been set back from Queen Square to Temple Meads, and Brunel had floated the idea of abandoning the river crossings in Bath on the same grounds. Now the directors, forced into a corner, made a decision that nearly scuppered their plans completely. They decided to build the line in two stages. Instead of asking parliament to authorize a line from Bristol to London, they would seek authority for two separate lines – Bristol to Bath and London to Reading – and deal with the section from Bath to Reading when funds permitted. On 18 October 1833, Brunel was told to "discontinue his survey between Reading and Bath, and to confine all further future expenses to the survey on the two extremities of the line."

In January 1834, a meeting was held at the White Lion in Bath to canvass support. Charles Saunders, Secretary of the Great Western committee in London, came down to speak:

> During an enquiry which lasted some six or eight months, it was shown that the railway is a practicable object, and that its completion will be productive of the most important advantages to the port of Bristol. It is well known that the trade of Bristol has materially declined; it is no surprise that the inhabitants of that city should take a step so well calculated to revive their commercial prosperity ... The capital which it has been estimated will be required for the completion of the whole line is £3,000,000, but on account of several minor undertakings of this kind having been unsuccessful, particularly as regards Bristol, there was initially some hesitation on the subject, and after the lapse of six weeks, there were only four or five thousand shares taken. It then became a matter of consideration whether the

> completion of the whole measure might not be made more feasible by first raising a number of shares sufficient to complete the portions of the line linking London and Reading and Bristol and Bath …

He then went on to extol the benefits the railway would bring to Bath:

> It has been seen by numerous examples that, wherever communication has been improved, towns have become larger and more prosperous. Bath is an acknowledged place of favourite resort and it is likely that the railway will double the number of families residing here.* A great many people come to Bath for the purpose of seeking health; the railway will enable them to reach Bath from London in four hours and a half, and without any fatigue; for it has been ascertained on the Liverpool and Manchester Railway that there is no fatigue in travelling of this kind. Now, if the number of residents is increased in Bath, who can deny that there will be an increase in trade; it might be said that an increase of the residents will increase the price of provisions; but this idea will be abandoned when it is considered that this anticipated ill effect will be obviated by the facility which the railway will afford for the cheap and rapid transport of agricultural produce.

Charles Saunders' sleight of hand in extolling the virtues of a railway that there were, as yet, no firm plans to build, while it ensured a rousing reception at the White Lion, did not fool everyone. Pamphlets and letters to the press soon started to appear, condemning the scheme:

> The Great Western Railway turns out on enquiry to be only a railway from London to Reading, and a railway from Bath to Bristol; in other words, it is an attempt to monopolise the two profitable ends of the line and leave the middle to take care of itself, not only without any certainty of the intermediate part ever being accomplished, but from the mode adopted laying the greatest obstacle in the way of its completion.

* *Charles Saunders' prophecy was not realized. While the population of England rose from twelve million to twenty-one million between 1841 and 1851, Bath's population hardly changed – rising from 53,000 to 54,000.*

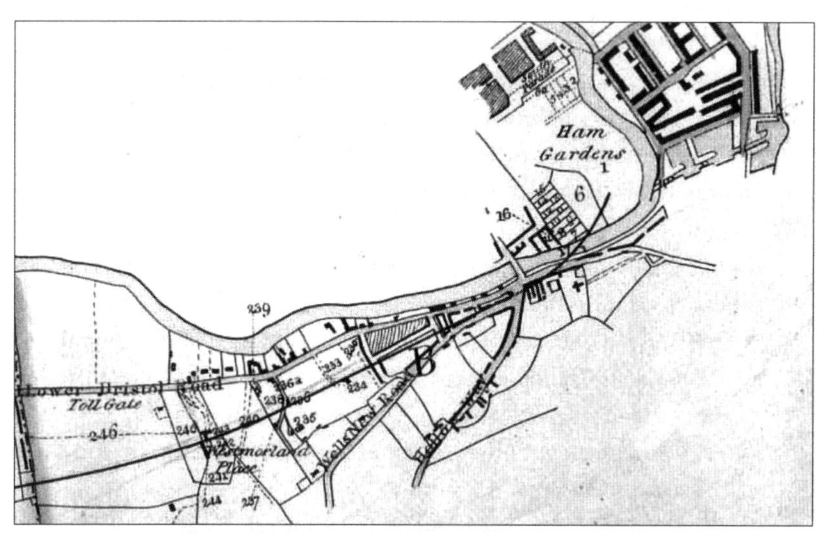

The Great Western originally planned to take the line from Bristol no further than Bath, and extend it to Reading when more funds had been raised.

Another pamphleteer described the railway as "a project wholly uncalled for, inasmuch as between the points now proposed to be connected, there are no manufacturers, no mines, no coal, nor any other species of trade which may not as convincingly and profitably be carried on by means of the existing communications, all of which both by land and water are of the very first order." However, opposition to the railway from landowners affected by the proposed line was far less than might have been expected. Between London and Reading, only 108 out of 458 were against; between Bath and Bristol, the figure was 32 out of 824.

The bill to authorize construction of the two ends of the line was deposited with the Commons, where it passed its second reading on 10 March 1834. The committee stage, which followed, was an epic 57-day struggle, from which the company eventually emerged triumphant. Although the House of Commons burnt down a few months later, destroying the committee's records, the Great Western published a short account of the proceedings, which was distributed to shareholders. Not surprisingly, all the witnesses quoted were in favour of the line, and the transcripts were heavily edited. Nevertheless, the following extracts give a vivid insight into the problems faced by tradesmen in Bath before the coming of the railway:

Mr Benjamin Collins, Butcher, in the neighbourhood of Bath:

"Is there not a considerable portion of meat consumed in Bath purchased at the cattle market in Bristol?"

"Yes, I should expect of pigs and sheep in the winter four months, two parts out of three that are killed at Bath are bought at Bristol."

"Do you know the amount of sheep the trade receive at Bath in the course of the week?"

"There is a great alteration in the course of a fortnight – some weeks 400 or 500; another week 250."

"How many pigs?"

"A wonderful sight of pigs, they are brought over from Ireland."

"Are sheep driven also?"

"One third of them are brought in wagons; the heavy sheep."

"How long are they on the road?"

"They will not come home in a day, they are left on the road in all directions."

"Have you seen sheep die on the road?"

"Yes, I have had them die to my sorrow."

"Have you lost them by theft?"

"Yes, since I have been in business I have had 73 stolen."

"Do you send meat from Bath to London?"

"Veal and pork; I have a son a salesman, at Newgate Market."

"Does the meat suffer from the time it is on the road?"

"Yes."

"Is not the meat very often injured by the travelling of the sheep?"

"Yes."

"Putting a large number of sheep in a small wagon, travelling at the rate of 20 miles an hour, would that hurt them?"

"No."

Mr James Shepherd, Grocer, Bath:

"What is the cost of the carriage of goods per hundredweight by the river?"

"Sixpence light goods and fivepence heavy goods."

"When the floods occur, and the passage is unfavourable, what is the time occupied between Bristol and Bath?"

"I have had goods detained frequently eight or nine days in the winter."

"Have you known instances of loss by pilfering?"

"Yes."

"Are you also in the habit of receiving goods in your trade from London?"

"Yes."

"How long are your goods generally coming by water from London to Bath?"

"By water six or seven days, and sometimes more."

"What is the price per hundredweight for the conveyance?"

"Two shillings and sixpence."

"Have you ever ordered goods from London to be sent by land, in consequence of the delay?"

"Yes."

"What have you paid per hundredweight then?"

"Six shillings."

"If the London market was brought nearer to you in point of time, should you derive any advantage in the purchase of your goods in that respect?"

"Very frequently."

"Is there frequently a great difference between the Bristol and London markets?"

"Yes."

"The difference of how much per hundredweight in sugars?"

"I have known it from three to four shillings in sugars."

"Have you ever given double orders from London?"

"Yes."

"That causes the employment of more capital in that direction also?"

"Yes."

"Is there any other inconvenience excepting a larger capital wanted?"

"Yes; we lose the chance of the markets, because by the time we get those things down, the market may be two or three shillings a hundredweight lower."

Mr Thomas Vesey, Tallow Chandler and Soap Maker, Box, near Bath:

"Tallow, barilla and rosin are necessary for your trade?"

"Yes."

"Where do you get them from?"

"Tallow from London, and barilla, rosin and palm oil from Bristol."

"How do they travel from Bristol?"

"I get them by water principally, except in flood time."

"Do those floods happen pretty often?"

"Very frequent in the winter."

"When the floods interrupt the passage of the river, you send your own wagon?"

"Yes."

"Is that cheaper or dearer than the river?"

"Certainly dearer."

"Should you send a wagon to Bristol if there was a railroad?"

"Certainly not."

"How does your tallow come from London?"

"By the Thames to Reading, and thence by canal."

"Do you find that a convenient mode of conveyance?"

"Very inconvenient, especially by the Thames."

Mr John Provis, Timber & Coal Merchant, at Chippenham, Bath and Reading:

"What is the time usually occupied in the voyage between Bath and Bristol?"

"One day to go down and another to come up, if it is good weather and not incommoded by flood, frost or drought."

"What has been the longest voyage from Bristol to Bath?"

"I had a boat detained a fortnight in Bristol, in bringing up a quantity of stone, by a flood."

"Some detriment has resulted to yourself by this delay?"

"Yes, it was a loss of three or four pounds to me, in the pay of the men and keep of the horses."

"Do you convey flour between Bath and Bristol?"

"Yes, a considerable quantity from Chippenham to Bristol."

"By the way of the Avon?"

"Yes."

"Is flour an article very liable to pillage?"

"We have had some stolen about six months since, which I was obliged to allow to the owner."

"That was a dead loss to yourself?"

"Quite."

Mr Samuel Provis:

"Were you formerly a carrier by water between Bristol and London?"

"I was."

"Between the years 1830 and 1832?"

"In 1831 and 1832."

"Was yours as large a carrying trade as that of any other person?"

"It was; except Messrs Betts and Drew, it was the largest."

"You are well acquainted with the navigation of the Thames and Avon?"

"Yes."

"What is the shortest time in which the voyage from London to Reading was performed?"

"Three days."

"Were the interruptions frequent?"

"Very frequent."

"From what causes?"

"From flood, short water, and frosts."

"When under the effect of those interruptions, what was the length of the voyage?"

"Sometimes it would extend to a fortnight or three weeks."

"Were the goods entrusted to you exposed to damage by wet?"

"Sometimes."

"And loss by robbery?"

"That was more general."

"I suppose the robbery would increase in proportion to the delay?"

"Yes."

"Were you frequently applied to to carry cloth from Bradford and Trowbridge?"

"We were, and we declined it."

"On what account?"

"On account of the risk of robberies."

Mr Thomas Cooper:

"Are you a proprietor of coaches on the Bath and Bristol road?"

"I am."

"How long have you been so?"

"Twelve years."

"How many coaches have you?"

"Four."

"Do you know the number upon the whole line including your own?"

"Twenty-two including the mail."

"What number of mails are there?"

"Four mails – two up and two down."

"Give me the average number of passengers by a four-horse coach."

"To the best of my belief about nine."

"That is throughout the year?"

"Yes, I think so."

"The average numbers of passengers by the mails?"

"I should consider about five – three inside and two out."

"The average number of passengers by a pair horse-coach?"

"I consider them about six."

Also called to give evidence was Henry Goodridge, who had surveyed the course of the line through the parishes of Twerton, St James and Lyncombe & Widcombe, and estimated the value of the land and buildings required by the railway at £21,500. He was asked for his opinion of plans for the skew bridge over the Avon at Bath. Having declared himself satisfied with them, he was asked what experience he had of bridge construction:

> I have constructed two; one over the Avon at Bath, which we constructed within the estimate; and I conceive from the amount of Mr Brunel's estimate, given to me, £12,000, that in all probability it may be completed for £2,000 less. The amount of our estimate for a bridge of 100 feet was £8,193; Mr Brunel having allowed £12,500,

> I conceive was ample; in fact, in all probability he may have £2,000 to spare.

The most authoritative witness was George Stephenson, who had designed the *Rocket* and built the Liverpool & Manchester Railway, and was known as the Father of the Railways. He praised Brunel's plan without reservation, declaring it superior to all rival schemes, and adding that his estimate of costs was very realistic.

George Burke, KC, who worked closely with Brunel in the promotion of the bill, and whose offices faced Brunel's on the opposite side of Parliament Street, gives a revealing portrait of Brunel at this time:

> To facilitate our intercourse, it occurred to Brunel to carry a string across Parliament Street from his chambers to mine, to be connected by a bell, by which he could either call me to the window to receive his telegraphic signals, or, more frequently, to wake me in the morning when we had occasion to go to the country together, which, it is needless to observe, was of frequent occurrence; and great was the astonishment of the neighbours at this device, the object of which they were unable to comprehend. I believe that at this time he scarcely ever went to bed, though I never remember to have seen him tired or out of spirits. He was a very constant smoker, and would take his nap in an armchair, very frequently with a cigar in his mouth; and if we were to start out of town at five or six o'clock in the morning, it was his frequent practice to rouse me out of bed about three, by means of the bell, when I would invariably find him up and dressed ... No one would have supposed that during the night he had been poring over plans and estimates, and engrossed in serious labours which to most men would have proved destructive of their energies during the following day.

The bill was eventually passed by the Commons, only to be defeated in the Lords. Lord Cadogan led the opposition to it, arguing that

> it is an incomplete measure. There is an immense difference between what the high-sounding title of the bill professes to

> accomplish, and what its provisions actually purport to do ... The railroad, according to the bill itself, is to extend only from London to Reading; from that place goods are to be transported by the Kennet & Avon Canal to Bath; and they are to be conveyed the remaining twelve miles from Bath to Bristol by another railway. I appeal to your Lordships whether it is right that the legislature should sanction a measure, the very enactments of which show that it is inefficient for the purposes it is intended to accomplish.

On the same day that the Great Western bill was defeated, the London & Southampton Railway received parliamentary approval. Although the Southampton company's plan to build a branch from Basingstoke to Bristol had been dropped two years earlier, the defeat of the Great Western bill now encouraged them to revive it. They appointed William Brunton chief engineer for the branch, and, a few weeks later, opened an office at 14 Argyle Street, Bath.

At this stage, with the Great Western camp in disarray, there can be little doubt that the London & Southampton Company could have seized the advantage. But they made a fatal miscalculation. When a meeting was called at the White Hart in Bath on 12 September, there seemed some confusion over the name of the proposed line. Was it the Basing & Bristol or the Basing & Bath? There was good reason for the confusion. William Brunton was one of the first to speak. He described the route the line would take between Bath and Bristol, keeping on the south side of the river and terminating in Somerset Square, behind St Mary Redcliffe Church. The station in Bath would be at the bottom of Prior Park Road. From there the line would run south-east through a tunnel under Claverton Down, to emerge at Monkton Combe, before following the course of the Kennet & Avon, and eventually branching off to join the Southampton line at Basingstoke. So far so good. His next comment caused uproar:

> At present the object will be confined to a railway between Basing and Bath, which I believe can be done at an expense of one million sterling.

Charles Saunders rose to reply, pointing out that the Great Western directors had offered to reach an agreement with the London

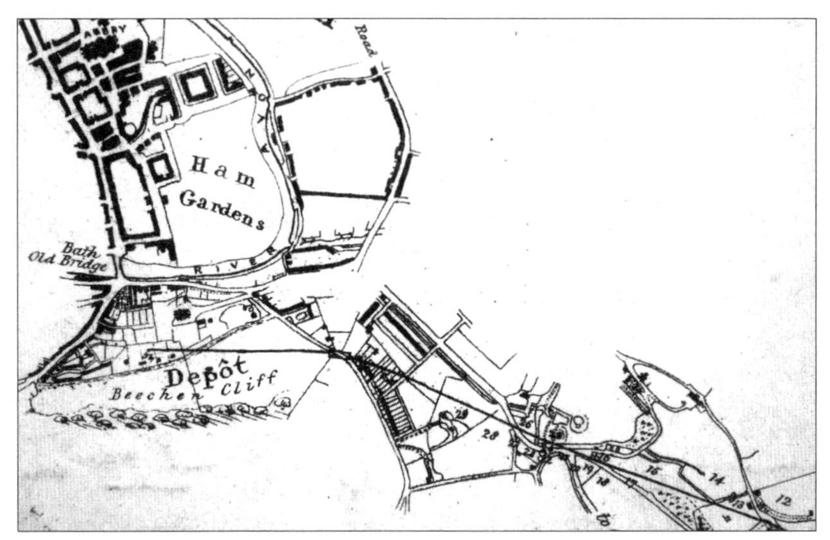

The London & Southampton Railway's branch from Basingstoke would have terminated below Beechen Cliff in Widcombe.

& Southampton Company, which had been declined, before going in for the kill:

> Imagine my surprise, after the eloquent appeal to the rights of Bristol, to find that the contemplated branch from Basing, so ingeniously advocated here today, will actually stop at Bath. The threat held out to the city of Bristol, that if the merchants will not at once coalesce to support a branch from Basing and to relinquish their own undertaking, they will be excluded from having a line taken to that port, is now to be realized.

Brunel then rose to address the meeting:

> He began by stating that he came forward in obedience to the call of the meeting, but, not having at all expected to be called on, he felt some difficulty in addressing them. He felt also, that gentlemen of his profession were not the best persons to speak on the merits of a line chosen by themselves, as they might be supposed to have a favourable bias towards it … He had been engaged, as they had heard, by the corporate authorities of Bristol, to survey the country

between Bristol and London, with a view to the adoption of the best possible line for a railroad communication between those cities. In doing so, his instructions were to select such a line as should embrace the greatest possible extent of public advantage, both in regard to its levels, and the number of important towns and districts through or near which the railway should be carried. He was wholly unbiased in his choice by any other instructions, and began his survey by re-examining a line which had already been selected by Mr Brunton, following the direction of the Kennet and Avon Canal. Pending this survey, he employed his assistants in taking the levels of a more northern line, in the direction of the Wilts and Berks Canal, and the result of the two surveys showed so manifest a superiority in favour of the latter that he at once decided on its adoption. Without entering into minute details of the comparative merits of the two lines, he would simply state to the meeting a circumstance of which many present were no doubt aware, that the Kennet and Avon Canal had a great number of locks to attain its summit level, so many as 29 within a distance of two miles: notwithstanding the great elevation this attained, the land is so much higher, that the summit level is of necessity carried through a long tunnel. The Wilts and Berks Canal, on the other hand, has but very few locks indeed, and the summit level is carried without cutting, over a flat country, the valley on the north side of the Marlborough Downs being upwards of 170 feet lower than that on the line proposed from Basing to Bath. This fact would sufficiently shew to the meeting the nature of the difficulties to be met with in the two lines; and he would leave them to draw their own conclusions from it. But it was not on the ground of the superiority of the levels alone that he was induced to adopt the northern line. It appeared also, from a calculation of the traffic on that line, as compared with one in a southern direction, that the former was by far the most considerable. The meeting would be able to judge of the correctness of the statement, when he told that for a distance of 75 miles from London it was in the direct line to Gloucester, would communicate with Stroud and Cirencester, would pass through Windsor, Maidenhead and Reading, within eleven miles of Oxford, and would afford facilities for making a branch of only nine miles in length, through a very level country, from Chippenham to Melksham, Bradford and Trowbridge ... He would

> here also state that even the engineers who were called to oppose the Great Western Railway in Parliament (of whom there were a great many), admitted that any railway which should be intended as the main branch to connect the West of England with the metropolis should pass in direction north of the Marlborough Downs.

The meeting, which had been convened by the London & Southampton to promote the branch from Basingstoke, ended in a rout. The resolution passed amid loud cheers was that "this meeting places the greatest confidence in the exertions [of] the directors of the Great Western Railway, in endeavouring to obtain the best possible line of communication between the cities of Bristol, Bath and London, and, as those gentlemen are principally connected with this neighbourhood, are identified with its interests, and not influenced by the wants or wishes of any other company, this meeting will not consent to support any rival scheme by which the efforts of the Great Western Railway may be rendered nugatory."

So it was that the threat from the London & Southampton was seen off. Just over a month later, on 23 October, another meeting was held at the White Lion, at which Charles Saunders gave an update on the Great Western's progress. The man who took the chair was to have a major influence on the route of the Great Western through Bath. Charles Wilkins not only owned two textile mills in Twerton, employing over a thousand people; he also owned most of the village. Brunel's initial survey of the line from Bristol to Bath had avoided Twerton, crossing the river twice in order to do so. Going through the village would have entailed the demolition of large numbers of cottages, the diversion of a turnpike road, and large-scale industrial disruption. Had Charles Wilkins opposed the railway coming through Twerton, which would, under the circumstances, have seemed perfectly reasonable, he could have held up work for months and involved the company in a great deal of unwanted litigation and expenditure. On balance, it seemed better to go to the expense of building two bridges, and route the line through the undeveloped land on the other side of the river, to save the aggravation.

If Brunel did not know Charles Wilkins personally, he would certainly have heard of him. His factories were among the biggest and most up-to-date in the West Country. Wilkins was also a captain in

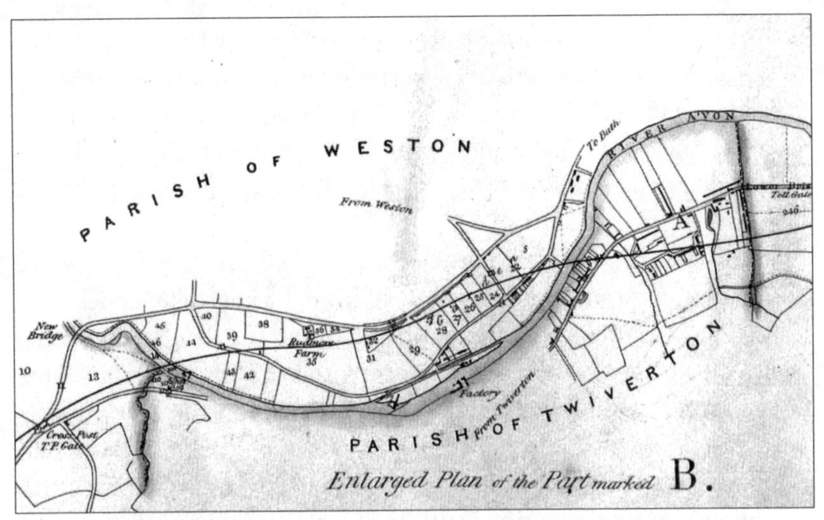

Brunel's first plan was to take his line through Lower Weston and avoid Twerton (or Twiverton as it was sometimes known).

the North Somerset Yeomanry. His presence at the head of his men at the Bristol Riots had only been frustrated because he had to deal with rioting in Bath. His chairmanship of the meeting at the White Lion is ample evidence that Brunel had not only met him, but had a great deal of respect for him. There was good reason for his high regard. Charles Wilkins had saved him the expense of the double river crossing by inviting him to build the railway through Twerton. The decimation of much of the old village this would entail was a minor consideration. Wilkins practically fell over himself to pull down properties in the way of the line – ever mindful of the generous compensation terms offered by the company. Brunel could hardly believe his luck: Wilkins, he informed his directors, "has allowed us the most perfect accommodation in allowing us to pull down such houses as were in our way before the line was finally determined and before the terms of purchase were agreed." When Wilkins was asked where the people whose cottages were destroyed would go, he suggested the arches of the viaduct that would slice the village in two. Brunel took him up on the idea, and a row of arches were turned into a terrace of two-roomed houses.

The reason for Charles Wilkin's eagerness was the long-term decline in the West Country's textile trade. The mills at Twerton had, to a certain extent, bucked the trend; when one of the factories burnt down in 1836, rebuilding started immediately. But difficult times lay ahead; competition from mills in the North of England was growing, and the railway – whether it went through Twerton or not – held incalculable implications for the industry. Wilkins needed money, and if the Great Western Railway were prepared to provide it in exchange for non-productive assets, such as people's houses, he was not going to turn it down. To be fair to Wilkins, his eagerness to help Brunel was probably not intended as an asset-stripping exercise. It is more likely that he viewed the railway as an agent which could transform the fortunes of his mills – and of Twerton.

There were two other obstacles to be faced before Brunel could bring the line through Twerton. First was the acquisition of land owned by the Kennet & Avon Canal Company, which had been bought for a canal from Bath to Bristol that was never built. They eventually agreed to sell it to him for £10,000 in June 1835. Second was the acquisition of the vicarage, through whose garden the line would run. This was owned by Oriel College, Oxford. "We have little doubt," wrote the college official entrusted with the matter, "that the bill will be carried, and we have declined joining the landowners who oppose it, or rather may oppose it if they receive money enough. We are trying whether we can prevail to have the railway carried not through the middle of the vicarage garden as at present proposed but at the lower part of the ground close to the path by the river. But I suspect we shall not succeed in this." They did not, and, in view of the proximity of the line to the vicarage, the company paid for a new vicarage to be built on land owned by Charles Wilkins.

FOUR
Parliament Approves

On 1 January 1835, the *Bath Chronicle* announced that

> an act will be applied for in the next session to construct the entire line between London and Bristol upon the disposal of 10,000 additional shares. Applications for shares may be addressed to … Messrs Mant and Bruce, Solicitors, 7 Northumberland Buildings, Bath.

Six weeks later, a correspondent wrote to the paper:

> If any doubt ever existed of the possibility of raising 10,000 additional shares for this great national undertaking, it must be entirely removed from the very spirited manner in which it has been supported in Gloucestershire and the West of England, Cheltenham alone having subscribed upward of 1,100 shares. This measure has been supported by the corporate bodies of Bristol and Gloucester; and by the principal merchants and bankers in those cities, and in the West of England. The apathy with which the inhabitants of Bath view the benefits to be derived by placing this elegant city within four hours and a half's distance from London is surprising, there being only 300 shares subscribed for, out of the 500 allotted to Bath. Surely if our rising rival, Cheltenham, thinks it worth while to support a railway, passing within 30 miles of the town, it must be more essential to Bath to do so, when the passengers from the railway will be taken up and put down within ten minutes' walk of the centre of the city.

Despite this apathy, three weeks later the *Chronicle* announced that, "the whole number of shares required by the company to sanction their application to Parliament has been subscribed for, and the bill for the new line of road was on Friday brought into the House of Commons by Lord Granville Somerset, and read a first time." On 19 March, the paper informed readers that "the bill for this grand undertaking is progressing successfully, and all but unopposed through the House of Commons ... Its success in Parliament [is] almost a matter of certainty."

In early June, the bill passed its second reading in the House of Lords by a majority of twelve, and passed into the committee stage. This was the opportunity for all manner of fatuous objections to be ranged against it. On 30 July, the *Bristol Mirror* reported that

> on Monday, Mr Serg. Mereweather opened the case on the part of the opposition, and occupied the whole day in a rambling and desultory speech; which, however, he did not conclude, but resumed and continued through Tuesday, promising to call witnesses on Wednesday. Mr Mereweather's speech continued to occupy the committee until Wednesday, when he concluded, it is supposed, from want of wind. Witnesses were then called, and the nature of their evidence was such as to satisfy every one that it was only a continuance of the game against time. One tried to prove that Eton, Windsor, and Windsor Castle would lose the Thames supply of water.

Two weeks later, it reported that

> the Great Western railway bill continues to occupy the attention of the committee of the House of Lords. Among the witnesses examined this week has been Dr Lardner, whose evidence was wanted for one purpose only, the very reverse of elucidation.

In late August, the preamble of the bill was passed by a majority of twelve, "notwithstanding the strong opposition that has been raised against it," and the committee adjourned for detailed consideration of its clauses.

Even now, the London & Southampton had not given up hope of building its branch from Basingstoke. Brunton finished surveying the line in February, and subscriptions were invited the following month. Sixty-five shares were snapped up in Bath, 80 in Trowbridge, 30 in

Staverton. Other towns were less enthusiastic. Frome, Bradford and Seend, for example, only managed five each, although Walter Long from South Wraxall put his name down for 50.

On 31 August 1835, however, the Great Western bill received royal assent, and the London & Southampton scheme for a branch to Bath was consigned to history.* The London & Southampton Railway, however, was to have a major, if somewhat indirect, impact on the future development of the Great Western. As railways had made the transition from horse-drawn mineral lines to steam-hauled inter-city routes, one thing nobody had seriously questioned was the distance between the rails – the gauge. Initially, there had been no standard measurement, with gauges varying between two and five feet. Gradually, as more ambitious projects got under way, and the same engineers were brought in to build them, one gauge – of four feet eight and half inches – became standard. By the early 1830s, when parliament authorized new lines, the bills generally stipulated that they should conform to this gauge. Brunel, as later became apparent, considered this gauge inadequate for high speed running; given all the other problems the Great Western had to face in getting their bill through parliament, he kept quiet about it. However, it did not escape his attention that, when the London & Southampton Railway was authorized, there was no mention of gauge in the bill. After the Great Western bill had passed the committee stage, with no further opportunity for objections to be raised, he pointed this omission out, and, claiming precedent, requested that the clause be dropped from the Great Western bill. This simple request, which was readily acceded to, was to have major consequences. A few weeks later, Brunel unveiled his plan for a broad-gauge railway to the Great Western directors. Although it would cost an extra £500 a mile to build, the investment would, he told them, be "amply repaid in the first few years of working." Dazzled, as so many were, by the force of his personality, they told him to go ahead and build it.

* *A similar line – the Bristol, London & Southern Counties Railway – was, however, promoted as late as 1902.*

FIVE

This Grand Undertaking

The parliamentary hurdle having been crossed, the Great Western Railway now had to be built. On 10 September 1835, the *Bath Chronicle* reported that "Mr Brunell [sic], the engineer, is now employed in making arrangements for the commencement of this grand undertaking. It is intended that the work shall proceed at both ends at once."

Fears that Bristol would miss out on the railway age, which had seemed so real a couple of years earlier, were forgotten as railway fever gripped the city and business confidence started to return. On 23 October, the *Bristol Journal* reported that, "another railway from this city to Exeter is announced, which will command immense traffic, as avoiding the dangerous and tedious navigation round the Land's End. It is also further contemplated to establish one between hence and Gloucester, eight or nine miles of which are already completed, so that in a short time Bristol will certainly have every chance of a revival of trade."

Some of the Great Western's directors started to get cold feet over the scale of the project, and its likely cost. When they voiced their concerns at a meeting that October, Brunel replied, "why not make it longer, and have a steamboat to go from Bristol to New York, and call it the *Great Western*?" Given Brunel's habit of playing his cards close to his chest, it was probably not a spur of the moment remark, but an idea he had cherished for some time, waiting for the right moment to announce it. Calculated or not, it was the signal for a new era in transatlantic travel. The *Great Western* steamship would, in fact, sail from Bristol to New York before the first train from London arrived in Bristol. Who but Brunel, as his directors squabbled about cost, with the railway still, as far as many were concerned, a dangerous novelty, would have conceived a plan for extending it to America? And who but Brunel could have achieved it?

As the preparations for building the line got under way, Bath's coaching inns were busier than ever, seemingly unaware that their death warrant had been signed. On 9 November, Lord John Russell, the Liberal leader, gave a speech at Bristol; the following evening the Friends of Reform gave a celebratory dinner at Todd's Riding School in Bath. Charles Dickens, then a political correspondent for the *Morning Chronicle* was sent to report on both events, with another correspondent called Thomas Beard.

On 8 November, Dickens wrote to his editor from the George & Pelican Inn at Newbury:

> We go down to Bristol today, and if we are equally fortunate in laying the chaise horses, I hope the packet will reach town by seven. As all the papers have arranged to leave Bristol the moment Russell is done, we have determined on adopting the same plan – one of us will go to Marlborough in the chaise with one *Herald* man, and the other remain at Bristol with the second *Herald* man to conclude the account for the next day. The *Times* has ordered a chaise and four the whole distance, so there is every probability of us beating them hollow.

As a result of these meticulous arrangements, the report of Russell's speech appeared in the following day's *Morning Chronicle*, beating the *Times* and providing a major coup for the young reporter.

Before leaving Bristol for Bath, Dickens wrote to his editor again, from the Bush Inn:

> The report of the Bath dinner shall be forwarded by the first Bath coach on Thursday morning – what time it starts we have no means of ascertaining till we reach Bath, but you will receive it as early as possible. ... Beard will go over from here tomorrow morning, and I shall come back by the mail from Marlborough. I need not say that it will be sharp work, and will require two of us; for we shall both be up the whole of the previous night, and shall have to sit up all night again to get it off in time. As soon as we have had a little sleep, we shall return to town as quickly as we can, for we have (if the express succeeds) to stop at two or three places along the road, to pay money and express satisfaction. You may imagine that we are extremely

> anxious to know the result of the arrangement. Pray direct to one of us at the White Hart, Bath, and inform us in a parcel sent by the first coach after you receive this exactly at what hour it arrived. Do not fail on any account.

On the night of the dinner, around 700 people gathered at Todd's Riding School in the Upper Bristol Road. Toasts were drunk to the King, the People and the Princess Victoria. "In giving this toast," reported the *Bath Chronicle*, "the chairman (William Hunt) dwelt on the peculiar interest which attached to it as proceeding from the Radical party, who had been the most prominent in shewing their attachment to the illustrious personage who was next in order of succession and in opposing the traitorous machinations of the Tory party, evinced in the secret machinations of the Orange Club." According to some of the Radicals, these treacherous machinations included a clumsy attempt to tarnish their reputations later that same evening, when "some loathsomely brutal rascals amused themselves with barking and cutting and tearing down many of the young trees in the Royal Victoria Park." The Radicals accused the Tories of doing it in order to discredit them. It is a story worthy of Dickens, but, unfortunately, one he seems never to have used.

Dickens' confidence that he would be staying at the White Hart proved short-lived. Perhaps there was a mix-up in the bookings; perhaps he simply assumed there would be room for one of the country's most promising political journalists. Whatever the case, when he got there, he found no room at the inn – hardly surprising, with 700 Liberal supporters in town for a celebratory dinner. It was the same everywhere he tried, until he was advised to try the Saracen's Head in Broad Street. The White Hart was one of Bath's most fashionable inns; the Saracen's Head was the haunt of ostlers, grooms and tradesmen. Even here, there was, as the landlady later recalled, "no room in the house proper, and he had to be sent across the yard to sleep above the outbuildings. At night the young man took his candle and walked across the yard, but just as he came to the outside of the room his light was blown out. He went back to the bar, relit his candle and just as he got to the steps again out went the candle." This he repeated several times, but, said the landlady, "the young gentleman never said a single swear."

It is hardly surprising that, when he wrote *The Pickwick Papers* a few months later, his depiction of Bath and of the White Hart was a savage indictment of snobbery with violence. He even took the name of the innkeeper of the White Hart – Moses Pickwick – for the principal character in the book. Despite this personal vendetta, *The Pickwick Papers* provides the most memorable description of Bath at the height of the coaching age, an age that was almost over. It also made its author one of the most celebrated authors in the country. When he returned to Bath many years later, to give a reading at the Assembly Rooms, he stayed at the best hotel in town – the York House. But he never forgot his first night in the city, over the outbuildings at the Saracen's Head, and he never forgave Bath for its treatment of him.

As 1835 drew to a close, Charles Dickens was not the only young man poised on the brink of a glittering career. On the day after Christmas, Brunel sat at his desk in his London office and confided his thoughts to his journal. The private diaries of great men often seem written with one eye on posterity, but rarely so blatantly as in this post-Christmas celebration of good fortune:

> *Saturday night. What a blank in my journal! And during the most eventful part of my life. When last I wrote in this book I was just emerging from obscurity. I had been toiling most unprofitably at numerous things – unprofitably at least at the moment. The railway certainly was brightening but still very uncertain.*
>
> *What a change – the railway now is in progress. I am their engineer to the finest work in England – a handsome salary – £2,000 a year – on excellent terms with my directors and all going smoothly, but what a fight we have had – and how near defeat – and what a ruinous defeat it would have been – it is like looking back upon a fearful pass – but we have succeeded – and it's not this alone but everything I have been engaged in has been successful:*
>
> *Clifton Bridge –*
> *My first child, my darling, is actually going on – recommenced work last Monday – glorious!!*

Sunderland –
Docks too going on well.

Bristol Docks –
All Bristol is alive and turned bold and speculative with this railway – we are to widen the entrances – and the Lord knows what.

Merthyr & Cardiff Railway –
This too I owe to the Great Western Railway. I care not however about it.

Cheltenham Railway –
Of course, this I owe to the Great Western – I may say myself – Do not feel much interested in this. None of the parties are my friends. I hold it only because they can't do without me – it's an awkward line and the estimate too low – however, it's all in the way of business and a proud thing to monopolise all the west as I do. I must keep it as long as I can but I want tools.

Bristol & Exeter Railway –
another too!! This survey was done in grand style – it's a good line too – and I feel an interest as connected with Bristol to which I really owe much – they have stuck well to me, I think we shall carry this bill – I shall become quite an oracle in committees of the house. Gravatt served me well in this B&E survey.

Newbury branch –
a little go almost beneath my notice now – it will do as a branch.

Suspension Bridge across Thames –
I have condescended to be engineer to this – but shan't give myself much trouble about it – if done however it all adds to my stock of irons.

I think this forms a pretty list of real profitable, sound and professional jobs – unsought for on my part that is given to me fairly by the respective parties – all … resulting from the Clifton

Bridge – which I fought hard for and gained only by persevering struggles and wise manoeuvres (all fair and honest, however). Voyons.

I forgot also Bristol & Gloster Railway:

After enumerating the capital tied up in each project and calculating the total as £5,320,000, Brunel continued:

A pretty considerable capital to pass through my hands – and this at the age of 29 – faith, not so young as I always fancy, tho' I can hardly believe it when I think of it, and then to amuse myself I am director of the Gt West [sic] American Steam Ship Company. The [Thames] Tunnel is going on as well.

I am just leaving 53 Parliament Street where I may say I have made my fortune or rather the foundation of it and have taken Lord Devon's house, No 18 Duke Street – a fine house – I have a fine travelling carriage – I go sometimes with my four horses. I have a cab and a horse. I have a secretary. In fact I am now somebody – everything has prospered, everything at the moment is sunshine – I don't like it – it can't last – bad weather must surely come – let me see the storm in time to gather in my sails. Mrs B – I foresee one thing – this time 12 months I shall be a married man – how will that be? How will that be? Will it make me happier – at any rate I shall not be [...]

SIX

The Digging Starts

In March 1836, the *Bath Chronicle* announced that, "in various parts of the line of road, preparations are making for the execution [of the Great Western Railway], particularly between Bath and Bristol."

On 8 March, Brunel visited Saltford. He wanted to build a tunnel under Saltford House, which was owned by Lieutenant Colonel William James, an opponent of the railway who was determined, if forced to sell his house, to get an exorbitant price for it. While looking around, Brunel worked out that he could reroute the line under the house next door. He negotiated with the owner and made him an offer of £700 for the house and land, which was accepted on the spot. In the event, the house did not need to be demolished when the tunnel was built, and it acquired the name Tunnel House, which it still bears today, along with the legend that Brunel once lived there. A tragic postscript to the story of this house is that a later owner, Lewis Wright, a writer and scholar, was killed while crossing the line at Saltford station on 15 December 1905.

On 7 April, the *Bath Chronicle* reported that

> the commencement of the works at the Bristol end of the line took place on Monday 21 March by William Roger, under the superintendence of Mr Parr, Agent, accompanied by several gentlemen from Bristol. We are happy to state that the works are now going on with the greatest spirit, there being at present 200 men employed, in addition to these 150 miners are now advertised for.

Two months later, just after work had started at Keynsham, "the workmen had to break up part of the old burying ground of the Abbey; they here found several bones in preservation, much more

Saltford Tunnel from the east, with Tunnel House above it and Saltford House on the right.

perfect than could be expected." On a stone in the wall of the Brass Mills at Saltford, an unknown hand chiselled an inscription:

BEGUN DIGGING THE RAIL ROAD JUNE 11 1836

On 18 June, Brunel sent his directors a progress report:

> *Contracts Nos 1, 2 & 3B extending further, canal feeder at Bristol to the Cross Post Gate Turnpike near Bath have been let and the works are now in progress of execution & the whole of this extent will according to the terms of the contracts be completed by the middle of February 1838 by which time the other parts of the line between Bristol & Bath may easily be finished without requiring the same degree of exertions which will be necessary to expedite the work upon these three contracts.*
> *No 1B which includes the greatest portion of tunnelling and generally the heaviest work which occurs between Bristol and Bath & extending from the feeder to the east end of a wood on the bank*

of the river commonly called Dr Fox's Wood, a distance of about two miles and three-quarters has been contracted for by Mr Ranger, the notice to commence the works was given on the 21st March last and from that day the works have proceeded with activity – the time allowed in the contract for the entire completion of the works will require 21st January 1838. The commencement of this contract involves much experience and laborious work without producing a corresponding apparent result, a great quantity of the best materials derived from the excavation have to be carried through the tunnels to the works at the other extremity of the line, and consequently the forming a heading or driftway through the line of these tunnels is the first and most important operation – and the period for opening these headings was limited on the contract under a heavy penalty ... In the Tunnel No 1 (the first from Bristol) two temporary shafts have been sunk so that the headings can be carried on at six places at once – one from each end and two from each shaft. In Tunnel No 2, one shaft has been sunk which gives four faces for the heading. In Tunnel No 3, which is the longest between Bath and Bristol, being upwards of half a mile, three permanent shafts have been sunk and two temporary ones, so that the headings can be worked at twelve different faces. At eight of these they are in active operation and the remaining four will be very shortly, the two shafts from which they will be worked being within a few feet of the required depths. At these headings the work has been carried on day and night, but I do not expect that they will be completed within the time fixed by the contract which for the tunnels Nos 1 & 2 expires on the 21st of next month. Time has been lost in this and in other parts of the work by the injudicious arrangements of the contractor's foreman. At my request he has been dismissed and the work has since proceeded more expeditiously and with greater advantage to the contractor himself as well as to the company. As I before observed, until these headings are completed, the progress of the work will not be very apparent. The cutting and the embankment at the west end of Tunnel No 1 is however proceeding with about 200 feet of the embankment being formed. A five foot culvert in this embankment has been finished and the foundations of an accommodation bridge in the meadows are in

progress, and the bridge itself will be completed as soon as a larger supply of stone can be brought from the quarry.
Preparations are making for commencing the bridge across the Avon. The excavation for the foundations is proceeding with, and they have begun driving the piles of the coffer dam. The contractor has obtained leave to form a temporary road along the banks of the river from above Netham down to the site of this bridge and has laid temporary rails for the carriage of the stone which is quarried in Dr Fox's Wood brought by the river to Netham Dam.
In the Nightingale Valley the contractor has established his principal workshop for the repair of wagons and tools.
In Conham Wood or Brickwood between Tunnels 2 & 3 nothing material can be done until the headings are complete.
In Dr Fox's Wood the embankment is proceeding, the excavation at each end consists of very hard sandstone. From this part it was always expected that we should obtain excellent materials for the construction of the Avon Bridge and the masonry generally, and we have no cause to be disappointed. At the west end particularly a quarry of very fine stone has been opened and is now working and an ample supply of good stone for the smaller work may be selected from the excavation at the eastern end.
Upon the whole, I consider that the works in No 1B are now proceeding satisfactorily. The contractor I think appears desirous of doing his work properly and with the exception of the inefficiency of the superintendent whom he has discharged I have no cause of complaint.
No 2B is contracted for by the same party as No 1B and the notice for commencement was dated 18th May and the whole is to be completed by 18th January 1838. This contract extends from the termination of No 1B to a short distance beyond the Keynsham Brass Mills – a length of about two miles and three furlongs. The principal works upon it are a deep cutting through the hill upon which Lodge Farm is situated and the embankment across the Keynsham Hams – the principal piece of masonry will be the bridge across the Chew and probably a short tunnel through a portion of the cutting which is expected to be of very loose material. The cuttings and embankments are commenced at each point upon

the line. The drains and temporary fencing are completed across the Keynsham Meads, the foundations for the Chew Bridge are being excavated and the work generally is proceeding satisfactorily, but there is nothing peculiarly worthy of remark.
No 3B, which extends from the termination of 2B to the turnpike road near the Cross Post Gate, a distance of about three miles, has been contracted for by Mr McIntosh. Some delay has taken place in commencing this contract in consequence of the refusal of Colonel Gore Langton or rather his agent Mr Brown to consent to a deviation from the parliamentary plan which I found it would be desirable to make and which I had reported he could not object to. Another small deviation which does not affect the line at the point where the works must be commenced has been since assented to by Colonel Langton.
The notice to the contractor dates from Wednesday next the 15th and the period for the completion will expire February 1838.
*The principal works upon this line consists of a long cutting through lias limestone, in the middle of which cutting occurs a short tunnel or covered way under the road at Saltford, and a rather heavy embankment across the Corston and Newton meadows – there is … of masonry upon this portion of the line worth mentioning … the contractor has taken possession of the necessary … ground and actually commenced work but of course I cannot as yet report any progress.**
When these contracts may be considered as securing the time of completion of the line between Bristol and Bath, the rest of the work may be commenced comparatively at our leisure. The necessary steps are taking however to get the whole of the line up to the depot at Bath ready to be contracted for in the course of the next month ….

I am, gentlemen, your most obedient servant,
IK Brunel

* *The lacunae in this paragraph are due to part of the manuscript having been torn off.*

One thing Brunel did not mention was a tragedy that had occurred near the line a few days earlier, when

> a poor woman named Sarah Cross, in the last stage of pregnancy, whose husband is employed on the Great Western Railway works, fell into the river at Crew's Hole, while dipping water, and was drowned. It appears that her struggles were for some time observed by some of the railway men, but they, supposing it to be a dog in the water, from seeing her long black hair in motion on the surface, rendered no assistance. The melancholy fact was established by her mother who having gone to her daughter's cottage, and finding her absent, proceeded to the dipping place, intending to help her home with the water, when she saw the bucket floating and suspected what had occurred. She instantly obtained assistance, and the body was soon taken up, but all means to restore animation failed.

SEVEN

Onward to America

By now, railway mania had taken hold of the nation. Joint stock companies were floated and the value of shares soared as a plethora of competing proposals was laid before an eager public. In February 1836, plans were announced for a line from Bath to Weymouth. By the end of June, the *Bath Chronicle* reported that "the survey of the lines of railway intended to be made by [the Bath and Weymouth Railway Company] has been for some time in progress and the results are highly satisfactory." By November, the company was ready to apply to parliament for authorization to build the line.

Opponents of the scheme were galvanizing themselves for action, however. In February 1837, a meeting of "landowners of Somerset" at the White Hart in Stall Street expressed

> its most unqualified disapprobation of the scheme, as involving a needless, wanton and uncalled-for invasion of private property, and an irreparable injury to many individuals, against the consent of nearly the whole of the large landed proprietors on the proposed line. The proposed railway is not required, or in the remotest degree necessary for any purposes of commercial or agricultural utility, as there are very few manufactories on the line, the country generally thin of population, and the whole of the travelling at present scarcely supporting one daily stage coach between Bath and Weymouth. There is at present a canal and railroad from the Somerset collieries to Bradford and other places laid down on the proposed plan, quite sufficient for the conveyance of coal, and by which coal is now carried at a less expense than the promoters of the present measure contemplate by their prospectus to carry it.

Although the bill was submitted to parliament, receiving its first reading in March 1837, it soon became clear that, in the face of such opposition, the company would not be able to attract enough support to proceed with the line. In May, the company called a meeting at the White Lion to announce the winding-up of the project. Captain Scobell, one of the directors said, "that though he now looked upon this undertaking as dead and gone, he thought that its merits had been underrated."

Other projects foundered on the rocks of indifference. In March 1837, for example, "the branch railway by which it was proposed to connect the town of Devizes with the line of the Great Western Railroad [was] relinquished in consequence of the feeble support given to the subject by the inhabitants of Devizes."

Meanwhile, on the Great Western, work continued. In June 1837, the *Bath Chronicle* announced that, "the greatest exertions are making by the Great Western Railway Company, and both officers and men are labouring day and night. No doubt whatever seems to be entertained but that it will be opened as far as Maidenhead by October. We understand that every part of the work is exceedingly well done."

In November 1837, workmen were digging a cutting near the Cross Post Turnpike west of Twerton when they discovered a tessellated pavement. Unfortunately, it was largely destroyed before they realized what they were digging though. The contractor made arrangements for the mosaic to be removed, and it later found a home in the waiting room at Keynsham station.

Brunel's off-the-cuff remark in October 1835 about extending the Great Western to America by building a transatlantic steamship bore fruit sooner than anyone expected. The *Great Western* was ready for her maiden voyage from Bristol to New York early in 1838. On 31 March, Brunel was accompanying her from the Thames to Bristol when a fire broke out in the engine room. It had been blazing for some time, despite copious amounts of water being thrown at it, when Brunel, hearing what had happened, rushed to the scene and attempted to go down to the engine room, using a wooden ladder with charred rungs. It gave way and he fell about 20 feet, knocking himself out and landing face down in several inches of water. Although he was rescued, he was badly shaken up. Over two months after the accident,

GREAT WESTERN RAILWAY.

'THE BEAUFORT.'
THIS NEW AND SPLENDID CONVEYANCE TO
LONDON!!
THROUGH Chippenham, Calne, Marlborough, Newbury, and Reading; and, by the Five o'Clock Train, from the
GREAT WESTERN RAILWAY STATION AT MAIDENHEAD;
LEAVES THE
LION HOTEL, BATH,
EVERY MORNING AT A QUARTER BEFORE EIGHT.
The BEAUFORT, on its arrival at the Great Western Railway Station, Maidenhead, proceeds, without the removal of Passengers' Luggage, to the terminus at Paddington, and from thence, through Oxford Street, to the BULL and MOUTH, Western Office, 40, Regent Circus; and BULL and MOUTH, St. Martin's-le-Grand, opposite the New General Post Office.
☞ *Superior four-inside Coaches to London, by the* OLD ROUTE, *in Eleven Hours.*
REGULATOR, Mornings, at Half-past Eight.—ROYAL MAIL, Evenings, at Half-past Seven, at Coach Fares.
W. LANE and CO., Proprietors.

An advertisement from July 1838.

he confided to Thomas Guppy that, "I am not particularly well in mind or body … I am still lame in the left foot and my back is weak. I don't write this letter without leaning back to rest and in consequence, I suppose, of the state of my stomach I am nervous, anxious and unhappy … An infinite number of things crowding in upon me, requiring attention and thought – all in arrears and I am quite incapable of getting through them."

The *Great Western* recovered from the fire more quickly than Brunel, setting sail for New York in early April, and taking 15 days for the journey. The first section of the Great Western Railway, from Paddington to Maidenhead, opened on 4 June. Despite being only 24 miles long, Bath's coach proprietors were quick to take advantage of the new line. London coaches travelled by road to Maidenhead, where they were loaded onto a truck and taken forward to Paddington by train, before completing their journey by road.

Less than a month after the grand opening of the Great Western, Victoria was crowned Queen. Bath celebrated in grand style. The streets of the city were lit by gas illuminations, turning night into day. An eighteen-gun salute was fired to mark the occasion, a gesture marred only by the bursting of one of the cannons, which seriously injured a nineteen-year-old employee at Stothert's works. The Victorian Age was born.

EIGHT

The People's Charter

The Victorian Age is often seen as one of unbridled progress, when so-called "Victorian values" were the order of the day, and a proper deference prevailed. While there certainly was progress, it was against a background of widespread social unrest. In the early years of Victoria's reign, Britain came to the brink of revolution, and Bath was at the epicentre of discontent. Its causes were multifarious, but its focus was, as it had been when Brunel had enlisted as a special constable in Bristol seven years earlier, lack of parliamentary representation. When the Reform Act was passed in 1832, it only extended the franchise to the middle-classes. In May 1838, a new People's Charter was drawn up, calling for "universal suffrage, no property qualification, annual parliaments, equal representation, payment of MPs, and vote by ballot." It was the rallying flag for a movement that was to shake the country to its foundations. Taking its name from the Charter, it was known as Chartism.

The publication of the Charter coincided with the start of a major recession. Elizabeth Gaskell later described its effects:

> For three years past, trade had been getting worse and worse, and the price of provisions higher and higher. This disparity between the amount of the earnings of the working classes, and the price of their food, occasioned in more cases than could well be imagined, disease and death. Whole families went through a gradual starvation. They only wanted a Dante to record their sufferings. And yet even his words would fall short of the awful truth; they could only present an outline of the tremendous facts of the destitution that surrounded thousands upon thousands in the terrible years 1839, 1840 and 1841 ... It need excite no surprise then to learn that a bad feeling between working men and the upper classes became very strong in this season

> of privation. The indigence and sufferings of the operatives induced a suspicion in the minds of many of them, that their legislators, their magistrates, their employers, and even the ministers of religion, were, in general, their oppressors and enemies; and were in league for their prostration and enthralment. The most deplorable and enduring evil that arose out of the period of commercial depression to which I refer, was this feeling of alienation between the different classes of society.

It was in this climate that Chartism, which started out as an essentially middle-class movement campaigning for parliamentary reform, was transformed into a mass movement with more generalised grievances. One historian – Élie Halévy – has gone so far as to assert that Chartism was not a creed but the "blind revolt of hunger." Nowhere was that hunger more keenly felt than in the weaving districts of the West Country, and particularly in Wiltshire. Bath, with strong middle-class support for the Charter, was only a few miles away. It was a potent combination, and with the charismatic Chartist leader, Henry Vincent, choosing Bath as one of his main stamping grounds, it is not surprising that the city featured so largely in the campaign. As one historian of the movement has written, "without Bath the Chartists of Wiltshire would have been poorly led; without Wiltshire the Chartists of Bath would have lacked the exhilaration of a mission field."

The first Chartist meeting in Bath was held at Combe Down on August 1838. A month later, Henry Vincent, addressed a meeting in the Orange Grove. The ultra-Conservative *Bath Chronicle* described this "gathering of rabble" as "a contemptible concern." The *Bath Figaro*, on the other hand, a subversive publication which folded when its editor was imprisoned for libel, recorded that the crowd was several thousand strong. A few days later, the *Figaro* reported a "great meeting of the working classes in Widcombe Fields," near Combe Down. The demonstration started in Ham Gardens, where Manvers Street and the railway station would soon be built. The crowd "filled up all the intermediate space as far as the Orange Grove," before marching in procession to Widcombe Fields, which they reached at three o'clock. This time about 20,000 people attended.

Demonstrations and meetings continued throughout the winter. Vincent established a newspaper in Bristol, called the *Western Vindicator*, to further the cause. On 5 March 1839, he

> rode over to Bath – the weather intensely cold. Found a meeting of the people was called for the Orange Grove in the evening … Although the night was cold several thousands of people assembled, amongst whom was a considerable number of ladies … I asked the meeting if they would stand firm by the Charter – and their loud YES shook the Abbey to its centre.

The *Bath Chronicle*, not surprisingly, regarded such demonstrations with disdain. On 28 March 1839, it reported that

> an attempt was made to hold a Chartist meeting in the Market Place, Devizes, on Friday last. A number of the good folks, however, of that town, not relishing the presence of the "physical force" vagabonds, got together and dispersed them.

A week later, "a party of Chartists visited Radstock, and, after having harangued the colliers in a most violent manner for a short time, disgusted with what they had heard, they drove them from the place."

A few days later,

> the Chartists held a second meeting [at Devizes]. There were present about 1,500, who came chiefly from Bradford, Trowbridge, Holt, Bromham, etc. Mr Vincent and Mr Roberts of Bath were the great men on the occasion. The speeches no sooner commenced than they were drowned by hootings, hissings, groanings and performances on cows' horns and other extempore instruments, which storm of disapprobation was raised by sundry inhabitants of Devizes and its neighbourhood …
>
> The Chartists then made an attack on the dissentients, which was the signal for a general rout of the former. The wagon on which the orators were perched was broken into a thousand pieces, and the whole party were put to most ignominious flight.

The affair at Devizes, which the *Chronicle* reported as though it was an episode from *The Pickwick Papers*, was in actual fact a serious attempt by a gang of armed ruffians, aided and abetted by certain elements of the Tory establishment, to inflict serious injury on the Chartist leaders, and anyone else foolhardy enough to get in the way. Had not the High Sheriff intervened to read the Riot Act, and the means been effected for the Chartist leaders to escape, it is unlikely that Vincent and his colleagues would have escaped with their lives. "If it had not been," Vincent later wrote, " for the very laudable and Christian conduct of a few of the Tories, myself and Roberts would have been killed."

Vincent returned to lick his wounds in Bath. The following evening,

> at seven o'clock an immense concourse of people assembled in the Abbey Green, to congratulate Roberts and myself on our escape. We went to the meeting, and were received with tremendous cheering.

Less than a week later, on 8 April, Vincent

> went to the Orange Grove at seven o'clock in the evening and found it swarming with people ... On entering the Grove I was loudly cheered. My friend Roberts was there with his gig. I mounted and briefly addressed the people, telling them to fall into procession, and walk through the city in an orderly manner – our place of destination was Twerton, a thickly populated place about one mile from Bath, the good people of which had convened a meeting to enable me to address them. On the road to Twerton, myself and Roberts were received with every demonstration of enthusiasm. The meeting was a very numerous one, there being from eight to ten thousand people present ... We addressed the meeting from the window of Mr Blackford, a regular straightforward, honest and determined Radical ... The greatest enthusiasm prevailed. We returned to Bath in procession and dispersed the people in the Grove at eleven o'clock.

The following evening, Vincent "walked to Batheaston with about 500 friends," to address a meeting composed of "about a thousand labouring men ... and a few of the tradesmen and farmers."

The next day, he "walked to Combe Down in the evening, in company with several Bath friends":

> We found about a thousand working men assembled. Roberts addressed them at great length ... I followed him ... The night was very cold, but the sturdy Chartists did not mind the cold, their hearts were warm with indignation against their country's oppressors.

A rally scheduled for Radstock the following day was called off after the Wells, Frome and Stoneaston troops of the North Somerset Yeomanry were deployed in the town.

In late April, trouble flared in Trowbridge after four women who had escaped from the workhouse at Avoncliff were arrested there. The *Bath Chronicle* described what happened next:

> As soon as the circumstance became known, a large number of women belonging to the Chartist associations assembled together and attempted a rescue; but the constables succeeded in taking the women to Devizes prison, together with a man who had struck the constables in the course of the affray. During the affray men and women paraded the streets with loaves of bread mounted on poles; some of them had firearms. Indeed the whole of the working classes appeared in the greatest excitement. The town is in a sad, demoralized state; and no wonder, when the very children are taught to treat with disrespect all who are in authority.

Two weeks later, the *Chronicle* reported that

> the Chartists are still very turbulent at Trowbridge. Scarcely any workpeople in the factories but contribute, some secretly but most openly, to the Chartists' Association. They have infected Holt, Bradley, Steeple Ashton, etc., and all the surrounding villages; and no person with a decent coat on his back can be seen without being hooted and insulted. The special constables are afraid to act, and the trade of the town is seriously injured. The children are paraded about with banners bearing mottoes: "Liberty or Death!" "We Want Justice!" "We will have our Right!" The children of the British School joined the procession in a body. They also the other day

> locked out the master and showed every mark of total insubordination. The chapels are very much thinned on Sundays, so are the Sunday schools; and the people instead attend Carrier's lectures and read Vincent's newspaper.

In the same issue, the *Chronicle* gave its readers a taste of Vincent's rhetoric:

> In a republican periodical, called the *Western Vindicator*, published at Bristol under the management of Vincent, the following paragraph appears: 'The Convention will soon issue its manifesto to the people. Then will begin the struggle – a struggle which will not, must not, cannot cease, until the people possess the whole of their rights, and all unequal privileges are destroyed. Let the meeting which is to be held in the vicinity of Bath on Whit Monday be a splendid and numerous display of the people's strength. Let every town and village within 15 miles send thousand of persons to attend it. Be cool, but yet determined in your proceedings. Deputations will attend from the National Convention. We have a full conviction that the meeting will be a proud display of the moral and physical power of the people."

This call to arms brought a robust response from the establishment. The following week's *Chronicle* described the measures taken to prevent a breakdown of order:

> On Monday, the city was the scene of much activity and preparation, in consequence of its have been publicly announced that on that day there would be a Grand Demonstration of Public Opinion in Favour of the People's Charter ... Notices were issued in the course of last week, expressing the determination of the magistrates to suppress all unlawful and riotous assemblages, and calling upon the inhabitants to attend at the Guildhall and enrol themselves as willing to act, when called upon, in the capacity of special constables ... In pursuance of instructions from Government, the Chelsea pensioners were also enrolled. On Monday morning there was an almost total cessation of business in the city, the persons who were to act as special constables having received summonses to attend at the

GUILDHALL, BATH.

MAY 9th, 1839.

WHEREAS Meetings have been held in the Neighbourhood of Bath, and in other parts of the country calculated to endanger the Public Peace ;—the well-disposed Inhabitants of this City, without distinction of Class, are invited by the Mayor and Magistrates to attend at the Guildhall, and Register their names and Addresses, as an expression of their readiness to serve in the capacity of SPECIAL CONSTABLES, when legally called upon so to do.

HENRY GORDON, Mayor.

GUILDHALL, BATH.

9th MAY, 1839.

THE MAYOR and MAGISTRATES of the City and Borough of BATH, in obedience to Her Majesty's several Proclamations, and with a view to preserve to all Classes of the Community the blessings of tranquillity and the equal administration of the Laws, HEREBY GIVE NOTICE, that they are firmly resolved to maintain the Public Peace, and suppress all RIOTS, MEETINGS for DRILLING, and other UNLAWFUL ASSEMBLIES, and to bring to justice all Persons guilty of exciting to acts of violence or intimidation, on any pretext whatsoever ; and they earnestly exhort the well disposed Inhabitants to refrain from attending Meetings of an illegal or questionable character, or otherwise lending their countenance to the enemies of the public peace.

HENRY GORDON, Mayor.

Preparing for trouble: from the Bath Chronicle of 16 May 1839.

> Guildhall to be sworn. These preliminaries having been arranged, the pensioners were stationed in the New Vegetable Market … and the other special constables were marshalled in sections in the large Banqueting Room at the Guildhall … The North Somerset Yeomanry were stationed in St James's Square, where the officers received the most polite attention from the inhabitants … A troop of the 10th Hussars marched into the city from Frome … The police force, which had been considerably augmented and armed with cutlasses, was kept in readiness at the police station … It had been announced that the Chartists intended to meet, for the purposes of forming a procession, on the North Parade, but they did not appear there, neither was their place of meeting known … About one o'clock a rumour began to spread that they had taken a field at Midford. The High Constables of the Hundred immediately rode thither to ascertain the precise spot, when they found that it was just beyond their jurisdiction, being within the county of Wiltshire. The place of meeting was marked by a banner mounted on a tree, bearing the inscription, "Peace, Law and Order" … When the demonstrators arrived on the ground at 3pm, they were found to consist of only a few hundreds, and the majority of these women and boys … Mr Neesome, a delegate from Bristol, addressed the meeting: "The day of oppression is nearly at an end. The cause we advocate is just and lawful. The people of England are determined to have their rights peaceably if they can, but otherwise if not ... Let every man who feels with me that he ought to have a voice in the making of the laws which he has to obey, and that he must therefore have universal suffrage or death, hold up his hand."

The meeting passed off without incident, although in other parts of the country, Chartists were now starting to resort to those non-peaceful means Neesome had alluded to. In Birmingham, there was a major riot in the Bull Ring, while in Newcastle around 6,000 Chartists, many of them armed, clashed with troops and special constables. Commenting on the deteriorating situation, the *Bath Chronicle* declared that it was "lamentable to reflect that there exists among the working classes of this country so large a mass of mental darkness as that which must be relied on by the knaves and rogues who form the moving power of the Chartist agitation." Charles

Dickens drew a chilling, apocalyptic picture of a night-time visit to the Black Country at the height of the Chartist disturbances:

> Night, when the smoke was changed to fire; when every chimney spirited up its flame; and places, that had been dark vaults all day, now shone red-hot, with figures moving to and fro within their blazing jaws, and calling to one another with hoarse cries – night, when the noise of every strange machine was aggravated by the darkness; when the people near them looked wilder and more savage; when bands of unemployed labourers paraded the roads, or clustered by torchlight round their leaders, who told them, in stern language, of their wrongs, and urged them on to frightful cries and threats; when maddened men, armed with sword and firebrand, spurning the tears and prayers of women who would restrain them, rushed forth on errands of terror and destruction, to work no ruin half so surely as their own – night, when carts came rumbling by, filled with rude coffins (for contagious disease and death had been busy with the living crops); when orphans cried, and distracted women shrieked and followed in their wake – night, when some called for bread, and some for drink to drown their cares, and some with tears, and some with staggering feet , and some with bloodshot eyes, went brooding home – night, which unlike the night that heaven sends on earth, brought with it no peace, nor quiet, nor signs of blessed sleep ...

In an attempt to stem the rising tide of unrest, the authorities sentenced large numbers of Chartists to imprisonment or transportation. Among them was Henry Vincent, who, in August, was given a twelve months' sentence for making inflammatory speeches and sent to Monmouth Gaol. This policy of containment seems to have worked for a time; on 17 October 1839, the *Bath Chronicle* expressed the smug – and somewhat premature – conviction that, "the Chartist agitation seems to have well nigh passed away."

Vincent's incarceration was the catalyst for the most celebrated Chartist rising of all, when hundreds of men marched on Newport one damp and dismal November night to demand his release. In reality, it was hardly worthy the name of rising; it was more of a shambolic rout, which ended, in the chill light of dawn, with 20 men dead on the streets of Newport. Nevertheless, it remains one of the defining moments of working-class history, and the suspicion can never totally be dispelled that, if the men of the Monmouthshire valleys had been more disciplined, better organized – if an inspired leader had arisen among them – the Newport Rising could have been the spark that ignited the tinder of resentment across the nation, with who knows what consequences. And, if Vincent, instead of being locked up in Monmouth, had been sent to Devizes or Shepton Mallet, who can say whether, instead of Newport, that catastrophic demonstration could have happened in Bath.

In the wake of the Newport Rising, there were more arrests across the country. Anthony Phillips and Charles Bolwell, Bath's Chartist leaders, were arrested at their meeting room in Monmouth Street. The country was in a state of high tension. At Radstock, nine men and three boys were killed at Wellsway Pit when the rope holding the cage which was taking them down a 750-foot shaft was cut through. No motive or culprit was ever identified. A few months later, the Queen and Prince Albert were shot at point-blank range as they left Buckingham Palace; fortunately for them, the would-be assassin was an appalling shot and they were unharmed.

Chartist meetings continued, though never on anything like the same scale as in the heady days of 1839. In January 1841, a rally planned for the Orange Grove was called off after the magistrates put up handbills declaring it illegal. After his release from prison, Vincent continued to make occasional return visits to the Bath area. In September 1841, he headed a torchlight procession through the streets of Bradford on Avon, although this time the crowd was numbered in hundreds rather than thousands. There were brief moments of excitement, such as one February evening in 1842, when an effigy of Sir Robert Peel, the Prime Minister, was paraded through the streets of Bath before being carried up to Beacon Hill and burnt. Chartists took part in the demonstration, but it was primarily a protest against the Corn Laws rather than attempt to further the cause of the People's Charter. On that chill November morning on the streets of Newport, the nation had come closer to revolution than it had done since the Gordon Riots of 60 years earlier, and it had drawn back in trepidation. The Chartists' demands did not go away, but their pursuit of them would never again shake the nation to its very foundations.

NINE

Navigators

Chartist demonstrations were not the only thing worrying the forces of law and order in the late 1830s. Whether or not railways were a civilising force was open to debate; the navvies who built them, however, were viewed with almost universal alarm. Navvies, or navigators, were nothing new; as Kellow Chesney points out in his study of the Victorian Underworld,

> for many years villages near canal workings had seen young men go off with the navigator gangs, as lost to home and friends as those who took the King's shilling. Over the years there had grown up a caste of specialised nomad labourers with their own habits and traditions; and although the railway boom vastly increased their numbers and spread them to every region of the country, it did not destroy … their sense of being a race apart.

There is no evidence that navvies were prominent Chartist supporters. Much of the unrest that characterised the Chartist movement was inspired by penury; the navvies were, by the standards of the time, far from penurious. As far as the establishment was concerned, however, they were, to all intents and purposes, outlaws, wandering the country, settling for a time where there was work, moving on when there wasn't, living by their own laws, observing their own standards, and owing nothing to anyone. Shanty towns were set up next to the course the line would take; fighting, whoring and hard drinking were endemic.

When Brunel's railway was being built, parts of Bath would have resembled the Wild West rather than the Queen of the West. When John Francis wrote an account of the social impact of the railways a few years later, he described a typical shanty town:

> Some slept in huts constructed of damp turf, cut from the wet grass, too low to stand upright in, while small sticks covered with straw served as rafters ... Others formed a roof of stones without mortar, placed thatch or flags across the roof, and took possession of it with their families, often making it a source of profit by lodging as many of their fellow workmen as they could crowd into it ... In these huts they lived; with man, woman and child mixing in promiscuous guilt; with no possible separation of the sexes ...Living like brutes, they were depraved, degraded and reckless. Drunkenness and dissolution of morals prevailed. There were many women but few wives; loathsome forms of disease were universal.

In November 1839, the *Bath Chronicle* published a pen picture of the typical navvy:

> The navigator appears to belong to no country, he wanders from one public work to another – now alone, then with a party of two or three; as long as he has sixpence in his pocket seems content, but sets so little value on the earnings of his slavish employment as never to be at ease unless in squandering them, although well paid for his labour. Go where he will, he finds some of his comrades whom he has met in some part of England before, and makes enquiries as to their mode of living, the wages they were paid since they last met, etc. His attire is peculiar. On his head he wears a kind of white felt hat, the brim of which is turned up all round, and generally a tobacco pipe is stuck in the band, which is of some glaring colour; a velveteen shooting jacket with white buttons, and scarlet plush waistcoat of large dimensions, with little black spots on it, sometimes a bright coloured neckerchief round his neck, and sometimes nothing at all; inexpressibles [breeches] of corduroy retained in position by a leather strap round the waist, and tied and buttoned at the knee; sometimes white stockings or grey worsted encircling most robust knees and high-laced boots of strong build complete his dress. His dicky or small smock frock is slung, when he travels, at his back ... In this he carries what else he has in the world, except the clothes he wears. In some things he makes an attempt at taste – in the dressing of the hair, by wearing one or more ringlets on each side of his face, upon which great value is placed. He knows no other pleasure or domestic

> comfort than is afforded in a public house or beershop, brawling or drinking with his companions after the toils of the day.

The *Bath & County Graphic* described the navvies working on the line near Batheaston:

> You met crowds of these burly giants as they walked along the road; they seemed a race by themselves, and had a language almost of their own. Saturdays nights and Sundays they were a nuisance, as they had on those days plenty of money and nothing to do. Scenes of disorder and fights were not unusual, a favourite spot for the latter being the meadow through which the footpath passes to the riverside. Here sometimes three or four battles royal were going on at the same time.

By 1846, when the navvies had long since left Bath to build lines elsewhere, the problem of the navvies had become so acute that a parliamentary committee was set up to look into it. One engineer told the enquiry that it was dangerous to approach them, "if they were in crowds or at all disposed to be unruly." Another reported that, "from being long known to each other they generally act in concert, and put at defiance any local constabulary force; consequently crimes of the most atrocious character are common, and robbery without any attempt at concealment an everyday occurrence."

The greater the amount of work required to build a particular stretch of line, the greater the potential for trouble. The major engineering works needed in the Bath area brought thousands of men into the city. As early as July 1837, the parishioners of Twerton petitioned the magistrates for 13 special constables "in consequence of fighting and drunkenness on the railway." Isolated villages near major engineering projects were even more vulnerable. With no rural police force, their only recourse was to the military, and that was very much a last resort. To build the long embankment at Christian Malford, east of Chippenham, hundreds of men had to be drafted in to an area populated by only a few dozen families. For some of the navvies, the opportunity was too good to pass up. In November 1839, the *Bath Chronicle* reported "serious disturbances in that part of the Great Western Railway which passes through Christian Malford, between the navigators and the village labourers ... Several of the labourers have been severely beaten, and robbed of their watches, etc."

Robbery with violence was a constant concern, even in Bath. Just after ten o'clock one evening in May 1840,

> as a young man named Hawkins was returning from Bathwick to Widcombe along the canal towing path, he was met by three men, having the appearance of navigators (supposed to have been employed on the railway) who, after separating so as to give him an opportunity of passing, immediately turned round and threw him down on his back. One of them then placed his knee on the chest of the young man, who immediately grasped him by the throat; but the others assisting their companion, he was soon overpowered, one of them covering his mouth, and threatening to cut his throat if he made any noise. The villains then turned out his pockets, from which they extracted a silver hunting watch and two shillings, with which they escaped. Notice was given to the police, but the robbers have yet escaped detection.

The navvies' shanty towns were the ideal place for someone on the run from the law to hole up. One of the Newport rioters, for whom wanted notices were posted, escaped detection for almost twelve months by fleeing to Bath and getting a job building the railway. When he was eventually tracked down by a police superintendent from Newport, he was working as a sawyer at the railway station. Had he been working on one of the more inaccessible parts of the line, however, it is possible that he would have escaped detection altogether.

Most of the trouble caused by the navvies, however, was among themselves. Fighting, although generally fuelled by drink, was frequently indulged in as a recreation, rather than as the result of a disagreement. This story, from September 1838, gives a frightening glimpse into how cheaply life was held among the navvies:

> An inquest was held at Corsham yesterday before John Edwards, Esq, on the body of Henry Hope, aged about 40; it was adjourned until 18 September in order to receive the medical evidence consequent upon a post mortem examination. It appears that the deceased had been drinking on Saturday last, at a beerhouse at Elly Green, with others,

> when a wager was made up for him to run with William Clarke a certain distance, for a gallon of beer. The race was won by Clarke. During the time the beer was being drunk the deceased continued wrangling, telling Clarke that if he could beat him at running, he could not beat him at fighting. After some time a fight took place in an adjoining field between Clarke and deceased, when, from the difference between the two men with regard to their state of ebriety, it was evident that the deceased had no chance, yet, although several persons were spectators, among whom was the deceased's own son, none attempted to interfere, even to act as seconds. The deceased was knocked down every time, and after 20 minutes was so beaten as to be unable to stand or speak. In that state he was left from seven o'clock on Saturday night until Sunday morning, when some person, passing by the spot, recognized him, and had him conveyed to his lodgings, where he died about one o'clock. The medical evidence given at the adjourned inquest proved that the excitement caused by the running, the drinking, and the fighting, produced the fatal result, the immediate cause being considered to be the fighting. The jury returned a verdict of manslaughter against William Clarke. The excitement produced here is considerable on the occasion, from the brutal manner in which the deceased was left in the field the whole of the night, and the delay in procuring medical attention after he was discovered and conveyed home, no one being sent for until twelve o'clock on Sunday. The deceased never spoke after the last round but one. Both parties are labourers on the works at the Box Tunnel. Clarke is a native of Atworth; the deceased was a native of Gloucester.

Despite this internecine fighting, navvies had a strong sense of tribal loyalty. Although the *Chronicle* characterized them as essentially solitary beings, wandering the country in search of work, their bush telegraph meant that the same men worked on projects throughout the country. A gang of navvies working for a particular contractor would, more likely than not, be made up mostly of men from the same part of the country, augmented by a few local recruits. When a contractor was dismissed or went bankrupt and the contract was re-awarded, it was common practice for the new contractor to recruit a new gang of navvies. This happened in April 1838, when Brunel, unhappy with the progress made by William Ranger between Bath and Bristol, took over part of the contract himself. He sacked the navvies working on a tunnel north of Keynsham, most of whom were from Gloucestershire, and brought in a gang from Devon. The *Bristol Journal* described what happened next:

> On Monday last, a number of navigators working on the Great Western Railway, amounting to upwards of 300, principally natives of the county of Gloucester, tumultuously assembled and made an attack on the workmen employed at Tunnel No 3, Keynsham, who are most of them from Devonshire and the lower parts of Somerset. The ostensible motive for the attack was a belief that the latter were working under price; to this was added a local or county feud, as the rallying cry of onslaught was "Gloucester against Devon." The result was a regular fight with various dangerous weapons ready to hand, such as spades, pickaxes, crowbars, etc. The contest was long and severe, in which several were most dangerously hurt, and one man was obliged to be taken to the infirmary, but no one was killed. The insubordination continued for several succeeding days, and was not repressed without the aid of the military.
>
> From further enquiries we learn that a jealousy has long subsisted between the Devon men and those from other counties, but the immediate cause of the late outbreak arose from the following circumstance. A few weeks ago the company arranged with the contractor to take the working of the tunnel No 3 out of his hands, and they then engaged a number of gangmen who were paid a stipulated sum per yard for the work done by their men. It appears that the Devon men have been long accustomed to the use of a ponderous instrument called a jumper for breaking the rock, and that they were thus enabled to execute more work, and accordingly gain higher wages, than the workmen from other neighbourhoods; and the Gloucester men being at least three times more numerous than the Devonians, the former came to a resolution of driving the strangers from the works. The consequence has been that during the past week very few men have been employed on the Great Western railroad in this neighbourhood. In several affrays there have been many heads broken, but we have heard of only one serious injury, upon a man called Richard Thomas, now in the Infirmary, who it is feared has received a severe injury of the spine.

The readiness with which navvies could buy alcohol had been greatly facilitated by an Act of Parliament passed in 1830. The Beerhouse Act, whose ostensible aim was to wean people away from gin palaces and encourage them to drink beer instead, enabled any householder to sell beer, for consumption on or off the premises, by paying an annual fee of two guineas. It was, as far as curbing drunkenness went, a dismal failure. A month after it became law, Sydney Smith wrote,

> the new Beer bill has begun its operations. Everybody is drunk. Those who are not singing are sprawling. The sovereign people are in a beastly state.

The number of licensed premises soon doubled, and, when the navvies arrived to build the first railways, nearby householders opened beerhouses to cater for them. Many provided accommodation as well; some, like the Tunnel Inn, near one of the shafts of Box Tunnel, were even run by navvies. At Hampton Row, where the canal had to be diverted to make way for the railway, four houses in a terrace of 14 became beerhouses. All but one closed when the railway opened. It was a similar story in Dolemeads and along Claverton Street. A few, like the Railroad Tavern – later known as the Railway Brewery – on the Wells Road, which opened in 1836 or 1837, survived until recently.*

The navvies were binge drinkers of epic proportions. In 1852, a porter at Bath station, who had worked with the navvies when the line was being built, said that, "drunkenness and fighting were carried on to an alarming extent; no teetotalism was known … with that class of men." There were rich pickings to be made by beerhouse keepers along the line, although the navvies were not averse to biting the hand that fed them. In August 1840, when the Bristol & Exeter Railway was built through Ashton near Bristol,

> the residents in the neighbourhood were considerably alarmed … by the outrageous proceedings of a large body of excavators, who broke

* *For more information on the beerhouses used by the navvies, see The Lost Pubs of Bath. For more information on the navvies' drinking habits see Awash With Ale.*

> into several beerhouses, from one of which they took two barrels of beer, the same quantity from another house, and five hogsheads and two barrels from a third. An application was made at eleven o'clock on Monday night ... for the assistance of the Bristol police to quell the disturbance. It appearing, however, that the inhabitants had allowed the matter to go on for two days without any attempt to stop it by the interference of the local constables, the request was not complied with.

The navvies did not confine themselves to makeshift beerhouses, however. If they fancied a night on the town, there were plenty of lively pubs in Southgate and Avon Streets to cater for their needs. Their exploits frequently landed them in trouble. This report, from February 1841, gives a flavour of what they got up to:

> John Baker, a railway labourer, was brought up to answer the information of a wandering minstrel, named Catherine Keller, a native of Germany, for a most outrageous and indecent assault upon her on Tuesday evening, at the Plough public house, Southgate Street. During a struggle which ensued in the apprehension of Baker, he received a fracture of the leg, and not being sufficiently recovered to admit of his being sent to gaol, the judgment of the magistrates will not be given until he is recovered.

Many of the ladies they encountered, however, were more than happy to receive indecent advances. In April 1841,

> James Burrell, landlord of the Crown and Thistle public house, Avon Street, was charged with keeping his house open during the hours of divine service ... Inspector Norcross stated that he was on duty in Avon Street, between the hours of three and four o'clock, when, on perceiving the door of the Crown and Thistle open, he went in and in one of the rooms he saw between 30 and 40 persons, railwaymen and prostitutes, assembled, and some of them had beer before them. Burrell admitted the charge, but pleaded in excuse that some of the party were lodgers and that he was ignorant of the law. Fined £5 and costs.

Prostitutes were about the only people who could outwit the navvies – at least when their defences were down. In December 1841,

> Sarah King and Mariah Hopkins were charged with stealing from the person of a railway labourer, named Matthew Leonard, a purse containing eight sovereigns, two half sovereigns and two half crowns. Leonard and another man named Whitelock had been sitting with the prisoners nearly all the day on Wednesday at the Plough Inn in Southgate Street, having first met them at the Bell in Stall Street. In the evening Whitelock missed a cheque for £40 from his pocket; but he could not discover by what means he had lost it. About seven o'clock, Leonard also missed his purse and money. An elderly woman saw Hopkins take the purse from his inside waistcoat pocket and hand it over to King at the door. She went out for a short time, and on her return accused them of the transaction, when King fell on her; a row ensued, which brought the police, when the prisoners were given in charge; but neither purse nor money was found on them.

With such rich pickings available, it is not surprising that the number of prostitutes in Bath soared in the late 1830s and early 1840s. Navvies, who were generally paid once a month, earned between four and eight shillings a day, compared with the maximum of fifteen shillings a week paid to agricultural labourers.

It is difficult to overestimate the impact the navvies had on Bath. When building work was at its height, there were between one and two thousand navvies in and around the city, together with wives and camp followers. The *Bath & County Graphic* later recalled what Bath was like in 1840 and 1841:

> There was one continuous line of work going on at the same time, gangs of men working day and night, driving and tunnelling through Box and Middle Hill; others building up the embankment by the Box Road; large numbers erecting the bridges at Bathford; others diverting the canal near to the Sydney Gardens, so that the rails should be laid in its bed. The skew bridge was being hurried forward without ceasing; large fires were kindled on it and on the banks of the river ... The field next to the Quakers' burial ground [on the border between Bathford and Batheaston] was covered with sheds

Working on the line in Bathwick, with St James's Bridge in the distance.

> for men and horses, a footbridge crossed the river from it, over which was an endless stream of barrows, men going and returning, wheeling materials for the bridge. Every cottage was crowded with navvies, as they were called.

But although navvies were often demonised in the local press, there was another side to the story. Many of them were skilled and dedicated workers in what was an extremely arduous and dangerous business. There was no job security and, if they were injured, no sickness benefit to tide them over. If they were killed, their wives and children were left without any means of support. Occasionally, newspaper reports let us glimpse a more benign side to the navvies. In October 1838, for example, an inquest was held at the Bell Inn beerhouse on the Lower Bristol Road "on the body of John Jennings, aged 24, an excavator on the Great Western Railway who died suddenly on Saturday last." The verdict was that he had died "from a disease of the brain. The remains of the deceased were followed to the grave by between 40 and 50 of his fellow workmen, the whole of whom wore white cockades in their hats."

There were also attempts by concerned citizens to help the navvies see the error of their ways, and to get them out of the beerhouses and into church. In January 1840, in a sermon at St Saviour's, Larkhall, parishioners were asked to contribute to a fund "to ameliorate the destitute spiritual condition of the men working on the railroad." Special services were held; in May 1840, it was announced that,

> for the spiritual benefit of the men employed upon the Great Western Railway, services will take place on Sunday afternoons at Batheaston church; in the evenings of the same day at the railway chapel, Temple Meads, Bristol, and at Thursday evenings at Box, in the schoolroom near the church ... Batheaston Church was opened on Sunday afternoon last, on which occasion there were assembled upwards of 150 railwaymen, who were extremely attentive to the prayers.

A "Railway Episcopal Chapel" was set up in the old poor house at Batheaston. An appeal for funds appeared in the *Bath Chronicle* on 4 June 1840:

> Considerable expense having been incurred in setting up an Episcopal Chapel, and further expense being contemplated to provide a home for railway boys, and a retreat for the men on wet days and Sundays, contributions are earnestly solicited by the Rev WC Osborn, BA, Chaplain.

A week later, it was reported that,

> on Monday last, about 100 men and boys employed on the Great Western Railway had a supper of beef, bread and cheese provided for them in the room underneath the Railway Episcopal Chapel at Batheaston. The building, originally the poor house, is divided into three floors. The middle floor is licensed by the Bishop for the purposes of a chapel, where service is performed on Sundays and Friday evenings, and the men are instructed in reading. The lower floor is intended as a retreat for the men on wet days, where they will be furnished with books and tracts. The upper floor the Chaplain

The former poor house in Batheaston.

wishes to convert into a dormitory for the boys engaged on the line, many of whom now sleep in and around the stables, or in or under the wagons, or by the side of the fires in the road.

On 19 October,

ninety of the railway men and boys employed on the line at Bathford and Box were assembled by their chaplain, the Rev WC Osborn, to partake of a supper provided for them in the room under the Railway Episcopal Chapel, Batheaston. While provision was thus made for their bodily wants, the chaplain failed not to give them such admonitions and exhortations as they stand so much in need of. Some of the resident engineers and other gentlemen connected with the railway company were present and ministered to the comfort of the men. We cannot doubt but that much good must result from the interchange of good feeling excited by such meetings. We beg leave again to recommend the above chapel to the warmest support of our readers, as being eminently calculated to work a large amount of religious good where it is most urgently required.

On Christmas Eve,

> a hundred men were assembled by the Rev WC Osborn at Batheaston to partake of beef, coffee, etc., provided for them at the expense of those friends who desire their temporal and spiritual good. They afterwards attended divine service in the Railway Episcopal Chapel. The Christmas evening was chosen by the Chaplain to entice the men from the beerhouses in the village, and in order that he might have the opportunity of impressing on them the vitally important considerations connected with the season.

It is impossible to imagine what life among the navvies was like – or how great their impact was on the communities they lived among. For beerhouse keepers and other tradesmen they provided a welcome source of revenue, but for many people they were unpredictable, dangerous outsiders, with unfamiliar habits. While the majority respected the communities they jostled up against, the shanty towns harboured a sub-class of violent, lawless vagabonds who knew little restraint, confident that the lack of an effective police force and an anonymity more or less guaranteed by their mode of living would generally protect them from the consequences of their actions.

TEN

In the Way of the Railroad

In December 1836, "notices to quit" were served on householders in the Dolemeads "in the line of the intended railway," so that "a viaduct extending from the Old Bridge to Raby Place" could be built. In Ham Gardens, four acres of Earl Manvers' land was bought by the company, who also agreed to build a street from South Parade to the station, to be called Manvers Street. This was to be maintained and kept in repair by the company until such time as buildings had been constructed along two-thirds of its length, when responsibility for its maintenance would revert to Earl Manvers. The street was intended for passengers and their luggage, either on foot or by carriage; carts "hauling articles of trade" were banned from using it.

Houses were also demolished in Claverton Street to make way for the railway. Originally, more were scheduled to come down, with part of the street turned into a tunnel under the line. When Brunel was questioned about this at the parliamentary enquiry, he declared that, because of the type of people who lived there, the more that were demolished the better.

"Is it the poverty of the people you object to?," he was asked.

"No, the class of people," he replied.

"They are not merely guilty of being poor, but something else?"

"Yes."

"Then your railway will operate as a great moral improver in the City of Bath."

Brunel was not alone in his opinion of Widcombe. Until 1836, when it became part of Bath, and the city's policemen extended their beat across the bridge, Widcombe was synonymous with lawlessness. Holloway, the road leading up the hill from the Old Bridge, was notorious as a haunt of beggars and vagabonds. But things were improving.

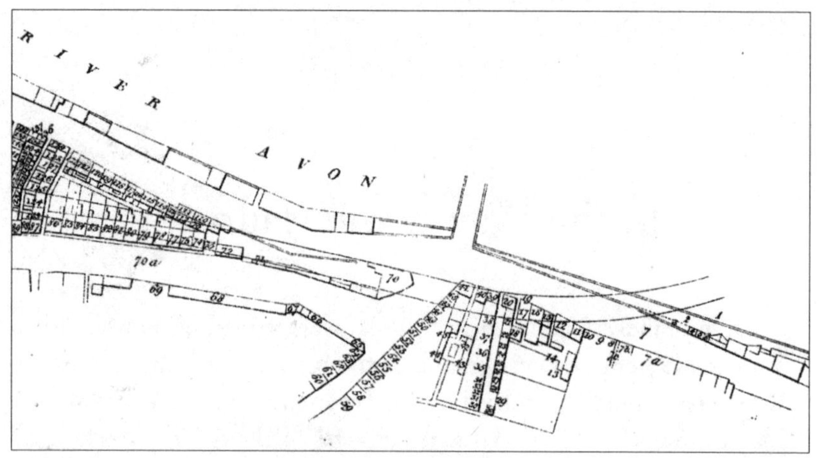

The course of the line through Widcombe, indicating the extent of the devastation envisaged by Brunel.

In late November 1836,

> the extensive and populous parish of Lyncombe and Widcombe was, for the first time, lighted with gas. The lamps are judiciously arranged; and, as the parish has hitherto been in a state of almost total darkness, the improvement is fully appreciated by the inhabitants. Now that the whole district is well lighted, and vigilantly watched by an efficient police, we have no doubt that the value of property in the parish will be considerably enhanced, and that many admirers of delightful scenery will be induced to look out for residences in a neighbourhood so eminently picturesque.

One of those affected by Brunel's plans for Widcombe was Thomas Peacock. The company offered £1,600 for his property, but he demanded £2,800. When an enquiry was held at the White Lion to assess his claim, however, he was awarded a mere £1,150. Another person affected was James Grant Smith. He owned the Angel Inn, which had already been cut in two when the Bath Turnpike Trust built the Wells Road. Now the railway was to take much of what remained, along with several rows of houses. Smith, who also owned the Anchor Brewery in Southgate Street, was one of the most influential men in the city, and a vociferous opponent of the railway. On 19 September

1838, a meeting to consider the plans "for carrying the railway across Claverton Street" was held at the workhouse in Widcombe. The *Bath Chronicle* reported that

> Mr James ... took the chair. He commenced the proceedings by stating the object of the meeting ... The railway company had, at considerable expense, given them every opportunity of judging the merits of each of the plans, for which the parishioners ought to be greatly obliged to them.
>
> Mr J English then requested that the notice calling the Vestry meeting should be read, which was accordingly done, Mr English repeating with emphasis the words, "and to decide which of the plans should be adopted."
>
> Mr English then rose and observed that ... he did not see how it was possible that the parishioners could be called together to decide on one of two plans, when it might turn out that both were objectionable. He did not believe the notice could bind the parishioners, but that they were at liberty to go into the subject at large. Mr English then proceeded to show what were the powers of the company and what indemnity the parish was entitled to.
>
> Mr Frere said that he was not at all acquainted with the legal points. He was there only as the engineer of the company, and if the law of the case was the only point to be discussed, he might as well employ himself elsewhere.
>
> Mr English said that what he had to advance was not with a view of throwing any interruption in the way of the proceedings, but as it was a question of law and fact, he had expected that some legal gentleman would have attended on the part of the company. The powers of the company were great, but when the legislature granted those powers it looked with a jealous eye on the interests of the public at large, and provided that the company should indemnify the public for any injury they might sustain. The 104th section of the Railway Act would not admit of two opinions. It provided that in all cases wherein any part of any road was found necessary to be cut through, raised, sunk, taken, or so much injured as to be inconvenient to the persons entitled to the use thereof, the company should, at their own expense, before any such road was cut through, raised, sunk, or injured as aforesaid, cause another

good and sufficient road to be made, which should be as convenient for carriages and passengers as the road taken or injured, or as nearly as might be. Mr English then contended that the road under the proposed tunnel would not be so convenient as the present road, inasmuch as six or seven feet of it would be taken away by masonry. He moreover objected to the tunnel, as being a nuisance on account of its darkness, from its extreme length, 140 feet.

Mr Frere said that the company were willing to do all that was required of them by the Act of Parliament in preserving the light to the side arches from the main arch.

At this stage of the proceedings, the attendance became so numerous that it was found necessary to adjourn the meeting to the green behind the house.

Mr English then continued, and contended that although the company had a right to cross a road by means of a bridge, they had no right to go along a road by means of a tunnel. The resolution passed at a meeting of the parish in 1835 was that no opposition be made to the crossing of Claverton Street by the railway provided an arch was made equal in every respect to the one to be made at the bottom of Holloway. Mr English then animadverted on the other plan proposed by the company, viz. the diverting the original road along Claverton Street, from a straight line as it is at present, to a curved road, going under the railway at about right angles to it, on the south side of Claverton Street by the old poor house. That road was to be only 20 feet wide with one footway of five feet wide. He also referred to the 8th section of the Act, which treated of the diversion of roads, etc., and showed that when a road was diverted it was required to be carried along by the side of the railroad, and he pointed to the new road at Twerton as an example.

Mr JG Smith ... directed the attention of the meeting to the proceedings required under the Highway Act, when a road was wanted to be diverted. He believed the present case would be one for a jury to decide, as the proceedings of the Vestry meeting would be invalid, for any person could go and appeal against the alteration at the Quarter Sessions. He moved that the meeting be adjourned to 1845.

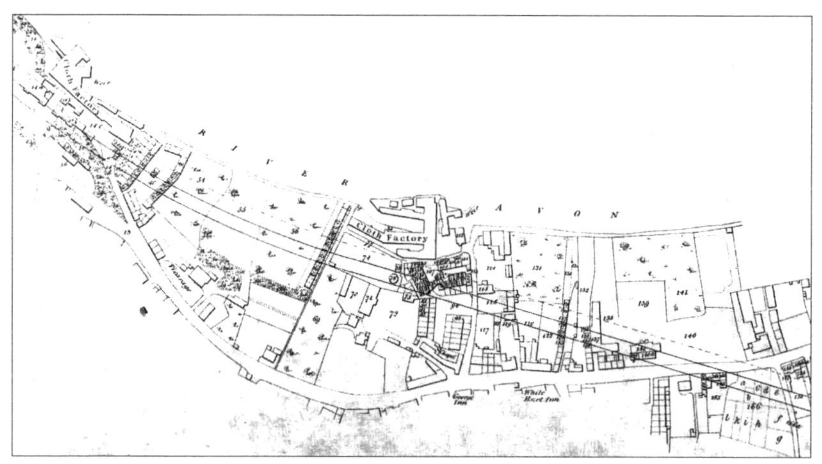

The course of the line through Twerton, as agreed by Charles Wilkins. The dotted line north of the railway indicates the course of the diverted turnpike.

Amid laughter, several people seconded the motion, and both plans were eventually rejected. The *Bath Figaro* later reported, in its "famous untruths" column, that

> it is not true that Mr Grant Smith dined on Monday with the directors of the Great Western Railway, and that he proposed as a toast, "Success to the Company."

The following year, the Bath Temperance Society announced plans to build a Temperance Hall in Claverton Street, a short distance from the skew bridge. Was their choice of location due to the moral turpitude of Widcombe's residents, to which Brunel had drawn attention, or was it perhaps due to the character of the men that Brunel had brought into the parish to build the railway?

Further up the line, at Twerton, the village had by now been transformed into a massive building site, courtesy of Mr Wilkins. The turnpike road was turned out of its course, cottages were knocked down, and, in digging up the lawn in front of the vicarage, workmen exposed the drains, from which the vicar's son caught cholera and died. There were a series of accidents on the line as well. On 20 June 1838, four men were building the arch work of Twerton Tunnel when the plank they were standing on broke and they fell to the ground. Henry Hillier received a compound knee fracture and had to have his leg amputated; Peter Holbrook received a compound fracture of the leg; William Bushell seriously injured his spine; and Thos Claveley received a head wound. There was, of course, no question of compensation or sick pay.

Just over three months later, on Wednesday 26 September, Mr WN Frushard, an assistant engineer on the line, was superintending the laying of the foundations of a bridge across the turnpike road at Twerton, when "one of the shear-legs [snapped] in raising the blocks, by which one of his ribs was broken." In early November, an inquest was held

> at the United Hospital on the body of John Marchant, who a few days since met with an accident on the Great Western Railway, caused by an empty wagon passing over his legs, and although he was but slightly bruised, locked jaw took place, from which he died.

There are no eyewitness accounts of the construction of the railway in Bath beyond the snippets provided by the *Bath Chronicle*: no records of the devastation of Dolemeads, Claverton Street and Twerton. Some idea of how total that devastation was can be gained from Charles Dickens' description of the building of the London & Birmingham Railway through Camden Town:

> The first shock of a great earthquake had, just at that period, rent the whole neighbourhood to its centre. Traces of its course were visible on every side. Houses were knocked down; streets broken through and stopped; deep pits and trenches dug in the ground; enormous heaps of earth and clay thrown up; buildings that were undermined and shaking, propped by great beams of wood. Here, a chaos of carts, overthrown and jumbled together, lay topsy-turvy at the bottom of a steep unnatural hill; there, confused treasures of iron soaked and rusted in something that had accidentally become a pond. Everywhere were bridges that led nowhere; thoroughfares that were wholly impassable; Babel towers of chimneys, wanting half their height; temporary wooden houses and enclosures, in the most unlikely situations; carcases of ragged tenements, and fragments of unfinished walls and arches, and piles of scaffolding, and wildernesses of bricks, and giant forms of cranes, and tripods

> straddling above nothing. There were a hundred thousand shapes and substances of incompleteness, wildly mingled out of their places, upside down burrowing in the earth, aspiring in the air, mouldering in the water, and unintelligible as any dream. Hot springs and fiery eruptions, the usual attendants upon earthquakes, lent their contributions of confusion to the scene. Boiling water hissed and heaved within dilapidated walls; whence also, the glare and roar of flames came issuing forth; and mounds of ashes blocked up rights of way, and wholly changed the law and custom of the neighbourhood.

By now, the enthusiasm with which coach operators had taken up the option of using the Great Western to carry their coaches between Maidenhead and London was waning. The time it took to secure them on wagons and unload them at the other end, not to mention time taken waiting for the train, all for a journey of 22 miles, meant that the journey often took longer than before. Some passengers were also unhappy about the arrangement, considering it unsafe. Contemporary illustrations show stage coaches being carried on open trucks, with nothing more than chocks and a couple of straps to prevent them rolling off, and coachman and passengers sitting on top. Quite apart from the danger of overbridges and exposure to everything the engine could blast forth, the centre of gravity of the coach was uncomfortably high. Even on the broad gauge, it could not have been a pleasant experience. Accordingly, in November 1838, the proprietor of the York House Day Coach announced that it performed the journey to London in ten hours "by the road only."

Safety, in the 1830s, was a relative issue. By modern standards, coaching was itself appallingly dangerous. Take, for example, two incidents that occurred at Pickwick in 1839:

> On Tuesday evening while the horses of the *Monarch* were waiting in the stable of Messrs Reilly at Pickwick for the arrival of the coach, one of them ... struck a candle out of its lantern by a toss of its head, by which means the litter was ignited, and the whole of the stable becoming speedily on fire, three horses were burned to death. (21 March 1839)

On Saturday morning, the *Beaufort* coach quitted the White Lion, Bath, for London, with its usual caution and regularity, but had not progressed to within a quarter of a mile of the Pickwick gate about eight miles from Bath, when, upon a slight descent, and the horses going at a moderate pace, the axletree broke short in two, and the coachman named Everett, one of the best whips on the road, was precipitated to the ground, and in the fall broke his leg just below the knee. By the concussion, one of the hinder wheels broke away from the coach, and ran with such velocity upon the causeway as to knock down an old woman who was accidentally passing, and in the fall the poor creature also had her leg broken. The passengers, most fortunately, were more frightened than hurt, and have escaped with a few bruises. They were taken to town by the *Regulator* Bristol coach. (17 October 1839)

ELEVEN

Through Sydney Gardens

Early in 1839, Brunel brought Michael Lane, who had worked for him as a bricklayer on the Thames Tunnel, to Bath to oversee the construction of the viaducts that would carry the railway across the city. The contract for building the Dolemeads Viaduct was awarded to David Aust, who also won the contracts for Bathford Bridge and for masonry work at Bathampton. Aust quoted £6,200 for the viaduct, £6,965 for the bridge, and £3,424 for the masonry work. The contract for St James's Bridge, east of Bath station, was awarded to William Chadwick from London, who quoted £11,500 for the work.

David Aust's record as a builder was an impressive one. He had built the viaduct for the Black Dog Turnpike Trust at Monkton Combe, St Michael's Church in Broad Street, and North Parade Bridge. This bridge was one in a series of bridges built in Bath in the 1820s and 1830s. In 1827, Goodridge built Cleveland Bridge. Three years later, a suspension bridge was built at Grosvenor. In 1834, Newton Bridge was widened and flood arches added. In 1835, James Dredge built a suspension bridge near his brewery on the Upper Bristol Road. In 1837, another suspension bridge was built further downstream, on the site now occupied by Windsor Bridge. North Parade Bridge was originally intended as a suspension bridge, but a design submitted by Mr Tierney Clark of London for an iron bridge was later accepted instead.

The contract for the most celebrated railway bridge at Bath went not to David Aust, but to a Mr Wilcox. This was the Skew Bridge west of the station. Unable to secure a satisfactory tender for iron to build the bridge, Brunel opted to use wood. Conventional wisdom – in England at least - was that, as far as bridge building went, the use of wood should be confined to ornamental bridges or swing bridges on canals. But Brunel would have been aware of the wooden bridges built

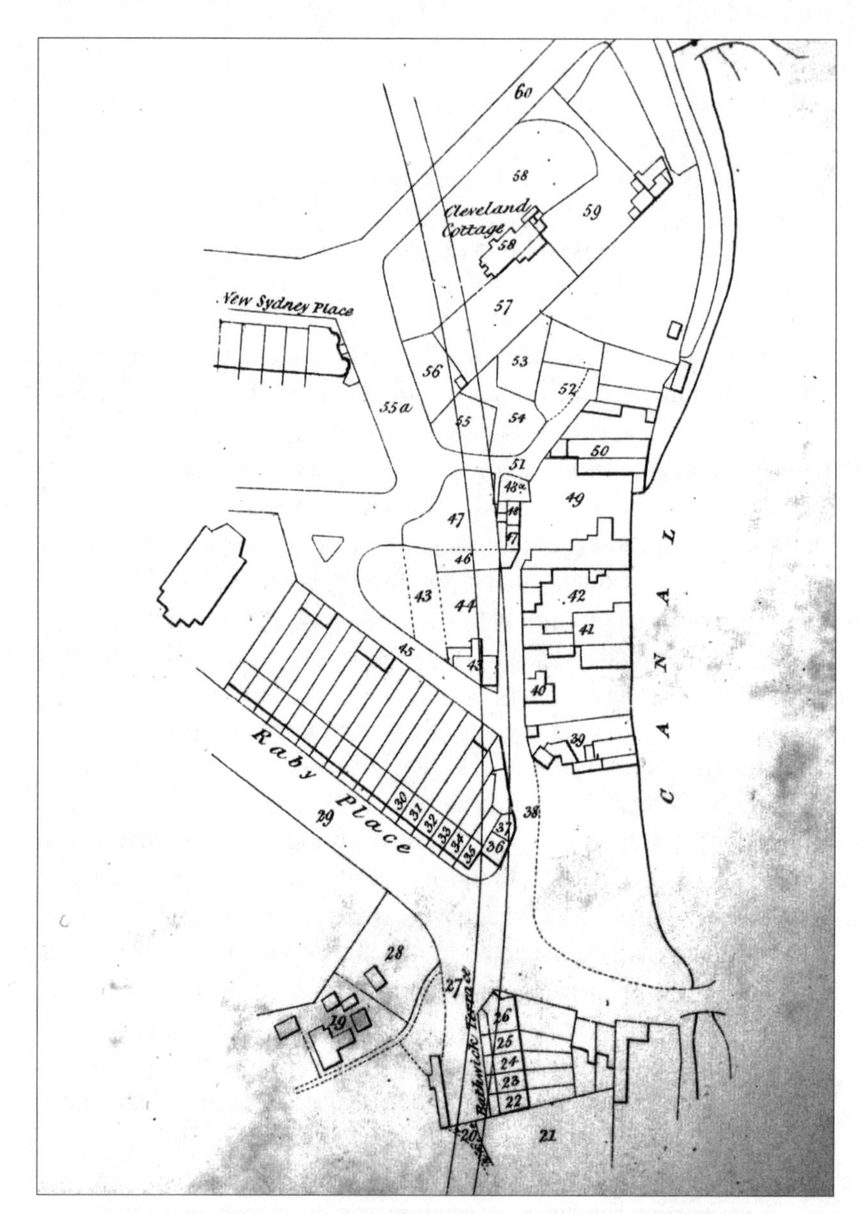

The course of the line through Bathwick Terrace and Raby Place.

in Switzerland built by Hans Ulrich and Johannes Grubenmann, which Sir John Soane had praised for their "sublime simplicity." Brunel had already built a large wooden road bridge over a railway cutting at Sonning in Berkshire. The success of the Skew Bridge project provided Brunel with the confidence to build the series of wooden viaducts that carried the railway over the deep valleys of Devon and Cornwall.

Work to prepare the way for the skew bridge, one of the most keenly observed civil engineering projects ever undertaken in Bath, started in August 1839, when "a mud barge [was] brought up for the purpose of clearing away the deposit at the bottom of the river, and thus deepening the stream where the barges pass."

In Bathwick, Brunel seems to have had fewer problems in persuading householders to sell up than he had had in Widcombe. A railway tunnel – or, as it was referred to in the company's minutes, Bathwick Covered Way – passed directly underneath the top house in Raby Place, as well as a pub – the Cleveland Arms – on Sydney Wharf. The house was demolished and rebuilt; the pub managed to survive – and was doubtless well patronised by the navvies engaged on this difficult stretch of line. The company also paid £2,650 for the houses in Bathwick Terrace, which the railway was to pass directly in front of. The contract for this stretch was awarded to John Vaughan, who had also worked on Beckford's Tower, for £5,664. Work started on it in October 1839.

Just as at Twerton, Brunel found one of Bathwick's major landholders only too willing to accommodate him. The course of the railway lay directly through Sydney Gardens, the only one of the city's eighteenth-century pleasure gardens to have survived. The Kennet & Avon Canal had already been built through Sydney Gardens, under Chinese-style bridges, through tunnels adorned with the presiding deities of Father Thames and Sabrina, in 1810. The proprietors had made the canal company pay two thousand guineas for the privilege, but all agreed the canal was an ornament to the gardens, especially as it was screened by ornamental shrubs and could only be seen from the bridges. Brunel's railway gouged a deep swathe through the gardens, destroying the tea house, the labyrinth, the sham castle, and blocking off the woodland ride that was one of the gardens' main attractions. The canal barges were drawn by horses, offensive only in the residue they sometimes left behind. Trains, on the other hand, would be drawn by whistling engines, belching steam, smoke and sparks, and covering everything, including the clothes of those who had paid to enter this sylvan retreat, with smuts of soot.

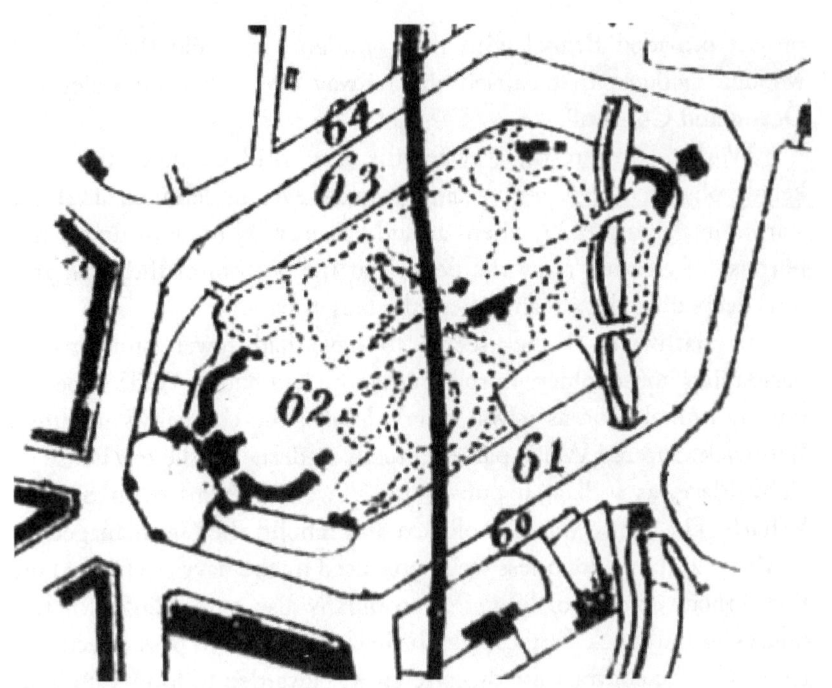

The course of the line through Sydney Gardens, with the canal on the right.

But Brunel did not force his railway through the gardens amid howls of protest, and after lengthy legal wrangles. In March 1839, for example, as plans were being drawn up for the navvies to enter this exclusive domain and lay waste everything in their path, the proprietors of the hotel and gardens held their annual dinner. This "not only comprised every delicacy in meat and vegetables that the season could supply, but was served up with that taste which has ever distinguished this hotel since it has come under the management of Mr Seymour. Mr Frere was present and acknowledged a toast to 'the success of the Great Western Railway.' A toast to the 'success of the Steamship Company and the *Great Western*' was acknowledged by Mr Godwin, Mr J Stothert and Mr Falkner."

The plain truth is that the gardens were strapped for cash, and the compensation paid by the railway company could not have been more welcome, even if it did entail their desecration. Once so popular, pleasure gardens had had their day, a relic of the eighteenth century fast giving way to the nineteenth century's version of *rus in urbe*, the

Brunel's sketch for a building in Sydney Gardens

municipal park. Bath's first park had been opened by the eleven year-old Princess Victoria in 1830.* The Royal Victoria Park, which was free, was devoted not so much to pleasure as to the study of the natural world and man's place in it. Pleasure, as far as the age to which Victoria gave her name was concerned, was not one of the primary objects of recreation, still less was it a virtue. Sydney Gardens had swings, mazes, and grottoes; Royal Victoria Park had the colossal head of Jupiter, bronzed lions guarding the gates and an obelisk dedicated to the Queen.

A few months after the opening of Royal Victoria Park, tenants occupying "gardens, cottages, etc., from the bottom of Grove Street to the extremity of Villa Fields" were given notice to quit, as it was intended "to dispose of the entire tract of ground into elegant

* *It is a cornerstone of Bath folklore that an incautious bystander commented on the thickness of her ankles, leaving her with the determination never to return to the city again. There is, however, not a scrap of evidence for this.*

A stage set for Brunel's trains: the line through Sydney Gardens.

plantations and walks, similar to Bath Park." So it was that Henrietta Park, a stone's throw from Sydney Gardens, came into being. The high-minded aims of the park's promoters were somewhat sullied when the park became a well-known haunt of prostitutes after dark.

Sydney Gardens had a succession of owners in the 1830s and 1840s, all of whom tried to adapt the gardens to changing tastes. It was Brunel, though, who left the only permanent mark on them. A lesser man would have tried to make the railway as inconspicuous as possible as it passed through, hiding it in a cutting or a tunnel. Not Brunel. He used the gardens as a stage set through which his trains would be seen to their best advantage. In imitation of the Chinese-style bridges over the canal, he built an iron bridge over the railway, along with a wide stone bridge. Not all of his plans for the gardens were realised, however. On 3 January 1840, he made one of his most enigmatic sketches. Simply headed "Sydney Gardens" it shows a single-storey building with overhanging eaves, possibly influenced by designs for Chinese pavilions such as that at Shugborough in Staffordshire. The likelihood is that it was intended as a tea-house to replace the one that had been destroyed by the railway, and would give visitors a grandstand view of the trains.

In April 1844, when the gardens were taken over by yet another proprietor, an advertisement tried to tempt people to come to the gardens by holding out the prospect of new walks "from which the railway trains may be seen passing." The following year the labyrinth was restored and a "Gothic Hall" was built. One of the first functions held there was a "temperance demonstration." The original promoters of the gardens must have turned in their graves. In 1851, with visitor numbers continuing to fall, another proprietor tried to reverse the decline by introducing statuary in imitation of that in Royal Victoria Park. A year later, Sydney Gardens was chosen as the location for a Crystal Palace, 144 feet long, 70 feet high and 48 feet wide, with a 96 foot transept, costing £6,000. Like Brunel's mystery building, it was never built, and before long the hotel was converted to a college and the gardens closed. Just over half a century later, the gardens were acquired by the council and reopened as a municipal park.

TWELVE

An Ornament to our Beautiful City

In the first week of September 1839,

> operations [were] commenced on that part of the line facing Hampton Row, on the banks of the canal, and many workmen have been employed in digging out the earth from the opposite field, preparatory to turning the course of the canal. The works in the neighbourhood of Wells Road, as regards the great archway and the coffer dam are likewise proceeding most rapidly.

The same month, Brunel made a preliminary sketch of what he described as the "Bath Depot," but which is now known as the station. In 1851, George Measom's official guide to the Great Western Railway described it as "a neat edifice, erected in the Tudor or Elizabethan style, with debased perpendicular windows and Romanesque ornaments." Apart from the addition of extensions to each side of the building, it is essentially the same today. It has been suggested that, by choosing a Jacobethan style for Bath station, Brunel was deliberately cocking a snook at the city's Georgian architecture. On the contrary, the style of the station was very much in keeping with the style of buildings that were going up in Bath at the time. At least nine churches had been built or rebuilt in and around the city in the previous 20 years – St Mary, Bathwick (1820), Holy Trinity, James St (1822), St Saviour's, Larkhall (1832), St Mark's, Widcombe (1832), Holy Trinity, Combe Down (1835), All Saints, Weston (1835), St John's, Lower Weston (1838), and St Michael's Twerton (1839). The grandest of all was St Michael's in Broad Street, designed by George Manners and built by David Aust. All were in Gothic style. Secular buildings, too, had moved away from Georgian conventions. South Hayes on Wells Road and the Gothic Villas on Entry Hill, built by Edward Davis in the early 1830s, or Oriel and Balliol Cottages on

Prior Park Road, built in the early 1840s, all demonstrate that Brunel's station was in the mainstream of current architectural design.

Classically-inspired buildings were still being built, however. The termini of the London & Birmingham Railway – at Euston and Curzon Street – were both in classical style, as was the hotel Brunel helped design at Bristol (now Brunel House) for passengers transferring from the Great Western Railway to the transatlantic steamships. The Royal Hotel opposite the station at Bath is in a similar style, and Brunel probably contributed to its design as well. Although the architect is unknown, it is likely to have been Henry Goodridge, not only because of its similarity to his work at Cleveland Place, but also because of his association with Brunel.

When Goodridge submitted a design for the Houses of Parliament, to replace the building consumed by fire in 1834, it was, according to the *Times*, who considered it "well done," in "the pointed style." Although Goodridge's plan was not adopted, the final design was also in a Gothic style. The reason for the success of the Gothic style in the nineteenth century was its iconic embodiment of solid virtues and, by harking past to a semi-mythical past, Britain's national identity. Classical style was all right for less important projects – such as hotels or houses, but for works of serious national importance – such as the Houses of Parliament or the Great Western Railway – only a style rooted in Britain's past glories would do.

Brunel would also have been aware of John Claudius Loudon's *Encyclopaedia of Cottage, Farm, and Villa Architecture and Furniture*, first published in 1833, and several times reprinted, with substantial additions. This was probably the most influential work on house design in the first half of the nineteenth century. It was not just an architectural handbook; it was part of a campaign by its author to improve the moral and physical health of the nation. The 1846 edition included drawings of stations built by Francis Thompson for the North Midland Railway in 1840. The largest of them, Ambergate, was in a Jacobethan style; the others were more Italianate. Loudon singled Thompson's stations out for especial praise:

> We cannot sufficiently express our admiration of the public spirit of the directors of the North Midland Railway, in causing the erection of such architectural gems along their line of works. They are great

JC Loudon's sketch of a villa in the castellated style.

> ornaments of themselves, and as they will be seen by many thousands of all ranks, and remain, it is hoped, for several generations standard models of cultivated design, they can hardly fail greatly to improve the general taste of the country. Even the mechanics who have worked at their construction must have had their ideas enlarged, and their taste more or less refined by them.

Looking through Loudon's *Encyclopaedia*, it is remarkable how many times one comes upon drawings reminiscent of Brunel's designs. The Italianate stations he built for the South Devon Railway, as well as the Jacobethan style buildings between London and Bristol, were almost certainly influenced by Loudon. One of Loudon's sketches, in particular, for "a small family villa in the castellated style," may have been where Brunel got the idea for the design of the viaduct west of Bath station. "It is not necessary," Loudon explains in an accompanying note, "that it should be accompanied by fortified outworks; but still the terrace walls, and other ornamental architectural appendages which accompany it, should either be in some degree marked by the liens and finish of fortified walls, or should imitate their ruins. Even in point of architectural harmony, the crests of such walls should be more or less embattled, like the parapets of the house." The main entrance to the building bears a striking resemblance not only to the original entrance to Temple Meads station, but also to the archways at the end of Claverton Street. The

The castellated viaduct at the bottom of Holloway.

Jacobethan style was maintained all the way to Bristol – at Twerton station, in the pointed arches of pennant stone, and in towers flanking the parapets of tunnels. The original skew bridge, its spandrels filled in with open screen work, with pointed arches and divisions similar to a Gothic screen, and its piers and parapets decorated with a strap motif, also continued the theme.

For the Victorians, improvement in taste went hand in hand with an improvement in morality. Great works of architecture were like great works of literature, inspiring those who came into contact with them to higher, more noble thoughts; this, it was firmly believed would inevitably lead to a improvement in the moral health and well-being of the nation. Loudon, like Brunel, was an intensely practical man, who realized that spiritual well-being went hand in hand with physical well-being. His last great campaign was to improve the layout and management of cemeteries, many of which, in the early nineteenth century, were perilously close to sources of drinking water and a danger to public health. The Abbey Cemetery at Bath, with its neo-Norman gateway and chapel designed by George Manners, was

Loudon's only direct contribution to Bath's physical and spiritual well-being, but his influence can be detected not only in Brunel's station, and in the castellated viaducts leading away from it, but also in many of the Gothic and Italianate houses lining the hillsides around the city.

Designs for the station were warmly received from the outset. When they went on display in December 1839, the *Bath Chronicle* stated that it would be

> another ornament to our beautiful city. By an advertisement in our columns it appears that the directors have secured a quarry for the supply of stone, the demand for which has been lately so much increased by their works. We trust that our spirited Bath builders will not allow this opportunity to escape, although the facility of procuring stone will no doubt introduce many competitors. Some of the most difficult works are already undertaken by our fellow citizens Messrs Vaughan, Aust and Lewis; but the arch over the river by the old bridge is being executed by a London builder; and the contractor for the works we before referred to at Holloway are Messrs Rennie & Co, who have here fully retained the high reputation they earned on the London & Birmingham Railroad. We shall be anxious to see who is successful in this competition.

A few weeks later, it declared that

> the progress of this immense national undertaking is beginning to be a work of the greatest admiration. Betwixt London and Bristol there are many points of observation shewing the wonderful daring and results of science which our forefathers could never have anticipated. The wonders of Egypt dwindle into nothing by the comparison. These are gigantic labours – without use, the monuments of pride and folly; here use, ornament, and durability try to surpass each other, and their several excellences are so adjusted as to show the foundation of future national prosperity beyond all power of calculation – not only the prosperity of trade by the rapid conveyance of merchandise, but the intellectual prosperity ... by bringing all parts of the empire into more frequent intercourse with large towns, and especially with the metropolis. The most costly portion of the line will be the tunnel at Box. This will ever be in

An early view of the viaduct from Broad Quay, showing the two large arches as originally built.

itself a magnificent proof of the skill and enterprise of the age: but these can never be truly estimated, without a knowledge of the overwhelming difficulties encountered in its progress. Of these no evidences will be presented by the work itself; they will be matters only of history. The company deserve high approbation, if not national gratitude, for their liberal endeavour, to make every point of observation an additional beauty to its locality. Even in Bath, the most beautiful city of England, where everything seems to harmonise in splendour, even here we find the line of works [add] to the general magnificence. The centrings of the arch over the Wells Road at the bottom of the Holloway have been removed, and erected at the place where the railway will cross Claverton Street. The arch and the two Gothic towers are pronounced to be excellent specimens of workmanship, and the entire viaduct, from the taste evinced in its design, will form, when completed, quite an ornament to the neighbourhood. At the tunnel near Bathwick Terrace the workmen have commenced the formation of a permanent way; and near

> Hampton Row great advance has been made during the last five or six weeks. At Hampton and the fields beyond, the cuttings and embankments are in a forward state. Close by the stone bridge between Hampton and Bathwick, the works are also beginning to alter the face of the landscape.

On certain parts of the line, changes to the face of the landscape were rather more dramatic than anticipated. On 23 January 1840, the *Chronicle* reported that

> the continual slipping of the earth embankment on the line of the Great Western Railway near the Victoria Public House at Patterdown [west of Chippenham] on the Lacock Road is assuming a serious aspect and threatens the safety of the above building.

The slipping of this and other embankments early in 1840 was due to a prolonged period of wet weather. In February, Brunel wrote to his directors to tell them that, although he had planned to open the line between Bath and Bristol in the spring, this would not now be possible:

> *At the Bristol extremity, the floods in the Avon have interfered with the supply of building materials; and at Bath and in its immediate neighbourhood the unprecedented continuation of a state of flood in the river for a long period and to within the last few days has rendered it impossible to carry on the works of the bridges or even of the station, the site of which has been flooded. Such a complete suspension of the works at some points and such delays at others [means] that certainly not less than four months additional time will be required for the completion of some of these works, the whole of which would otherwise have been finished within a month or two of the present time, which must delay the opening to the end of the summer instead of the spring. The works of the station at Bristol, including the viaduct and offices, are rapidly advancing; but at Bath the causes I have referred to have prevented till within the last few days anything more than the commencement of the approaches.*

Between these two extremities, all the principal works – the tunnelling, cutting and embankments – are so far completed that, had the weather permitted it, the ballasting and permanent way would have been by this time in a very forward state. The excavation of the tunnel is everywhere opened throughout, and the only work remaining to be done to them consists of the formation of the permanent drains and the finishing of detached parts of masonry, which in the general progress of the work had been injured or condemned, and the completion of one of the tunnel fronts. A few weeks will complete everything but the permanent rails, but many parts of the line, long since prepared, have not been in a state to allow of men or horses passing over them without destroying that portion of the forming which the rains had allowed to be completed, so that not more than two and a half miles of ballasting have been actually finished.

Work on the station at Bath had also slipped well behind schedule, and, in March 1840, the directors "resolved, that in consequence of the unsatisfactory progress of the work at the Bath depot, it is necessary that the same be forthwith taken into the hands of the company for completion."

THIRTEEN

Open to Bristol

On 1 July 1839, the line had been extended from Maidenhead to Twyford. In February 1840, the Bath, Exeter and London mailcoach was carried on the railway for the first time. On 30 March 1840, the section between Twyford and Reading was opened. The *Bath Chronicle* informed its reader that the maximum speed on the inaugural run was a staggering 58 miles an hour. Just over two months later, on 1 June, the line was opened to Steventon, and on 20 July to Faringdon Road (later renamed Challow). As the railway came ever closer, and journey times to London were slashed, a series of mishaps provided ammunition for those who were convinced it was an invention of the devil. In May 1840, the Bristol mailcoach caught fire when sparks from the engine landed on it. Fanned by the wind, parcels and luggage to a value of around £500 were soon consumed, despite the guard frantically blowing his horn to attract the attention of the driver. For the passengers, hurtling along at speeds of up to 50 miles an hour, with their stagecoach on fire, it must have been terrifying. In the early days of the Great Western, fires were commonplace. A month later, another mailcoach caught fire, between Twyford and Reading, and, in the last week of June, there were fires on two goods trains.

On 9 April, the *Bath Chronicle* reported that

> the works connected with the new bridge for the Great Western Railway over the Avon, near the Old Bridge, in the prosecution of which so many difficulties, owing to the wetness of the season, have arisen, are now advancing rapidly and satisfactorily. We shall soon see the stream spanned by new arches, and the flat land between them and the tunnel near the foot of Bathwick Hill will speedily be traversed by a continuation of the viaduct which now forms so prominent an object on the Lower Bristol Road. The progress now

NOTICE! NEW ROUTE!

WHITE HART HOTEL & COHCH-OFFICE.

THE Public are respectfully informed, that on and after MONDAY NEXT, the 14th inst., the

(White Hart)

LONDON DAY COACH,

At 20 Minues before 9, Morning,

WILL COMMENCE RUNNING, VIA DEVIZES AND SWINDON,

To the FARINGDON STATION

OF THE

GREAT WESTERN RAILWAY.

M. PICKWICK, Proprietor.

Bath, Sept, 10.

☞ Coaches to all Parts Daily.

(By Appointment.)

OMNIBUS—*To and from every Train, at the Bath Station of the Great Western Railway.*

FARE—6d. Each.

ROUTE — Glo'cester Inn, Paragon-buildings, Broad-street, Castle and Ball, New Bond-street, Union-street, Stall-street, and WHITE HART HOTEL.

An advertisement from 17 September 1840.

making is so marked that even casual observers may see a difference from day to day. We hear that the large sums paid in wages to the great number of railway labourers employed in the lower part of our city have caused, by their disbursement among the tradesmen of that neighbourhood, much briskness of business – a very acceptable accession at the present time of general dullness.

Three weeks later, the *Chronicle* reported that

> the foundation of the pier in the centre of the Avon having been properly laid, operations have been commenced on the Widcombe side of the water. In the Ham Gardens the erection of the arches on which the Bath depot will be situated is being rapidly proceeded with, while some steps have been taken towards erecting the viaduct across the Dolemeads and Pulteney Road. The tunnel at the top of Raby Place is likewise being finished in a very rapid manner. Towards Hampton the works are of a heavy character, and the utmost dispatch is therefore observable in that quarter. The workmen have made great progress in the necessary excavations for turning the course of the canal immediately opposite the Cleveland Baths. The embankments for the permanent way are here in a forward state while near Hampton Church, and in the meadows beyond, the contractors have been very active, and operations have commenced throughout the extent of the line to Bathford.

On 21 May, it announced that

> the permanent way has been laid down in the neighbourhood of Keynsham to a considerable extent, and the locomotive engine is at work. Between Keynsham and Bristol the road is all formed, and, except for finishing off the head of No 3 tunnel, is in a perfect state. The beautiful elliptical gothic arched bridge across the Avon near Bristol station is now completed, and presents a most splendid appearance. The work does infinite credit to the contractors, Messrs Wilcox & Son.

A week later, the *Chronicle* regaled its readers with the first part of "a Walk on the Great Western Railroad from Bath to Bristol," which went as far as Newton St Loe. Unfortunately, subsequent parts never appeared, possibly due to complaints from the railway about sightseers, inspired by the article, taking a weekend stroll along the line. A shortened version of it appears below, with the strict proviso that on no account should readers attempt to try it for themselves:

From [the Old Bridge] the road proceeds, for a considerable distance, through the gardens below South Hayes, near which the arches are succeeded by an earth embankment; then we find ourselves getting quite into the country, were it not that the road enters a "deep cutting," which means that an elevation of the ground, not sufficiently great to render a tunnel necessary, has had a trench driven through it, the bottom of which forms the level of the road. The sides of this trench shut out all view of the surrounding country, which is very beautiful. The slopes of the cutting have already become clothed with grass and wild flowers, but it must be confessed that there is little here to please the eye. We have railway and nothing else. Long lines stretch before us until their parallelism is lost in the vanishing point, and everything which meets the gaze bears witness to the operation of the inevitable square and level, so that the lover of the picturesque finds himself sadly discomposed. But we must remark, before going any further, that we should be doing great injustice to those who are engaged in the construction of the railway, if we were not to state that they have manifested a constant desire to avoid, as far as possible, deforming the face of the country. Trees have been spared wherever practicable, and the masonry of the work has been executed so as to harmonise with neighbouring buildings and other objects …

[We soon pass under] three handsome stone archways, over which pass as many parish or private roads. After leaving the second of these archways we emerge from the cutting into the open fields and are presented with delightful views of the adjacent scenery … We soon arrive at the village of Twerton with its huge factories and bustling inhabitants, many of whom bear token, in the blue dye which stains their faces and apparel, of the employment in which they are engaged – the manufacture of cloth … The factories form almost the entire support of the village, and … the large number of persons employed in them have the great advantage of working under one of the best and most considerate of masters – Mr Charles Wilkins, Esq.

We should remark that between Bath and Twerton the road is in a condition to receive the coating of broken stone, etc, preparatory to laying down the permanent rail … The railway here crosses a recently abandoned portion of the Bristol Road (now only used as

The shorter of the two tunnels at Twerton, looking east, with Charles Wilkins' mills in the distance.

leading through Twerton to some villages beyond) over a curiously constructed "skew arch," which is well worthy of examination for its singularity of structure; the courses of stone, when looked at from a distance, more resembling the timbers in the sides of a ship than a piece of masonry. The railway is continued by the side of the new piece of turnpike road to Bristol on massive stonework at a considerable elevation above the said turnpike. We soon arrive at a noble gothic archway, flanked by massive turrets, and looking like the portal of some huge feudal castle. This archway is partly for the support of a portion of the garden in front of Mr Wilkins' house, which is situated by the side of the railway ... and partly for the purpose of carrying a road from the house into the Bristol Road. Beyond this archway the precipitous hill along the north side of which the railway runs is secured against the possibility of "land slips" by imposing masses of masonry of great height and immense solidity, which cannot fail to excite the admiration of the spectator ... A little further on is perceived another Gothic archway, similar in general effect to the last, darkly yawning as if wishing to swallow up

The castellated portico of the long tunnel at Twerton, looking west.

whatever might have occasion to approach its wide and gloomy jaws. This is the entrance to the first tunnel between Bath and Bristol. It is no petty perforation, low-browed and narrow, such as those through which pass some of the older canals, and the first constructed railways, but a spacious excavation 30 feet high, some 20 feet wide, forming a noble arch of nearly 300 yards through. The tunnel is slightly curved, and dark only in the middle, and then only a little. Water drops slightly from the top in two or three places. A powerful current of air was rushing through on the day when we made our inspection; but whether this is actually the case or not we are not able to say[?] … Emerging from the tunnel, we have a sweet view of the neighbouring country … To the right may be observed that most excellent establishment Partis College, and Mr Beckford's tower is seen looking proudly down from its elevated site on Lansdown … We soon proceed under another arch, and find our way leading for some distance through a deep cutting, a part of which forms the site of the Roman villa discovered some time since … [We then pass] though a kind of vault, over which is carried a diverted piece of the Bristol turnpike road, supported by diagonally placed beams of iron, the interstices of which are curiously filled up with brickwork … Having passed under the old road to Bristol, the railway enters on the extensive embankment which traverses for two

> miles that beautiful part of the Avon valley which lies between Newton and Kelston. This embankment is a work of very great magnitude, and inclines us to think with somewhat less of wonder of the Pyramids and other great constructions of the ancients ... Along the banks of the river we see places used for landing, from rafts and barges, the timber and iron railing to be used for the completion of the road, and which materials are here and there seen piled in large quantities by the waterside.

The day of the opening drew near. On 23 July 1840, the *Chronicle* reported that "the permanent rails are now laid from Bath nearly to the terminus at Temple Gate." Only at the line's extremities was major work still outstanding. At Temple Meads, the foundation of two or three arches supporting the terminus started showing signs of weakness. The solution was to load them with several hundred tons of earth, and, after they had sunk about eight or ten feet, build them up again to the required height.

On 30 July, the *Bristol Standard* declared that

> we can state from the best authority that the line will be opened from hence to Bath in about three weeks from the present time. Everything progresses very satisfactorily in regard to the preparatory arrangements. Mr Brunel is now on the spot, and is pushing the work forward with great rapidity, and the utmost activity prevails in every department. One locomotive is at present being tried on this part of the line; and in the course of the next week ... four other engines will be placed on the rails for the same purpose.

A week later, the *Standard* reported that,

> as the period approaches for the completion of the line from this city to Bath, public interest seems to increase, and our generally quiet townfolk, shaking off their old apathy and conquering their well-known aversion to those novelties yclept improvements, are stealing out in thousands watching the progress of the works, not a few biting their nails at the thought that they have suffered a good investment to pass by unheeded. This line now possesses in a high degree public confidence in Bristol, and when fairly opened to Bath, Bristol will

> send forth her thousands, whirling along the beautiful banks of the Avon, to visit the sister city. We opine this will prove the most profitable portion of the line yet opened, and we shall very soon be enabled to dispense with the old road and all its cumbrous apparatus, its slow movements and many disappointments, and avail ourselves of the new order of things and go ahead, steaming it in about fifteen minutes ... We had much pleasure in inspecting a powerful locomotive engine for this end of the line, manufactured by Messrs Stothert & Co of this city. This is the first specimen of this kind of engine work manufactured south of Manchester ... The beauty of the workmanship we have never seen surpassed by any of the far-famed engineers of the north, and we doubt not that but that the *Arrow* will be found to distance all competitors. Together with a tender this engine was placed on the line on Tuesday. She is expected to attain a speed of 90 to 100 miles per hour.

On 13 August, the *Bath Chronicle* announced that

> an experimental trip on the line from Bristol to Bath will be made on the 24th inst. In addition to the locomotive, which we noticed in our last as being on the line, three more engines have arrived this week – one from London and two from Liverpool. Three of the carriages have also arrived from Oxford. As the period approaches for the completion of the line from this city to Bristol, public interest seems to increase. The traffic on this portion, where upwards of eight coaches now traverse daily, can scarcely be calculated.

Five days later, "the *Meridian* and tender did the distance from Saltford, through Keynsham, to the entrance of no 3 tunnel, nearly four miles, in the incredibly short period of three minutes."

On 20 August, the *Bristol Standard* informed its readers that

> the opening of the line to Bath is definitely fixed for Monday 31 August. Several experimental trips have been made during the last few days, in all cases attended with successful results. On Thursday one of the engines went at a speed of 60 miles an hour, or a mile a minute ... On Friday a powerful locomotive drew the enormous weight of 24 wagons loaded with gravel for the ballasting of the line.

> The progress of the works at the Bristol terminus is very satisfactory and progresses as rapidly as possible. The interior now presents a view the most interesting, and conveys a good idea of the magnitude of these undertakings, and the vastness of the traffic which calls them into existence. Taking up our position at the starting point underneath the grand shed, with a roof of larger span than that of Westminster Hall, we behold the rails from a single point, radiating in every conceivable variety of direction, with "turn tables," on which the massive and ponderous carriages and engines will be shifted from one line of rails to another, with as much ease as though they were children's toys. A little further on, we perceive the carriage depot, about 200 feet in length, and about 40 feet in breadth, which has been constructed in a few weeks, and is roofed with zinc ... The arrival of carriages has continued within the last few days, and there are now upwards of 25 on the line, many of them first-class carriages, fitted up in a very splendid manner with every regard to comfort.

A week later, it reported that

> during the past week many splendid runs have been made on the line by the powerful engines already here. On Friday we saw a locomotive, which took a large party of gentlemen, including Mr Brunel and some of the directors, at the rate of 60 miles an hour from hence to Bath, and on their return the distance was done in sixteen and a half minutes, exclusive of stoppage. Another engine, the *Lynx*, not previously tested, was placed on the line on Tuesday, and performed exceedingly well. The locomotives on this line, from the greater width of gauge, are of larger construction than those of any other railway, and are also of greater power. The *Arrow*, the splendid engine manufactured here by Messrs Stothert & Co, is of 60 horsepower, but can readily give a power equal to 100 horses, and with its tender laden with coke and water, is of the enormous weight of 32 tons.

Meanwhile, work continued to get the skew bridge ready in time for the line's opening. On 12 August, Edward Greenland, one of the labourers working on the bridge, was taking down the centring "when one of the massive timbers, which had been removed to a short distance, fell upon his leg and broke it in three places." On 27 August, the *Bath Chronicle* wrote that

> the sharp, shrill scream of the steam whistle and the rapid beatings of the locomotive engine – new sounds to our city – now give daily notice to our fellow citizens that the railway between Bath and Bristol is on the eve of actually being opened. The preparations for this event have been carried on with astonishing vigour and rapidity ... The achievements which labour and skill can perform have been particularly exemplified at the works in Claverton Street. To those who have been in the habit of passing the spot day after day it has appeared as if piers and arches were rising out of the ground by force of magic. Count the arches as you went by at evening – and lo! in the morning, another arch, bringing the railway one stride nearer to the river's brink. The beautifully scientific skew bridge is rapidly approaching completion and all the difficulties which were opposed to its progress, during the past winter, by the heavy floods which continually baffled and delayed the workmen, are now forgotten in the triumph of success ... The cast-iron standards for the support of the roads, and the longitudinal timbers on which the permanent rails are to be laid are nearly all in their place. The masonry on each side of the water is now almost completed ... When the structure is finished, and the piles and scaffolding are removed, it will present a very imposing appearance, and, from the peculiarity of its construction, it will no doubt be greatly visited, both by residents and strangers, as an object of considerable curiosity ... The depot cannot be finished in time for the opening on Monday, but temporary offices are being rapidly constructed. During the past week, several experimental trips have been made by the directors accompanied by Mr Brunel, and large quantities of timber and other materials required for the works have been conveyed from Bristol to Bath by one of the company's powerful engines. Relays of men are now employed on the works day and night ... Several fresh arrivals of carriages have taken place ... and there are now about 40 on the line, those belonging to the first class being fitted up in the most splendid manner ... Crowds of spectators every day assemble to witness the progress of the line, so soon to be finished in its whole length from Bristol to London, after an almost incredible exhibition of skill and

Bath station from Manvers Street.

> labour – and enormous outlay of capital – and, we are sorry to add, a destruction of human life which, though not more than is proportionate to the extent and nature of the work, cannot but excite the most melancholy feelings when we bear in mind the grounds which there are for fearing that too many of those who have been thus sent to their dread account have gone down to the grave "unaneled – no reckoning made." It does lessen the sadness with which this wear and tear of life cannot but be viewed, to know that a large number of the accidents which have occurred may be traced to the neglect of those who have fallen victims to use common precaution and to avail themselves of the safeguards which the conductors of the works have provided wherever required.

On 30 August 1840, Manvers Street, leading to the as yet unfinished station, was opened. The next day, at twenty minutes to nine on the morning of 31 August, the first train from Bristol steamed into Bath:

> The most astonishing efforts had been made to get the work into a state of sufficient forwardness by the above time. At the Claverton Street bridge, and within a short distance, upwards of 1,000 men had

been labouring during the week, throughout the 24 hours. The scene was altogether a most impressive one. Wherever an artisan could be useful – *there* was one busily employed, and stones and timbers seemed to be literally growing together. At night, the work presented a most singular and imposing appearance. The workmen carried on their operations by the light of numerous huge fires, which not only illuminated the immediate neighbourhood, but threw into the sky a red and lurid reflection which could be seen several miles off. Thousands of our fellow citizens visited the works, for the purpose of looking on the novel and striking spectacle which they furnished. And it was well worthy of an inspection. The glare of the fires, brightly mirrored in the bosom of the river – the columns of smoke continually rising into the air – the busy figures moving about in all directions, as they took each his part in the business of the night – and the dense crowds assembled to witness the various operations, afforded altogether a fine field for the studies of the painter, and furnished abundant food for the most interesting reflection. We are sorry to add that "Sunday shone no Sabbath day" on the works – a needless and most unjustifiable desecration …

The first experimental trip between Bath and Bristol … took place on Friday the 21st … The party consisted of five of the Directors … attended by Mr Brunel, Mr Clarke, the superintendent, and some other officers of the company. In consequence of the rails not being quite finished at the station in Temple Meads, it was not easy to get a carriage upon the line at the engine house and the party were therefore content to "take their places" on the engine and tender. The engine selected for the first part of the journey was the *Arrow*, the first Bristol-made locomotive … The start was made from a point nearly opposite to the engine house, at 20 minutes after four o'clock, and after threading the darksome passage of Tunnels Nos 1, 2, and 3, and skimming over the new embankment at Fox's Wood, the engine was stopped at the Keynsham station at 4.30. Here the Directors alighted, and after a delay of eight minutes, they started again on the other line of rails, with the *Meridian*, a fine engine from the manufactory of Messrs Hawthorn & Co of Newcastle. As the engine flew onwards, the party were greeted with hearty cheers from bands of workmen and spectators at different points, and, after making a short stoppage near the Cross-posts bridge to take up the assistant engineer, Mr Frere (who, we regret to hear, had lately met with a severe accident from a fall), the Directors completed their trip to Bath at the Oak Street viaduct at 4.53. After staying some time to inspect the progress of the bridge over the Avon, the party again took their places on the engine, and the start was made at 5.32. A short stoppage was again made at the Cross-posts bridge, and then the Keynsham station was reached at 5.45. Here the Directors again took flight by the *Arrow*, which landed them safely at the engine house in St Philip's in ten and a half minutes. In consequence of the numerous workmen still at work on the line, it was not thought prudent to make any trial of speed; but our readers will see that the trip was performed to Bath in 35 minutes, including two stoppages, one of these of eight minutes, and the return trip in twenty-three and a half minutes, including one short stoppage. Such a rate as this must be quite sufficient to secure an abundant traffic as soon as the line is opened to the public. We think it not amiss to add, at a time when public attention is painfully excited by dreadful casualties on other lines, that though nearly two millions of passengers have passed over that part of the Great Western line already open to the public, not one individual has lost his life or any serious accident occurred. This is in great measure to be attributed to the width of gauge which renders it all but impossible for the carriages to run off the rails, and which, whilst it is productive of a vast superiority in speed, ensures also a superiority on a point of infinitely more importance – that of safety. When completed, there is no doubt that this line will rank as the very first in the kingdom.

And now to speak of the opening on Monday. Contrary to general expectation, there was no procession or other public ceremony ... Our reporter repaired to the station in Temple Street, Bristol, in order to start by the first train. The Union Jack was displayed on the depot, and numerous flags were so disposed as to give an air of great gaiety and animation to the spot ... As the time of departure drew nigh, passengers began to arrive in rapid succession, and, at a few minutes before eight, the train, consisting of three elegant first class, and five second class carriages, was nearly filled. The arrangements of the company were admirable; not the slightest confusion occurred, and all was ready for the start by eight o'clock, when the bell was rung and the *Fireball* engine was attached to the train. At ten minutes past eight it was in motion, and glided beautifully off with gradually quickening speed until it was lost to the sight of the spectators who had assembled at and around the depot. Thus commenced the first regular railway journey between Bath and Bristol …

As the train proceeded towards Keynsham the scene became extremely animated. Thousands of gazers of all classes had gathered together at the various places affording good views of the line, and enthusiastically evinced their admiration and delight. The Keynsham station was reached in fourteen minutes. Here there was a stoppage of three minutes for the purpose of taking up and setting down passengers, after which the well-filled train proceeded rapidly towards Bath, the country on each side of the line displaying countless groups of spectators anxious to get a glimpse of the new and surprising mode of travelling.

The train reached this city in exactly 30 minutes, exclusive of stoppages, from the time of leaving the Bristol depot. For the sake of safety on this, the first day of actual travelling in the ordinary sense, the great speed which will be generally attained on the railway was very properly avoided … At the Bath end of the line a large multitude of spectators had congregated to witness the opening. Stall Street, the Bristol Road and Claverton Street were densely thronged, and all the thoroughfares from which a view of the line could be obtained, and most of the elevated positions around the city, were crowded with curious gazers. There was a large concourse of strangers from the neighbouring country who kept the whole of the city in a considerable bustle until night. Merry peals from the Abbey bells, and occasional discharges of firearms, marked the day as one of especial rejoicing. Many of the shops were closed and large numbers of our fellow citizens made "a whole holiday" of the occasion.

As the train came in sight of the various assemblages of spectators they greeted its appearance with hearty cheers which the engine-monster seemed to acknowledge with loud snorts of satisfaction. The crowds which gathered to witness the arrival and departure of the first trains did not diminish during the day … The bridges across the line were favourite positions, as they afforded the opportunity of seeing the carriages coming and going for a

Early days on the Great Western as re-enacted in 1925.

considerable distance. Two or three of the engines were decorated with small flags which had a very pleasing appearance as the trains rushed rapidly through the air, keeping them in almost a fixed position, as if by the means of a powerful gale of wind. The passengers in the various carriages added to the animation of the proceedings by the continual waving of hats and handkerchiefs.

As was to have been expected, a large number of our fellow citizens visited Bristol on this occasion, and there was an abundant ingress into Bath of our Bristol neighbours. The numbers that started from the Bath station during the day were, as nearly as we have been able to ascertain, as under:

FIRST CLASS PASSENGERS	720
SECOND CLASS DITTO	2030-2750

And the amount received was, from

FIRST CLASS PASSENGERS	£90
SECOND CLASS DITTO	£176-£266

That most of these passengers were attracted by the novelty of the occasion is evinced by the fact that no very great diminution was perceptible in the numbers of the travellers by the stage coaches. During Tuesday and yesterday, the competition of the railway was more felt by the old conveyances. Mr Lane of the White Lion Coach Office, Mr Reilly of the York House, Mr Pickwick of the White Hart, and Mr Clarke of the Greyhound, have started omnibuses, etc, to convey passengers to and from the railway station at 6d each, thus judiciously making the best of circumstances, and getting all they can out of their gigantic rival.

We will now give a few disjointed particulars connected with the events of the day.

A numerous party, including some of the railway directors and others officially engaged in the undertaking, on arriving by the first train from Bristol, partook of a splendid breakfast at the White Lion.

The fastest trip during the day was accomplished in 20 minutes, and the longest in 30 minutes, exclusive of stoppages.

There were four engines on the line during the day — the *Fireball*, the *Arrow*, the *Lynx* and the *Meridian* – all of them fine specimens of machinery. The carriages are of splendid construction: those of the first class being fitted up with an attention to luxurious comfort which, we are told, coachbuilders are not in the general habit of putting even into gentlemen's carriages. The second class carriages also afford very excellent accommodation. The road itself has proved to be of the most admirable character as regards smoothness of travelling. When the trains are fairly off there is a total absence of the unpleasant jerkings and bumpings which are felt by passengers on other lines, and which indeed were experienced on the Great Western between Maidenhead and Paddington, until removed by an alteration in the principle of laying down the rails.

The company's guards and porters (habited in neat dresses of green, with badges upon the right arm bearing the initials GWR) were extremely active and attentive. Although there was now and then some small delay in the starting of the trains during the day, and a little mishap or two of other kinds, everything went off in the most admirable manner. No accident occurred either to life or limb, which, considering the newness of the arrangements of this great

A broad gauge train passing through Keynsham station.

undertaking and the extensive assemblage of spectators at all points along the line from which a view of the trains could be obtained, is a circumstance calculated to excite much surprise and to reflect the highest credit on all concerned … It was somewhat apprehended that, in consequence of the great rapidity with which the works at and near the Claverton Bridge were executed, in order to allow of the opening on Monday, some disaster would occur. There was, however, not the slightest ground for fear. The most careful precautions had been taken, and the result has fully proved that the calculations made by those to whom the execution of the work was entrusted were in every respect correct.

The *Bristol Standard* provided its own version of events:

We were at the terminus in Temple Gate shortly after seven o'clock on the eventful morning. Numerous stragglers were already in the neighbourhood, and many had placed themselves on the summit of Pile Hill, eager to enjoy the sight of the first-started train. Precisely at 7.30, the boarding which had closed up the passengers' entrance at the northern gate fell inwards and formed a platform leading to a gravelled path, over which we were the first of the public who walked towards the booking office. Having paid our money we proceeded up a flight of stairs which led us to the passengers' starting platform forming one side of the building. The railway guards, dressed in handsome liveries, were in constant attendance, and with the utmost promptitude the passengers were shown into the carriages. The first class carriages are divided into six sections; the sections being subdivided into two compartments, each affording ample room for four persons. The second class conveyances are also divided into six sections, each of which is adapted to carry 12 individuals; they are covered at the top and have open sides.

The locomotive which had the honour of conveying this the first railway train that ever left Bristol was the *Fireball*. The train soon arrived at the tunnels, which form the only unpleasant part of the ride; as in two of them the passengers were for a short time in complete darkness. Approaching Bath, the scene, which towards the centre of the journey had become less animated, began to assume a more lively appearance. The passage across the Avon over the extraordinary timber bridge near the entrance into Bath was made with the greatest caution. Confident assertions had been made that it would not be in a fit state to permit the passage of the train by the day fixed for the opening of the line; but the unremitting exertions of Mr Brunel and those immediately under him so hastened the work that it was completed in time, though we understand that the last rail was not laid till seven o'clock on Monday morning. It is said that Mr Brunel and Mr Wilcox, the contractor for the bridge who had betted largely that the structure would be in readiness, won considerable sums of money on the occasion. Arrived in safety at the Bath station, the passengers gave expression to their joy by utterance of a loud cheer, which was warmly and cordially responded to by those on the platform and the surrounding multitudes.

Here, as well as at the Bristol terminus, we were struck with a novel description of signals, consisting of a large disc perforated with holes on the top of a pole, which is made to present its edge to the line of railway when the approaching trains may with safety proceed to the station, and, when any obstruction exists, its face is presented. At night coloured lights indicate the same information.

"The day terminated," wrote one relieved onlooker, "without disturbance, and during the evening in the cities of Bath and Bristol there was but one demonstration – that of festivities and pleasures."

Jubilation was not universal, however. Among those who were less than delighted at the coming of the railway were those whose livelihood depended on carrying people or goods by road or water. "Several stage coaches," reported a correspondent in Bristol, "have announced they will still continue to run, and although Jarvey's face was less cheery than of yore, he proposes it will be long before the last of his race will be seen on the Bath Road, as many persons will prefer glorifying in the beauty of a set of smoking bays to being whirled along by a pot of boiling water."

Others bemoaned the desecration of the countryside. William Wordsworth was one of the most prominent anti-railway campaigners; some, like Mr Berkeley, the Member of Parliament for Cheltenham, had less poetic reasons for their opposition. "Nothing," he wrote, "is more distasteful to me than to hear the echo of our hills reverberating with the noise of hissing railroad engines, running through the heart of our hunting country, and destroying the noble sport which I have been accustomed to from my childhood."

Those who bemoaned the coming of the railways were outnumbered, however, by those who greeted them ecstatically. They were not simply exhilarated by the sensation of travelling at speeds hitherto possible only by jumping off tall buildings; they saw the railways, as Brunel did when queried about knocking down buildings in Claverton Street, as the harbinger of a moral revolution. The railways would sweep away the tired, old system, with all the human misery it entailed, and usher in a golden age of unbounded progress. The Reverend Edward Stanley, Bishop of Norwich, argued that, although "the realities of the age" were "not propitious to the aspiration of the poet,"

> they afford abundant matter for the study, the admiration, and the delight of the philosopher. They abound with scientific wonders, they manifest the rapid march of intellect, they exhibit man competing with man, and nation with nation, in glorious rivalry for pre-eminence in art, science and literature, in conquering prejudice, and in advancing the "end and aim" of creation – human happiness.

> Of all the promoters of civilization, the railway system of communication will be amongst the foremost in its effects, for it cannot fail to produce many and mighty changes in manufactures, in commerce, in trade and in science …

He then went on to describe his first journey on the Liverpool & Manchester Railway:

> No words can convey an adequate notion of the magnificence (I cannot use a smaller word) of our progress. At first it was comparatively slow; but soon we felt that we were GOING, and then it was that every person to whom the conveyance was new, must have been sensible that the adaptation of locomotive power was establishing a fresh era in the state of society …
>
> The most intense curiosity and excitement prevailed … Enormous masses of densely packed people lined the road, shouting and waving hats and handkerchiefs as we flew by them. What with the sight and sound of these cheering multitudes and the tremendous velocity with which we were borne past them, my spirits rose to true champagne height …

For others, like Walter Thornbury, the poetry of railway motion was more than adequate compensation for the passing of the coaching era:

> Men see no poetry in being shot as from a cannon, or passing from Bath to Bristol with the speed of a planet on a tour, or a fallen star bent on pleasure … Know, O insensate man, that that sound of the engine is like the champ and tramp of a thousand horse: it might be Tamerlane riding to conquest: it might be Alaric thundering at the gates of Rome … We are gliding on golden rails that the sunset shines on, and we are just about to thread an arch. When we lean back, and the great smoke-clouds that roll around us grow crimson in the sunlight, we shall seem as if we were in the aerial car of Indian mythology. Like a white banner flies the engine's smoke – and away it rolls – stooping to join the great white fog that has no wings, and sits and broods yonder about the damp autumn fields. Through dark caves of tunnels – through dull barrennesses of high and bare

GREAT WESTERN RAILWAY.

ALTERATION OF TRAINS BETWEEN BRISTOL AND BATH.

Horses and Carriages being at the Stations ten minutes before the time specified for the departure of the trains, will be conveyed by Railway between Bristol and Bath Stations.

Hours of Departure, regulated by Bristol time, until the whole Line shall be opened, Daily, (Excepting Sundays).

UP FROM BRISTOL.	DEPARTURE FROM Bristol.	Keynsham	Saltford.	Twerton.	Arrives at Bath.	DOWN FROM BATH.	DEPARTURE FROM Bath.	Twerton.	Saltford.	Keynsham	Arrives at Bristol.
	H. M.	H. M.	H. M.	H. M.	H. M.		H. M.	H. M.	H. M.	H. M.	H. M.
To BATH, A.M.	7 0	—	—	—	7 23	To BRISTOL, A.M.	8 0	—	8 10	8 16	8 26
— —	8 30	8 40	—	8 51	8 56	— —	9 30	9 34	—	—	9 55
— —	9 30	—	9 45	—	9 55	— —	10 30	—	—	10 45	10 55
— —	11 30	11 40	—	11 51	11 56	— P.M.	12 30	—	12 40	12 46	12 56
— P.M.	1 30	1 40	1 46	—	1 56	— —	2 30	2 34	—	—	2 55
— —	2 30	—	—	2 50	2 55	— —	3 30	—	—	3 45	3 55
— —	3 30	3 40	—	—	3 55	— —	4 30	—	4 40	—	4 55
— —	4 30	—	4 45	—	4 55	— —	5 30	5 34	—	5 46	5 56
— —	5 30	5 40	—	—	5 55	— —	6 30	—	6 40	—	6 55
— —	6 30	—	6 45	6 51	6 56	— —	7 30	—	—	—	7 53
— —	8 30	8 40	—	—	8 55	— —	9 30	9 34	—	9 46	9 56

ON SUNDAYS.

UP FROM BRISTOL.	Bristol.	Keynsham	Saltford.	Twerton.	Bath.	DOWN FROM BATH.	Bath.	Twerton.	Saltford.	Keynsham	Bristol.
	H. M.	H. M.	H. M.	H. M.	H. M.		H. M.	H. M.	H. M.	H. M.	H. M.
To BATH, A.M.	8 0	8 10	—	8 21	8 26	To BRISTOL, A.M.	9 0	9 4	—	9 16	9 26
— —	9 0	9 10	9 16	—	9 26	— —	10 0	—	10 10	10 16	10 26
— P.M.	2 30	2 40	2 46	2 54	3 0	— P.M.	3 30	3 34	3 42	3 48	4 0
— —	5 30	5 40	5 46	5 55	6 0	— —	6 30	6 34	6 42	6 48	7 0
— —	8 30	8 40	8 46	8 54	9 0	— —	9 30	9 34	9 42	9 48	10 0

Further Particulars, and Train Bills, may be had on application at the Company's Offices, and at the Railway Stations.

By order of the Directors,

CHAS. A. SAUNDERS,
THOMAS OSLER, } Secretaries.

Trains between Bath and Bristol in February 1841.

embankments – we rush with the force of a steam-catapult or a huge case-shot that is never spent – like a battering ram – in a long race, for this steam-horse, with fire for blood, never wearies. Swift round curves, and swift up low hills – swift past village church and park and farmhouse and wood – over river – along moor – past fat and lean, rich and poor, rock and clay, meadow and street; for this mad horse never wearies.

In the weeks following the opening of the line, Bathonians and Bristolians slowly began to adjust to the unwonted proximity of their two cities. Some were quick to exploit the potential of the railway. James Ivatts, of the Royal Gloucester Hotel at Clifton, advertised railway excursions from Bath, with carriages meeting every train and conveying visitors to "view the unrivalled scenery of rocks, woods and water, as well as the suspension bridge."

On 10 September 1840, the *Bristol Standard* published a somewhat exaggerated survey of locomotive performance:

> Since the opening of the line we have had frequent opportunities of testing the superiority of the wide gauge, and ascertaining the greatly increased speed attained thereon, beyond what we have experienced on those of the northern lines at present open to the public. Whether this speed is attributable to the longitudinal bearings, and the greater width of rail adopted, or in part owing to the much greater power of the locomotive engines employed, we are not aware. Certain it is, however, that we have travelled in some parts of this distance at a rate exceeding 60 miles an hour, and with a steadiness which prevented any uncomfortable sensation from passing over the ground at this extraordinary speed. We have great pleasure in saying that the swiftest engine on the line is the *Arrow*, manufactured in our own city ... On one occasion the *Arrow* brought a train down from Bath in 13 minutes, and steam was shut off at the entrance of No 2 tunnel, the train afterwards coming up to the terminus, a distance of one and three quarter miles, by its own momentum. A speed was here attained equal to 100 miles per hour, for a part of the distance, which is very far beyond that of which any other railway has yet been found capable

Today, it is generally accepted that the first locomotive to break the 100 mile an hour barrier was the Great Western locomotive, *City of Truro*, which reached 102.3 mph down Wellington Bank in Somerset in 1904.

Three weeks after the opening, the line between Bath and Bristol suffered its first fatality:

> A frightful and fatal accident occurred on the Great Western Railway yesterday afternoon, It appears that a cow keeper named Robert Ruddel, aged 80 years, had been in the habit of crossing the line in pursuit of his avocations, at the Gravel Pits, Keynsham, and on this occasion he was induced, at the request of one of the police, who knew that he was deaf and feeble through his great age, to sit down on a post until after the five o'clock up train from Bristol, which was momentarily expected, should have passed. He, however, unfortunately left his seat too soon, and got between the rails just as the train came in sight, and, notwithstanding that the whistle of the engine and other signals were used to warn him out of the way, he

> did not move, and the whole train passed over him, causing his instant death and terrible mutilation. No blame whatever can be attached to the company's servants.

Incidents that today would warrant a full-scale enquiry seem to have been accepted as part and parcel of running a railway. Most common were derailments. This report, from the *Bath Chronicle* of 17 September, is fairly typical:

> The five o'clock train from this city to Bristol was detained an hour on Thursday last, in consequence of one of the carriages slipping off the rails. The turntables at this end of the line not being completed, the trains, after their arrival from Bristol, have to be taken back to the "pointers," a short distance along the road, for the purpose of being removed to the other line. On crossing the intersections the accident happened. A large body of the company's servants immediately rendered every assistance, but it was nearly six o'clock before the carriage was replaced on the line. About a quarter past five the train from Bristol came in sight, but in consequence of the admirably arranged signals the steam was let off, and the engine stopped before it arrived at the obstruction.

That week's *Chronicle* also carried a report of a more serious accident, which highlights how ineffective the brakes on early locomotives were:

> On Sunday evening an accident occurred on the Great Western Railway near the depot at Bristol, which, though unaccompanied with any serious injury, caused a consternation among the passengers of no ordinary nature. In order to render our account of this occurrence intelligible to our readers, it is desirable that we should convey to them some idea of the formation of the line in the immediate vicinity of the place where it happened. The engine house, that is the place where the engines are taken for the purposes of being repaired, cleaned, etc., is situated about a mile from the depot, a little to the north of the main line, and from the purposes of running the engines from the main line to that on which they are conveyed to the engine house, moveable points are placed, called

switches. When the engine has crossed the intersections where the switches are situated, it is the duty of the switchman, a responsible person appointed for the purpose, to see that the points or switches are so placed as to admit the transit of the trains to the main line. On this occasion, however, this duty was omitted, and hence the accident which we have to detail. The particulars are as follows: The eight o'clock train, consisting of eight crowded carriages, left the Bristol terminus at a few minutes after the appointed hour, drawn by the *Lynx* engine, with the tender in front. After proceeding about three quarters of a mile, during which a speed was attained of the rate of about 12 or 15 miles per hour, the engine, in consequence of the switches being left open, ran off the main line on the one leading to the engine shed. The engineer immediately saw the mischief, and quickly let off the steam and applied the break [sic]. The conductors and guards being also on the lookout, found the train running off the main line, and immediately applied their breaks also. The unusual anxiety evinced by these officers, together with the harsh grating sound occasioned by the sudden application of the breaks, gave the first intimation to the passengers that something was wrong. An alarm soon spread from carriage to carriage, and the enquiry had scarcely been made "What's the matter?" when the tender of the *Lynx* engine came in contact with the *Arrow* engine. The violence of the concussion shattered the tender and did serious damage to the *Arrow*, but to what extent we have not been able to ascertain. An indescribable terror came over the passengers, who were thrown from their seats and huddled together in the greatest confusion. The shrieks of the females, mingled with the shouts of some of the men, created the greatest confusion, and, amidst the general hubbub, repeated exclamations of "We are all killed" could be distinguished. Several of the females fainted, and remained unconscious of what was going on; others had their bonnets crushed; and scarcely any of the passengers escaped without a blow of some sort or other. Beyond these matters, however, we are happy to add that no personal injury was sustained. It is very fortunate that the *Arrow* was stationed on the line, for coming in contact with that engine the speed at which the train was going was materially checked; had this not been the case, the train must have gone some yards further, where, we understand, there is a large opening made, for the purpose of

> forming a turn-table. Had the engine run into that place the probability is that the lives of the engineer and the fireman, if not of other persons, would have been sacrificed. It not being considered safe to proceed to Bath with the *Lynx*, that engine was removed, and the *Fireball* attached to the train. A delay of about an hour took place, when the train was conveyed to the main line, the signal of "all's right" was given, and the passengers were conveyed in safety to Bath, which place was reached about a quarter to ten o'clock. In the meantime, considerable uneasiness was manifested in this city in consequence of the non-arrival of the train at the usual hour. We hear that, immediately after the accident occurred, the switch man, through whose neglect the accident happened, decamped, and was not to be seen any more that night. We understand he will be brought before the directors for examination, and those gentlemen will, no doubt, punish him to the extent of their power for culpable remissness.

Despite what would today be regarded as appalling levels of danger, the Great Western's safety record was an enviable one. On 1 October, the *Bath Chronicle* reported that, since the first stretch of line had opened over two years earlier, over a million and a half passengers had been carried "without any accident, fatal or otherwise." For those who still maintained the superiority of horse-drawn transport, this report of a coaching accident in the same issue would have brought little comfort:

> On Saturday evening as the *Mercury* Birmingham coach was passing through Bath, the horses took fright near the top of Milsom Street and galloped rapidly by the White Hart Inn, where they ought to have stopped. By the time they reached St James's Church they became so frightened by the confusion and noise which they occasioned, that they dashed along with increased fury till they arrived at the corner of the Old Bridge on the Widcombe side, and here the coach, coming in contact with the pavement, upset with a frightful crash, throwing the passengers in all directions. The scene in Southgate Street at the time the coach passed through is described as having been one of an alarming nature. The horses swerved from side to side, upsetting the fruit carts and apple baskets, and placing

> in extreme jeopardy the lives of those who were passing. One or two persons were knocked down, but not severely injured. On the coach there were seven or eight passengers, who were more or less hurt. One man was conveyed to the General Hospital, as was also a female.

In the context of such incidents, rail travel must have seemed positively benign, even though reports such as the following continued to appear with alarming regularity:

> There was a delay of some hours in one of the trains yesterday week, arising from some carriages having been placed on the rail, on which the train was travelling. No accident, however, occurred, notwithstanding rumours to the contrary. (26 November 1840)

> An accident, fortunately unattended by any serious consequences, occurred on the Bath and Bristol line on Saturday. It appears that a new engine named the *Antelope* had recently been placed on the line and in the course of its journey on the above day, when near the Twerton station, one of the tubes connected with the boiler suddenly burst, in consequence of which the train was unable to proceed further. In a short time, however, another train came up, and the disabled engine was drawn to the Bath station, and the carriages were almost immediately afterwards propelled to Bristol. (17 June 1841)

FOURTEEN

Fear and Loathing in Bathwick

Although the line from Bath to Bristol was now open, much work needed to be done before the line to London was complete. The major obstacle was Box Tunnel, but the section eastwards through Bath also presented formidable engineering challenges. For the army of labourers who had struggled to get the skew bridge finished in time, there was no respite. They were redeployed on works whose completion was now a matter of the utmost urgency. On Christmas Eve, 1839, the Great Western directors had instructed the secretary "to call Mr Brunel's attention to the urgent necessity for letting the works that remain to be constructed between Hampton Row and the Bath Depot." Contracts had been awarded; all that now remained was for the work to be completed. Because of the need to get the work finished as quickly as possible, corners seem to have been cut, especially with regard to safety, and the accident rate soared.

The *Bath Chronicle* of 13 August 1840 carried news of no less than three fatal accidents:

> A very young man, named John Allen, one of the drivers on that part of the Great Western Railway now constructing by the side of the canal on the road to Bathampton, was on Thursday night brought to the United Hospital, having met with a frightful accident. His foot slipped and he fell, when the whole train of tram wagons went over his right arm and thigh, completely smashing both limbs. The loss of blood was so great that he died soon after he had reached the hospital. The funeral service of Allen on Sunday morning, in Bathwick Churchyard, was attended by a very large body of his fellow workmen on the railroad. The men were all uniformly dressed in clean smock frocks, and each wore a white bow in his hair. A few of them appeared to be deeply affected by the calamitous accident

which had brought a remarkably fine youth to a very early and most unexpected death.

Another accident, which proved fatal, happened on Friday afternoon to a man named John Dingle, whilst he was at work on the Great Western Railway near Bathford, by the falling in of a quantity of earth. The poor fellow was conveyed to the United Hospital, where he lingered until Sunday night.

On Tuesday afternoon, another accident, which terminated fatally, occurred on the line of the Great Western Railway between Middle Hill and Bathford to a youth, aged 15 years, called William Atkins. It appears that the deceased was engaged with a train of loaded tram wagons, which, moving unexpectedly, passed over both his thighs, completely crushing them. The sufferer was removed to the United Hospital, where he died within a few hours.

On the afternoon of Saturday 22 August,

a shocking accident which occurred on the railway at the Dolemeads Viaduct instantaneously put a period to the existence of George Matthews, a mason employed on that part of the works. The men engaged at the spot had nearly completed the centre of an arch, and, while a piece of timber was being hauled up, a portion of the scaffolding gave way, and the whole mass fell with a frightful crash. At this moment the unfortunate deceased was passing under the intended archway, when a heavy beam came in contact with his head, which was so frightfully shattered by the blow that not a vestige of his features could be distinguished. We understand that the deceased has left a wife and four young children.

A day earlier, William Chadwick, the contractor building St James's Bridge, narrowly escaped serious injury, while on the bridge inspecting the progress of the work:

Whilst in conversation with one of his men (and standing at the time on the highest part of one of the ribs), he lost his balance. He immediately made an attempt to regain his position, and in doing so unfortunately stepped over the beam, when he was precipitated into the water, a depth of 30 feet. In his fall he came in contact with the

Navvies at work in Sydney Gardens.

> woodwork which is erected for the purposes of the undertaking, and then pitched violently upon the piles of the coffer dam, into which he fell. From this perilous situation, however, he was speedily extricated, and being placed in a boat was conveyed on shore. He was senseless for a short time, but soon recovered his consciousness.

On 8 September,

> two men named Ward and Greedy, who had been at work on the railway, near Sydney Gardens, were taken to the United Hospital, having received serious injuries from the falling in of a quantity of earth work. Greedy was buried a long time, and when extricated from his perilous situation it was feared that life was extinct, but animation was restored. We regret to state that the poor fellow has sustained a dislocation of the hip and other severe contusions. His companion also had his thigh broken.

Just over a month later, on 16 October, John Tapp was sawing stone on the viaduct at Dolemeads, when "a box containing stones, while being drawn to the top of the masonry, fell upon him and injured him so severely that he died in half an hour after being taken to the United Hospital."

Five deaths in just over two months was an appalling record, but there was no health and safety enquiry, no compensation paid to the victims' families, no official reprimand for the contractors. Nevertheless, working practices may have been tightened up, for there were no more serious accidents until the following midsummer's day, when John Hewitt was at work, near Sydney Gardens,

> beneath a plank which was stretched across the line, when, on another labourer passing over it, the plank suddenly gave way at one end, and falling upon Hewitt's head, fractured his skull and jaw severely. The sufferer was taken to the United Hospital, where he lingered until [5 July], when he died in a state of delirium ... The deceased has left a widow and three children.

One of the largest works between Bath and Box was the bridge over the Avon at Bathford, the contract for which had been awarded to David Aust. Similar in design to the controversial bridge at Maidenhead, which Brunel's critics had insisted would collapse once the centrings were removed, it not only carried the railway but also a public footpath. Initially, it was suggested that it could also carry a road. In July 1840, a petition was drawn up to that effect:

> To the Surveyors of the Highways of the Parishes of Bathford and Bathampton in the County of Somerset:
>
> Gentlemen,
>
> We the undersigned inhabitants ... beg leave to draw your attention to the following facts:
>
> That the ford which connects your two parishes, and which, if properly repaired, would be an accommodation to the public, is now useless for want of repair.
>
> That a bridge is about to be built over the Avon by the Great Western Railway, near the meeting of the three turnpike roads leading from Bath to Devizes, Chippenham and Bradford, and that a private footway is to be provided over such bridge for the use of the Lord of the Manor of Bathampton and his tenants.

The bridge over the Avon at Bathford.

> That such way, if converted into a carriage road and thrown open, would afford a very great accommodation to the inhabitants of this parish and the public in general, especially as the distance from the point where the three roads above named converge to Bath would be very considerably shortened, and a communication opened with the new Warminster Road.
>
> Under these circumstances, we would respectively [sic] but urgently represent to you the propriety, if not the duty, of your making such arrangements with the directors of the Great Western Railway and the Lord of the Manor of Hampton as will secure to the public a free carriage road over the intended bridge.

The *Bath Chronicle* threw its weight behind the project, pointing out that

> the old foss road from Bathampton to within a short distance of the old ford is in good repair – that it communicates with the new Warminster Road – that the Great Western Railway are willing to

> enlarge the bridge about to be erected at Bathford, so as to allow a 20-foot carriage road, independent of the railway, if the necessary funds can be raised – and that such a road would be a very great accommodation to the public ... There is, however, no time to be lost, as active preparations are making for the construction of the railway bridge.

It is needless to add that the road was never built, needless too to remind present-day residents of Bath what a lost opportunity this was, and what a useful link the road bridge would have provided. As it was, the only way from Bathampton to Bathford (except by ferry) was via Cleveland Bridge until 1872, when the Bathampton Toll Bridge opened.

On 24 September, the *Bath Chronicle* gave further details of building works in Bath:

> Those who are inclined to wonder how the immense stones of which Druidical and other monuments of remote antiquity are constructed could have been taken from their original situations and placed in their present positions, may have their surprise considerably qualified by witnessing the transporting, by limited and ordinary means, of the huge masses of oolite which are now almost every day brought down Widcombe Hill, from the quarries on Claverton Down, for the construction of the works connected with the Great Western Railway. We saw the other day at Widcombe Crescent a number of persons assembled round a wagon and on drawing near to ascertain the object of their curiosity, we found that they were gazing on a Brobdingnagian monolith, 15 feet long, four feet thick, and weighing not much short of ten tons. It was dragged down the hill by seven horses. The road to Claverton Down has during the last year been subjected to so much wear and tear by the wagons carrying stone for the railway, that some time since a turnpike bar was placed at the top of the hill, for the especial benefit of the persons engaged in these extraordinary haulages.

A week later, it was reported that Mr Lewis, who had been awarded the contract for the station at Bath was "advancing with great rapidity," joists having been laid for the first floor. At Keynsham, however, work on the station was running late, due to the negligence of the unfortunate Mr Fripp, who had been appointed to oversee the project. On 12 October, Brunel wrote to him in a fit of Gallic pique:

> *Fripp,*
> *Plain gentlemanly language seems to have no effect upon you. I must try stronger language and stronger methods. You are a cursed, lazy, inattentive, apathetic vagabond and if you continue to neglect my instructions I shall send you about your business. I have frequently told you, among other absurd, untidy habits, that of making drawings on the backs of others is inconvenient. By your cursed neglect of that you have wasted more of my time than your whole life is worth. Looking for the altered drawings you were to make of several things at the station and which I have just found – they won't do. I must see you on Wednesday. Let me have no more of this provoking conduct or of the abominable and criminal laziness with which you suffer contractors to patch and scamp their work.*

Fripp was not the only one who prompted Brunel into penning white-hot missives. A few months earlier, he had visited Stothert & Slaughter's works in Bristol, and seen a cracked cylinder fitted to an engine destined for the Great Western Railway. The cigar wedged between his teeth must have been chewed to shreds as he scribbled this monumental piece of invective:

> *The flaw was so large that it could not escape the attention of the most careless observer … I do not believe that a workman would have thought of using it in the most contemptible, worst mannered shop in England – except with fraudulent intention – yet I find such a thing in that which you profess to put perfection of workmanship and materials and upon the success of which the reputation of your house depends … Your foremen are utterly neglectful … They are so grossly ignorant as to suppose that they could succeed in defrauding the company … Your workmen are spoilt, they have learned that they may scamp their work. All confidence on my part is completely destroyed and I should neglect my duty to the company if I did not now withdraw the order.*

Skew Bridge as originally built.

However, as the locomotive in question, *Dart*, was delivered five months later, it appears that the firm managed to mollify Brunel and persuaded him to reinstate the order.*

In October, "a handsome pierced parapet [was] placed on the skew bridge of the Great Western Railway at Claverton Street, and which gives the structure a greatly improved appearance." The *Bath Chronicle* offered the opinion that, "when the scaffolding about this bridge is removed, and it has been cleaned and painted, it will be one of the most beautiful as well as curious erections of the kind which this country contains." The scaffolding was removed the following January, and the erection stood forth "in all its singular beauty. Those of our readers who have not seen it," enthused the *Bath Chronicle*,

> will find an inspection very gratifying. We question whether the country contains a more curious specimen of bridge architecture on

**This was the second locomotive built by Stothert & Slaughter for the Great Western, the first being* Arrow. *They lasted for 23 and 29 years respectively. Curiously, both* Arrow *and* Dart *were names borne by locomotives used at the opening of the Liverpool & Manchester Railway in 1830.*

> the same scale. Viewed as a whole, it has an elegantly light and airy appearance – so light and airy, indeed, that, at first glance, it seems hardly strong enough to bear the weight of the heavy trains continually passing over it. But when its details are examined, immense strength is found united to grace of outline; the solid ribs of closely compacted timber, and the bolts and bars of toughly wrought iron, which lend their powerful aid, effectually convince the spectator that the bridge is far more than equal to any service which can ever be required of it. An excellent view may be had of all the mechanism of the bridge from the towing path which passes under it. Looked at thence, the interior of the structure bears some resemblance to the large wooden roofs under which ships of war have of late years been built in the government dockyards. The best general view of this pleasing effect of art is from the Old Bath Bridge, whence the acute angle at which it crosses the stream, and the perspective of its arches, have a very striking aspect. We have heard lovers of the picturesque complain that, however beautiful the railway bridge may be, it has, in conjunction with the formal line of railway leading from it, sadly marred the very splendid prospect of Bath which is beheld from the edge of Claverton Down, just above Macaulay Buildings, the railway having interfered with the view of the Old Bridge, which, as seen from the above spot, was a very pleasing feature of the landscape, especially just after sunset on a fine day, when its outline rested darkly against the bright water behind it, and the lustre of the evening sky streamed through the arches, giving them a distinctness which they possessed at no other time of day. As some set-off against this particular deterioration of our scenery, it may be mentioned that the curved line of arches over which the railway passes through the lower part of our city materially improves the appearance of that neighbourhood, as seen from the higher parts of Bath – especially from Bathwick Hill and its immediate vicinity – beheld from which the new works have a very pleasing effect.

One of the most difficult sections of line that still remained to be completed was at Hampton Row, where the Kennet & Avon Canal had to be diverted to make way for the railway. Originally, the line was going to be built north of Hampton Row, near the river, but in 1836 it was decided to route it to the south. The reason for the change is

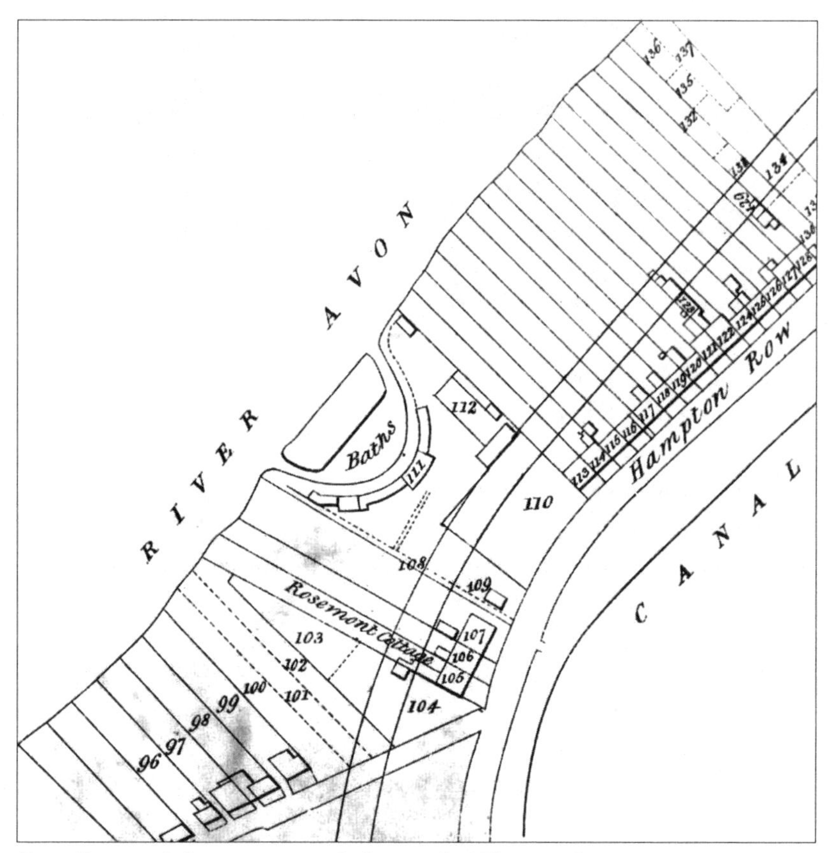

Brunel's original plan was to route the line north of Hampton Row

unknown, but it was probably because Brunel, having re-examined the route, considered that an embankment at this point would not only be difficult to construct, but, as it lay on a hillside liable to flooding, be inherently unstable. A viaduct similar to that at Twerton would have been necessary; given the lie of the land, even that would not have guaranteed stability. The only course the railway could take to the south of Hampton Row was already occupied by the canal. Brunel's solution was to move the canal further south. As the ground south of Hampton Row rose sharply, this meant that the canal had to be separated from the railway by a high retaining wall.

The operation to divert the canal was fraught with difficulties. The first major setback occurred on 15 November 1840, when

> the works of the Great Western Railway, near Hampton Row, [were] considerably damaged ... by an irruption of water at the side of the canal, close to the operations. The removal of a great quantity of earth, for the purposes of carrying on the works, was partly the cause of the flow of the water; and a barge, heavily laden, passing by, increased the pressure of the water against the bank, and accelerated the accident. It is stated that it will cost the contractors a large sum to rectify the mischief which has been done.

This was not the first time the canal had been breached at Hampton Row. Three years earlier, on 29 March 1837,

> the inhabitants of Hampton Row were alarmed by a threatened inundation from the canal. Suddenly the water found vent through the bottom of the canal through the bank, caused, as is supposed, by the giving way of a covering to a sewer or some other subterranean channel. A great body of water poured into the road, which was fortunately prevented from doing much injury by Mr Sumsion, who was on the spot, cutting a quantity of turf and earth, by throwing which and some hay into the hole, the latter was quickly sucked in by the force of the water, and the vent thus stopped.

FIFTEEN

Floods and Sabbatarians

On 17 December 1840, stations opened at Twerton and Saltford, and the line from London was extended to Wootton Bassett Road. On 7 January 1841, a signalman in No 3 Tunnel, between Keynsham and Bristol, was found asleep "with his light so placed as to act as a signal" when the six o'clock train from Bath passed through. He was committed to Shepton Mallet gaol for one month with hard labour.

Perhaps this incident prompted the editor of the *Bath Chronicle* to call for tougher safety measures on the railways, adding that he did not believe "that railway travelling will ever, or can ever be, as safe as the travelling by coaches and horses, on the common roads." Unfortunately, his comments coincided with the sort of weather conditions that continue to prove the superiority of rail transport to this day. "On Thursday evening," reported the *Chronicle*,

> we had a very heavy fall of snow, which was very general. The coaches from London experienced great difficulties in their journeys. The Bath mail, on coming down Marlborough Hill, had to pass through snow as high as the springs of the coach. At half past two in the morning, the same mail, the *Age*, and another coach, were brought to a standstill about three miles this side of Marlborough, the snow having drifted in places to the height of 15 feet. At half past six the mail made an effort to proceed, a passage having been cut through the fields, the drifts of snow having rendered the road impassable, and it was one o'clock pm before the mail arrived in Bath. The above coaches were dug out of the snow six times between Calne and Marlborough. The Bristol Mail, from London, did not arrive till ten minutes to three in the afternoon of Friday, being eight hours and a half after its time. The Devonport mail was compelled on its journey to London to stop all night at Mere, seven

> miles from Wincanton, as no post horses could be obtained. The snow had here accumulated to a depth of from 15 to 20 feet, and the guard was obliged to wait until daylight, when he made his journey across the fields to Basingstoke. At Stonehenge Hill, where a new road has been made, the foundations have all been washed away, and the mail, with other coaches, had to take a circuitous route through a by-road.

The snow melted even more quickly than it had fallen, causing the Avon to burst its banks:

> The effects of the flood were, as usual, the most severely felt in the Dolemeads, where, in consequence of the poverty of the inhabitants, houses with four rooms very generally contain as many families … On Monday, after the water had left their houses, the inhabitants were seen occupying them, wet as they were, without having a spark of fire, and exposed to the cold wind, making its way through the broken windows, from which the rags which had stopped them up had been washed by the flood. We regret being obliged to add that many of the inhabitants of the Dolemeads had gone to bed the preceding night in a state of intoxication habitual to them, and had they not been roused by those who were differently situated, we should not now be able to announce that no loss of human life took place. We have heard of one instance in which a man and his wife, both inebriated, were only awakened by the piercing screams of their four little children who were becoming covered with water in an adjoining bed.
>
> Many strong walls were washed down by the torrent; houses have been partly demolished; and other damage of various kinds has been done along the river's banks. The most serious individual loss is that sustained by Mr Chadwick, who holds the contract for building the St James Bridge over which the railway is to pass from the Ham Gardens to the Dolemeads. A temporary wooden bridge, which had been thrown across the river, for the accommodation of persons concerned in the railway works, was carried away and was floated with great violence towards St James bridge. The works of this bridge were in a state of considerable forwardness. The abutments were already erected, massive piles were driven into the

> bed of the river, strong centrings were fixed, and all was ready for the masons to throw over the arch. The temporary bridge came into contact with these centrings and carried them away with a tremendous crash. The large mass of woodwork was hurried swiftly down the river. It received a check at the skew bridge, against which a portion of the wrecked materials lodged; the remainder was taken onward by the stream to the Old Bridge where a large accumulation was effectually stopped, greatly impeding the rush of water through the arches (which were almost buried by the flood) and thereby imminently endangering the stability of the structure. As soon as practicable, the timbers washed against the bridge were secured by chains and ropes, until the subsiding of the waters should allow of their being taken away. Mr Chadwick's loss by the injury done to the works at St James's Bridge amounts to about £400.

The flood came on top of several weeks of bad weather, which had brought work on the line to a virtual standstill. It was a desperate time, with navvies laid off, wandering the streets of Bath looking for odd jobs or begging for money. For one, at least, the lay-off proved fatal:

> A coroner's inquest was held on Thursday evening [7 January] at the Bell public house in the Lower Bristol Road on the body of John Edwards, a railroad labourer, aged 32, who died, on Wednesday last, at his lodgings in Wood Street, as was supposed at the time, from want of the necessities of life. He had been out of employment five weeks with the exception of two days' work the week previous. He was ill three or four days; and both he and his wife were in the state of the most deplorable wretchedness. A few hours before his death, application was made for him to the medical officer of the Union. Mr Lloyd, on making, by order of the coroner, a post mortem examination, stated his opinion to be that cold and want of nourishment had caused the man's death. It was proved, in evidence, that no application for relief had been made to the relieving officer, the only reason for which given by his wife was the hope of a change of weather, and his then being able to go to work. Verdict: Died from want of the common necessaries of life. The deceased has left a widow and one child, about a year and a half old.

In February, Brunel updated his directors on the progress of works in the Bath area:

> *In the immediate neighbourhood of Bath much still remains to be executed on one contract. The diversion of the Kennet & Avon Canal, in the progress of which very serious difficulties had occurred, caused principally by continued wet weather at a critical period of the works, requires most attention; the retaining wall, however, is nearly completed, and when the course of the canal is diverted, which will shortly be done, the construction of the railway itself at this point is a simple and easy operation.*
> *With the exception of this one point, the works are in a sufficiently forward state between Bath and Bathford. At Bathford the bridge across the Avon is much in arrears, but the necessary means have been and shall be adopted for securing its early completion.*
> *From this point to the Box Tunnel, the works are in a forward state; the long embankment requires but a small additional quantity for its completion, and we are commencing to form the surface preparatory to ballasting.*

The issue of navvies working on Sundays had been simmering ever since they arrived in Bath. In July 1838, the *Chronicle*

> received some communications respecting an impression which has gone abroad, that the labourers on the Great Western Railway pursue their occupations on Sundays as on other days. This impression must owe its origin to the fact that a few men are employed on the tunnellings, etc, in which no cessation can, without danger, be allowed to take place, and the continual prosecution of which is a work of absolute necessity. We have made a careful enquiry into the subject, and we are happy in being able to state, on the best possible authority, that no Sunday work whatever is performed on the railway, excepting that which is strictly indispensable. We may add that it is contrary to the interest of the contractors that work should be done on Sunday, as the men who are employed on that day always expect and obtain a higher rate of wages.

However, those who made it their business to make sure no one worked on Sundays did not let the matter rest, and, on 3 September 1840,

> one of the labourers employed on the Great Western Railway was fined by the borough magistrates for pursuing his ordinary calling on the preceding Lord's Day, being the day before the opening of the railway to Bristol. Two other labourers were not satisfactorily identified, and two others against whom summonses were issued could not be found. The proceedings were instituted by the Lord's Day Observance Association.

Having drawn blood, the local chapter of the Lord's Day Observance Society turned their attention to the running of trains on the Sabbath. In January 1841, they sent a petition to the directors of the Great Western Railway, expressing the "anxiety and alarm" with which they viewed "the running of railway trains upon the Lord's Day, whereby the servants of your establishment are compelled to violate a Divine command, and others who undervalue or disregard its authority are provided with increased facilities for spreading the contagion of their evil example through all the surrounding neighbourhood." While they were prepared to admit

> the many and important advantages which, in commercial and other points of view, may result from the completion of so splendid an undertaking as that of the Great Western Railway; nevertheless, they cannot but at the same time deeply lament that those advantages, however great, will be more than counterbalanced by the evil consequences which must inevitably accrue if this vast work of human art is thus made the instrument of dishonouring Almighty God, as well as of extensive and continually increasing demoralization among the community at large.

Not only did trains continue to run on Sundays; in April, it was announced that the diversion of the canal at Hampton Row was to take place on a Sunday. For Melmoth Walters, the Secretary of the Lord's Day Observance Society, and one of the guiding lights behind the Railway Episcopal Chapel at Batheaston, this was tantamount to

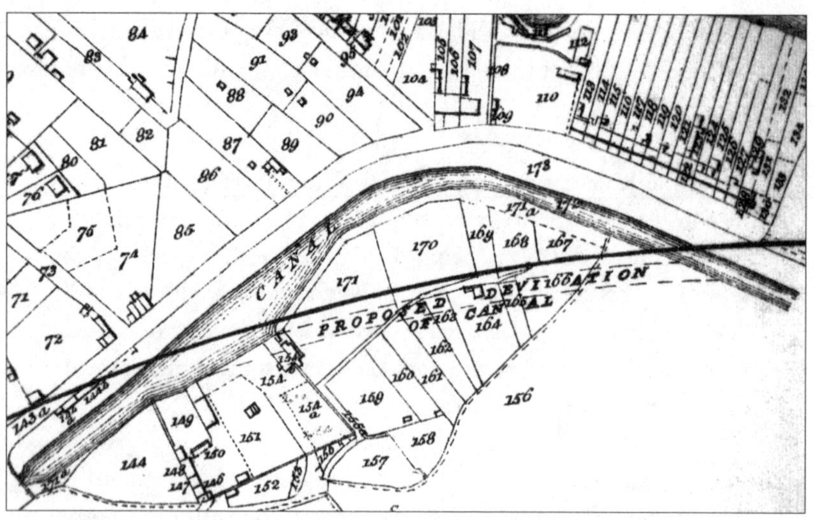

The canal diversion at Hampton Row.

a declaration of war. On Wednesday 7 April, he appeared before the mayor and magistrates to inform them that

> it was the intention of the Great Western Railway to have the water of the canal diverted into the newly-made channel, and that the operation was to be commenced by the workmen on Saturday night, and to be continued all day on Sunday, by which a number of men would be deprived of their day of rest. Mr Walters said there would be crowds drawn together there from curiosity, and it would be a day of profanity; and as it was with great difficulty any proceedings could be taken against the men in such cases, after the law was violated, owing to their refusing to give their names, he would suggest to the magistrates that they should attend in person, and convict on their own view.

The mayor took the complaint seriously and visited the site on Sunday, where he "caused many of the men to be dismissed; but others persisted in their work." That was not enough for Mr Walters, however, and the following week,

> Morris Perry, a railroad labourer, was summoned at the instance of Melmoth Walters, Esq, secretary of the Lord's Day Society, for

> pursuing his worldly calling on the Sabbath … John Webb, a tythingman [constable], stated that on Sunday, the 4th instant, he proceeded to the works of the Great Western Railway, at the canal, near Sydney Gardens. On his arrival there, he saw between 50 and 60 men at work, and among them was Morris Perry. Henry and William Oldham, contractors, were then charged with also pursuing their worldly calling on the same day, which, having been fully proved, and the charge admitted, the mayor took occasion to remark that he thought their conduct was not all justifiable, and, as they had not proved necessity, which the law admitted as a justification of Sunday labour, he could not allow the offence to go unpunished. He said the company were most to blame; but this did not excuse the men for continuing their work on the Sabbath, for it was evident that if they were to resist there would be an end to the evil. The defendants were fined five shillings and costs.

Morris Perry resurfaced 16 years later when the branch to Bradford on Avon was being built. Navvies were once again camped out in the fields near Batheaston, and one night a large crowd of them gathered to watch a bare-knuckle fight between two navvies. When two constables tried to break it up, one of them was knocked to the ground and killed. Although evidence as to who had struck the fatal blow was inconclusive, Morris Perry was sentenced to death on the grounds that he had shouted out, "the constable be ****ed, I don't care for any constable." The sentence was later commuted to transportation for life. Given Perry's hotheadedness on that occasion, it is likely that Melmoth Walters was able to single him out because of the vehemence with which he responded to the request to keep the Lord's Day holy.

The Great Western Railway agreed to pay the canal company £20 an hour for disruption of traffic. As it was closed for 383 hours – over two weeks – this worked out at £7,660, far higher than the £3,850 it cost to physically divert the canal. One legacy of the project was a large "heap of rubbish deposited at Hampton Row." This remained there for over two years, before a gang of workmen took it away and used it "in widening and supporting the narrow embankment across the meadow immediately beyond Hampton Row, near the River Avon."

SIXTEEN

Open to London

On 21 April 1841, Brunel sent another missive to the hapless Mr Fripp, this time threatening physical violence:

> *A long time ago I gave you instructions respecting certain details in the rooms at Bath station. Notwithstanding this I have to attend to every detail myself. I am heartily sick of employing you to do anything that, if I had ten minutes to spare, I would do myself. If you go over to Bath on Friday and can be ready with the outlines of the finished rooms you may still save me some trouble – if you wish to do so. If not pray keep out of my way or I will certainly do you a mischief, you have tried my patience so completely.*

One of the details to which Brunel gave his attention was the design of the lamp posts at Bath station. It seems incredible that, with responsibility for the biggest civil engineering project in the country, he could find time for such an incidental feature, and speaks volumes about his obsessive drive for perfection.

Meanwhile, preparations were being made to extend the railway from Wootton Bassett Road to Chippenham, 13 miles from Bath. In late April, work started on Chippenham station "in a field called the Wall Ground, north of the town, the intended entrance being through the once extensive timber yard of Mr John Provis." Provis had been among those who gave evidence before the committee of the Commons in support of the railway in 1834. On 13 May, the *Bath Chronicle* reported that the line was

> very nearly completed as far as Chippenham; and there seems no reason to doubt that it will be opened to that town by the first of June. As far as Wootton Bassett, the permanent rails are nearly all

Brunel's design for lamp posts at Bath station

> down; and the experimental train is expected this week. The works in the neighbourhood of the latter place has [sic] been proceeding with extraordinary rapidity; and there have been several accidents. One man had four ribs broken, from a piece of timber falling on him; and another a leg so badly fractured that immediate amputation was deemed necessary.

On Whit Monday, 31 May 1841, the line to Chippenham opened, along with a branch from Swindon to Cirencester.* It was now possible to travel from Bath to London in five hours. The weeks leading up to the opening of the final section of line were truly an Indian Summer for Bath's coachmen, who operated a shuttle service between Bath and Chippenham. There had already been an explosion in the number of people travelling between London and Bristol. Travellers from London to the far South West and South Wales, who had previously taken routes avoiding Bristol, now went via that city, to go forward by coach from there. For some, it was the novelty of riding behind a steam locomotive that attracted them; for most, though, the time saved was the main consideration. The day the line opened to Chippenham was, as the *Bath Chronicle* recorded, the busiest yet:

> In addition to the excitement caused by the processions, etc, of Whit Monday, the Market Place and the road leading to the station presented on this day an unusually busy appearance, from the continual running of the coaches from and to Chippenham. Many of the coaches which only performed one journey a day are now increased to two, and one to three times a day – an arrangement which will continue until the whole line is completed. It is a singular fact that, notwithstanding the numerous coachmen who are now "out of collar," as they technically term it, the supply was not equal to the demand; and in one or two instances coachmen who drive on other roads, and who usually remain in Bath all day, took the heavily laden vehicles to and from Chippenham. In consequence of this temporary revival of the good old days of coach travelling, that species of conveyance is quite "up in the market."

* *The branch to Cirencester was built by the Cheltenham & Great Western Union Railway, which was later absorbed by the Great Western.*

St James's Bridge from the north.

But this brief revival in the fortunes of the coaching trade had no more than a few weeks to run. In late May, the centrings of St James's Bridge were removed, and rails were laid between Bathampton and Bathford. Bath station was nearly ready to open. The *Chronicle* declared that it "will form a very striking object when finished, and will not only be a great ornament to the locality in which it is situated, but it will also be worthy of the stupendous undertaking with which it is connected." The opening day was set for 30 June. On 28 June, Sir Frederick Smith, the Government Inspector of Railways, travelled over the line between Chippenham and Bath and found it far from ready. That evening, he wrote to Charles Saunders:

> Sir, With reference to your notice of it being the intention of the Directors of the Great Western Railway to open on the 30th instant that portion of the line which will connect Chippenham with Bath, and thus complete that magnificent work which will afford railway communication between the metropolis and Bristol; I have to acquaint you that I have inspected the portion of the line in question,

The railway east of Bath, with the Grosvenor Suspension bridge in the background.

and while I desire to express my unqualified praise of the finished parts of the railway, it is necessary that I should point out to you those works which will require to be put into a more complete state before the contemplated opening. These consist chiefly of fences, ballasting and bridges ...

It would, if practicable, be desirable that, before the opening, the parapet along the top of the retaining wall, between the canal and the railway, as well as the balustrade to separate the railway from Sydney Gardens, be built ... The balustrade and wing walls of the entrance of the Box Tunnel are still incomplete, as is the coping of the Ashley Green Bridge. The bridge for the parish road near Sydney Gardens, the approach to the adjacent iron bridge, and the coping and approach of the bridge east of it, are unfinished. It is of great importance to the public safety that, if these bridges should not be finished before the opening of the line, the strictest orders should be issued to prevent any obstruction being thrown on the rails in the course of the operations for their completion.

The permanent way is yet far from finished, but as the embankments are complete, and the cuttings, with few exceptions,

Two early views of the station from Beechen Cliff.

cleared out, it may be possible to lay the remainder of the rails by the 30th, but I am desirous of recommending that great attention may be paid to their being properly screwed down to the timbers, in which I at present observe a deficiency.

The ballasting is generally scanty, and especially at some of the outer curves on the lofty embankments. This point wants particular care.

The station from the east.

> I am glad to find that it is the intention to remove some earth which is still in one of the cuttings by means of an extra line, so as to avoid those chances of accident which would exist if for that purpose either of the permanent lines of rails were to be used...
>
> I can only sanction the opening of this portion of line with the clear understanding that your Chief Engineer satisfies himself, by a personal inspection, before the running of the first train, that all the points which I have mentioned have received that degree of attention which is essential to the public safety; and I earnestly hope that for a few days the rate of speed may be moderate over the newly laid portions of the line...
>
> In conclusion I would call to your recollection that the signal posts have not yet been put up.

At three o'clock on the morning of 30 June, Sir Frederick went over the line again with Brunel. Most of the points he raised had been addressed in the intervening 24 hours; for those that had not, he was prepared to take Brunel's assurance that everything would be done to ensure the safe running of the trains. The opening could go ahead.

GREAT WESTERN RAILWAY.

OPENING THROUGHOUT.

NOTICE is hereby given that the LINE will be OPENED THROUGHOUT to BATH, BRISTOL, and BRIDGWATER, for the Conveyance of Passengers, Parcels, Carriages, Horses, Goods, and Cattle, on WEDNESDAY NEXT, the [illegible] instant.

There will be an alteration of the Trains on and after that day, particulars of which may be known on application for Train Bills after Saturday, the 26th inst., at any of the Company's Stations.

The 9 o'clock Down Train to Bristol will be discontinued, instead of which a Train will leave Paddington at 11 o'clock, A.M., for Bath and Bristol.

LONG TRAINS will run as under:—

	h. m.	FROM PADDINGTON.
A.M.	8 0	o'clock to Cirencester, Bath, Bristol, and Bridgwater.
,,	10 0	,, Cirencester, Bath, Bristol, and Bridgwater.
,,	11 0	,, Bath and Bristol.
noon	12 0	,, Cirencester, Bath, Bristol, and Bridgwater.
P.M.	2 0	,, Cirencester, Bath, Bristol, and Bridgwater, with a Train from Bristol at 7 o'clock to Bridgwater.
,,	5 0	,, Cirencester, Bath, and Bristol.
,,	8 55	,, Mail Train to Cirencester, Bath, Bristol, and Bridgwater.

TRAINS to PADDINGTON from

Bridgwater at	a.m. 11 30	p.m. 1 30	p.m. 3 30	and	p.m. 11 30	Mail Train
Bristol at ...	a.m. 7 0	a.m. 10 0	noon 12 0	p.m. 1 0	p.m. 3 0	p.m. 5 0, a.m. 1 0 Mail.

The Journey to Bridgwater will be performed in about 5½ hours, and the Fares by Railway—1st Class, 38s.; 2d Class, 26s. 6d.

By Order of the Directors,

CHAS. A. SAUNDERS,
THOMAS OSLER, } Secretaries.

June 25th, 1841.

Finally open: the first trains between London and Bath.

The first train from Bath to London left at 7.25am, arriving in the capital at 11.20. If the same journey had been undertaken just three years earlier, London would not have been reached until around half past five. The first down train from Paddington left at 8.00am and arrived in Bath at 11.45. The fastest train was the 10.00am from Paddington, which arrived in Bath at 1.35pm. There were seven passenger trains a day each way on weekdays, and three on Sundays. There were also two goods trains each way on weekdays, leaving Bath at 4.00am and 10.30pm, and London at 4.30am and 9.30pm. These appeared in the public timetables because they – and only they – conveyed third-class or goods-train passengers in uncovered trucks. Later, parliament forced the railway to convey third-class passengers on other trains as well. Once the line was open throughout, London time was kept at all the stations on the railway. Timetables warned passengers that this was about four minutes earlier than Reading time, eight minutes earlier than Chippenham time, and eleven minutes earlier than Bath and Bristol time. Gone were the days of mailcoach guards keeping watches set to different times, to regulate their arrivals and departures. Now, thanks to the Great Western, everything conformed to what came to be known as railway time. Brunel had not just built a railway, he had not only moved Bath closer to London; he had conquered time.

In 1837, as William IV lay seriously ill at Windsor, news of his condition took a day or more to reach Bath – officially that is. Rumours travelled somewhat faster. On 15 June 1837, the *Bath Chronicle*, after relaying the court communiqué, added:

> To the above we regret to add that the Bath coaches, on their way down yesterday, heard very unfavourable accounts from Windsor, as they passed Salt Hill.

When the men of Monmouthshire marched on Newport two years later, rumour, for a time, was all there was. Newport had fallen; the Chartists had been driven off, but were regrouping and were expected to return at nightfall; the fire of rebellion had spread, Birmingham would be next, the whole country was up in arms; the Queen was preparing to leave the capital. It was several days before the truth of what had happened became known.

A down train running into Bath over St James's Bridge in mixed gauge days.

Now news could travel not only at the speed of steam, but at the speed of electricity. In December 1839, an "electro-magnetic telegraph" had been introduced between Drayton and Paddington, operated by two boys from the Deaf & Dumb Asylum in the Kent Road. As the railway crept ever westward, so the telegraph followed. "It is contemplated," reporters were told as they inspected the arrangements for this technological marvel, "that information of any nature will be conveyed to Bristol and an answer received in London in about 20 minutes." It was, quite simply, the greatest leap forward in the history of communication, to which all subsequent developments have been mere refinements.

For good or ill, Bath would never be the same again. Some of what lay ahead, such as the demise of the coaching trade, was predictable, but much was unknown. The city was entering uncharted waters. But, instead of devoting the whole of the following day's *Chronicle* to a celebration of Brunel's stupendous achievement, not only did the editor consign the news to a short paragraph; the reporter got his name wrong:

> Considerable speculation has been afloat during the week, touching the probability of the entire line being open yesterday. From the

> unfinished state of the works, particularly in the neighbourhood of this city, it was generally considered that it would not be possible to accomplish this object within the stated time. The most strenuous exertions, however, were used, and by keeping very large bodies of men at work night and day the directors were enabled to carry their intention into effect. The line was opened yesterday. The chief engineer, JK Brunel Esq [sic], accompanied by Mr F Smith [sic], the Government Inspector of Railways, passed over the line with an engine and feeder, to prove its condition yesterday morning at three o'clock and returned again at eight o'clock. The opinion of Sir F Smith was not entirely feasible to the completeness of the works, but we hear that he consented to its being opened on Mr Brunel guaranteeing its safety. Several trains passed over the line to and from London during the day. We have not heard of any accident occurring on the occasion, excepting that the engine which propelled the down train from town, which arrived at about a quarter past three o'clock, got off the rails near the station. It was, at the time of this occurrence, going at so slow a rate, as to occasion no consequence, beyond a delay of about an hour. The engine, on being replaced on the rails, proceeded with the train to Bristol.

Even by the standards of the day, it is an incredibly shoddy piece of writing, scribbled down by an overworked reporter with no time to check his facts or correct infelicities of style. It was not intended, however, as a snub to Brunel. The railway may have come to town, but a General Election was being held at the same time – and this was no ordinary election. In an age where political contests were routinely marked by civic disorder and drunkenness, the Bath election of 1841 was notable for the scale of the disturbances that accompanied it. Ever since, it has been known as Bath's Drunken Election.

SEVENTEEN

The Drunken Election and Other Sundry Misfortunes

It is remarkable that, with only a small minority of Bath's citizens – uniformly well-to-do – entitled to vote, one of the most radical politicians in the country became Member of Parliament for the city. JA Roebuck was not only committed to an extension of the franchise; he had republican sympathies and advocated a fundamental overhaul of the constitution. He had also written the preamble to the People's Charter in 1838. Needless to say, the *Bath Chronicle* regarded him with undisguised contempt, calling him a "rabid little reviler" and a "noisome sample of political vermin."

The campaign that led to his election, along with follow Radical, Lord Duncan, in June 1841, was reminiscent of the Chartist demonstrations two years earlier. Most of those who took part were not eligible to vote; denied the opportunity to express their views by ballot, they took to the streets to make sure their voice was heard. On 17 June, the *Chronicle* reported outbreaks of violence as Radical and Conservative bill stickers tore down each others posters, while Duncan and Roebuck's supporters stencilled their names in yellow on buildings owned by Tory sympathisers. The Conservative candidates were also "greatly obstructed in their canvass by numbers of low blackguards who … followed them from street to street, offering them all kinds of insults, and proceeding, in some cases, to the commission of personal outrage."

On 1 July 1841, the *Bath Chronicle* carried news of the Radical victory:

> The Bath election has terminated in the defeat of the Conservative candidates, and our city now enjoys the bad distinction of having for its members a thick-and-thin supporter of the present unprincipled administration, and an advocate of all that is wild and reckless in

> legislation ... If anything more were needful to make those who have any regard for principle feel rejoiced that they do not share the triumph of the ... liberal majority, it would be furnished by the brutal violence with which the liberals have conducted themselves during the election. From the time that the Conservative candidates commenced their canvass ... a Conservative, known to be such, has not been able to go through the streets without the certainty of insult, and the risk of personal violence.
>
> The nomination for the city took place on Monday. At an early hour in the morning the radicals began to muster, and were the first to parade the streets with music, banners, etc. After they had been through the principal streets, in order to collect the members of the different trades' societies, the whole proceeded into Pulteney Street, where they arranged themselves in marching order. The numbers were certainly very great, but they were composed of all sorts, sizes, and descriptions. At the head of the procession was an immense banner, having inscribed on it, "Duncan and Roebuck – Foreign Wheat Duty Free – Sugar Duty Free" ... The engineers and iron founders had a banner, with a roebuck in the centre. A railway engine and tender was inscribed, "Stop it who can," and the reverse of the banner exhibited a ship in full sail, with the motto:
>
> True as the winds, and boundless as the sea
> Should intercourse between all nations be.
>
> The juveniles' banner – "Our fathers are contending for our rights." The Painters' Arms – "May God protect us and our cause protect." The Twerton Weavers had a banner bearing their arms, and the inscription, "May trade and commerce flourish."

The Radical supporters assembled in Great Pulteney Street, filling nearly the whole street, before marching to the hustings. When the Conservative procession from Queen Square reached the hustings, most of the space was already taken. Jostling soon turned to blows, as Tory banners were ripped asunder. When the Conservative candidates appeared on the hustings they were pelted "with missiles of various descriptions." Lest this be thought of as some little local disturbance, it is worth pointing out that the *Chronicle*, never one to exaggerate in these matters, estimated that there were between twelve and fifteen thousand people present. Demonstrations, marches,

News of a mass radical demonstration in Great Pulteney Street overshadowed the opening of the line from London.

window-smashing, muggings and punch-ups continued sporadically for the next few days. No wonder the *Chronicle* reporter was so exhausted when he covered the opening of the railway. No wonder, too, if some people wondered whether the brave new world promised when the railway arrived was all it was cracked up to be.

The opening of the railway did bring at least one benefit – the departure of the navvies. On 22 July, the *Chronicle* reported that

> a vast number of the workmen who have been for a length of time employed on the works of the Great Western Railway at Corsham have lately left for Southampton and other places to seek employment, in consequence of the line in the above named parish being near completion.

It was the same all down the line. Beerhouse proprietors and those who had supplied the navvies with food or accommodation might have regretted their departure, but most people gave a sigh of relief.

The completion of the railway had altogether more serious consequences for William Todd, who had worked as a draughtsman on the project for three years, lodging at 5 Henry Street. He was deeply in debt, and, when his contract was terminated, unable to find other employment, he took his own life.

The first of Bath's coaching inns to close in the wake of the railway's arrival was the Elephant & Castle on Monmouth Street, which was advertised for sale in August 1841. Some still hoped against hope that the coaching trade would survive. Operators offered reduced fares in a desperate bid to attract custom. In early September, a new coach, the *Emerald*, started running to London from the Greyhound Hotel. "To those who prefer this form of transit," enthused the *Bath Chronicle*, "this will be held as a great accommodation as the journey is performed with great expedition." But it was a lost cause. In January 1843, when the *Emerald* was overturned on its way to London, "by coming into contact with a cart," there was only one passenger on board, Mr Stockman, a coiffeur from Milsom Street.

There were still some who held out against the railway a little while longer. In January 1844, a lady from Wiltshire wrote to a friend describing a journey from Wiltshire to London:

> I have arrived in town, after an adventurous journey by road. My state of mind would not permit me to travel by rail, for Mr Brunel is no hero of mine, since he has destroyed posting, put down coaches and compelled people to sit behind his puffing monsters. Two days since have passed since Belinda and I left our home ... You could not imagine that we two women were allowed to take a lengthy journey on deserted roads with the bare possibility of getting horses. I had hoped that we should make London before night, but there was always the possibility of a fog. Just think of the awful risk of damp beds, and no one sleeps at inns since the railway has been cut. "We shan't get to Reading before three, unless we get horses," said Belinda as we seated ourselves in the barouche, "and we shall certainly have to sleep on the road." We admired the country, noted the heavy frost, and talked over our neighbours' affairs until we came to the end of the first stage ... We drew up at the Golden Lion [at Marlborough] which ten years since was one of the busiest inns on the road. The inn looked deserted – no ostler, no horses ready saddled as in the times when we were children and landlords took a real pride in their stables. We looked at each other in consternation. "Any horses?" shouted Richard. The landlady, a slatternly person in curl-papers, came out in a slip-shod way. "No," was plainly written on her face.

She seemed surprised to see an old-fashioned travelling carriage and four. "No, milady, we are new people. We are just come into the house. The people afore us was ruined. Since the railroad came this way nobody wants horses." "Will you please to alight, milady," said the elder postillion, a man of about 55, still called a boy; "we'd take you on another stage if so you'd bait an hour. The horses would be fresh enough." There was no alternative, so we descended and followed the landlady into the guest rooms ... The hour passed, and once again we took our seats, this time not so excitedly. We were now on the worst stage, a particularly hilly one, and the surface of the road been neglected by the turnpike trust. "Ah," thought I, "they will never make another cutting, they will not undertake systematic levelling or throw another bridge across a hollow. Thirty years from now the roads will be as bad as they were in our grandfathers' days ... So we jogged on to the end of the next stage. We stopped only a few yards from another inn, the Red Lion [at Hungerford]. Here we found slightly better comfort, for the inn is on a cross route and still boasts a two-horse coach, and we were fortunate enough to secure a change of horses which carried us to Newbury, where we made a halt until further horses could be obtained from a livery stable. On, once more, two stages to Reading, and then another change. The light was failing; what with delays and bad cattle, it was dark when we drew near a small tavern eight miles beyond. The inn in the village seemed busy enough; the landlord said it was a great struggle to keep things going, but he protested on the cleanliness of his rooms and the aired state of his beds. With wondering steps we followed the woman-waiter upstairs into the bedroom and waited in misery while she lit the fire. The woman said it was "the worst grate in the house, only after a bit it would burn up." It was cold comfort for two women who had spent the day under such difficulties. We made preparations for dinner, and on this being announced we made our way to the coffee room ... We found an old-fashioned mahogany table in the centre of the coffee room large enough to hold 20. There was a sideboard covered with all sorts of utensils that bumped, rattled and shook like one of Mr Brunel's trains every time the woman-waiter stamped about. At last came the mutton, smoking hot and tender, followed by a pudding tasting strongly of onions. This dinner, such as it was, compensated for all the injuries we had gone through ... Next morning we packed into the barouche and in three stages reached London, not experiencing any difficulty with horses.

It was not only on the Bath Road that inns were deserted and landlords were ruined. With clerks, porters, ostlers, drivers, waiters and chambermaids dismissed, a sepulchral calm descended upon once busy inns in the heart of Bath. Some dwindled to a couple of bars, kept in business by a handful of regulars, while upper rooms were shut off, abandoned to dust and decay. One by one, they slipped into oblivion, to be pulled down or converted into shops or warehouses. The decline of most of them went unrecorded. An exception was the White Hart, where Dickens had once been shown the door. He would have had no trouble finding a room in 1846, when the landlord sent this letter to the mayor and corporation:

> Gentlemen,
> The very great change that has taken place in the business connected with the White Hart since railway travelling has come into operation entirely puts it out of my power to provide the large rent I am now paying.
>
> Stage coaches which formerly brought so large a business to this house are now almost entirely swept away. Posting is also so much reduced that the trifling and uncertain earnings are insufficient to meet the expense of maintaining the reduced number of horses. The coach house and stables appropriated to private carriages and horses are nearly always empty, so few persons now travelling with those vehicles. The falling off in the business of the hotel from these causes, particularly that of the sleeping department, is a truth in support of which abundant evidence can be given, and in this altered state of affairs it is impossible for me to continue the occupation of the White Hart at its present enormous rental without certain ruin to myself and family.

The White Hart eventually closed in 1861 and was demolished six years later.

Stagecoaches were replaced, on the streets of Bath, by horse-drawn omnibuses and cabs, plying to and from the station. Such was the competition for business that the safety of passengers and pedestrians was often disregarded. As early as August 1841, the *Bath Chronicle* expressed concern about "the furious rate at which the omnibuses drive through the Orange Grove, Walks, and Pierrepoint Street on their way to the railway station, by which much danger arises to persons ... crossing the road." Accidents were common. One afternoon in 1848, for example,

> as Robert Frost of Park Street Mews was driving a gentleman in his fly to the two o'clock down train, when near the Literary Institute, the Greyhound omnibus passed on its way to meet the same train. A collision ensued, the omnibus coming against the fly at so furious a rate as to throw the driver from his seat. He lay insensible for some time but the gentleman escaped uninjured. The fly was much damaged to the great annoyance of Frost, who has no other means of supporting his family.

A more serious incident occurred in September 1852:

> The York House omnibus was proceeding empty to the railway station [when] the horses, on reaching the bottom of Broad Street, became frightened and started off through the Market Place at an alarming speed. The driver, William Hennick, a clever whip, avoided a collision with the vehicles and pedestrians who happened to be passing, and managed to check the animals in the Orange Grove; but before the conductor, who promptly descended, could seize their heads, they started off again towards the station. Hennick, with great coolness and skill, cleared all the corners of the zigzag course to the station, though going at full gallop, and as the strength of the animals was not exhausted on nearing the station, he determined to turn them up the incline leading to the Goods Station, rather than attempt to proceed through Dorchester Street, towards the main thoroughfare of the city. Unfortunately, however, a fly obstructed the way. Hennick, therefore, made another strenuous effort to stop the horses, when some part of the harness broke, the horses fell forward, the vehicle suddenly stopped, and Hennick, being unseated by the jerk, was thrown off with great violence, on the kicking horses, one of whom had got a leg fixed between the wheel and spring of the

> vehicle. Hennick was found to be insensible, and was removed in that state to the Bath United Hospital and is now recovering; the horses sustained very little injury. We rejoice in being able to say that no other accident happened.

On the railway, too, the catalogue of mishaps continued:

> On Friday afternoon [9 July 1841], as the four o'clock train was nearing Bridgwater, it came in contact with a barrel of tar, which had been placed too near the rails, either accidentally or by design. The collision knocked off a great number of the massive iron steps along the sides of the carriages like carrots, and the passengers and carriages were plentifully besprinkled with tar.*

> A labourer on the Great Western Railway was on Tuesday week [31 August 1841] accidentally killed on the line between Corsham and Chippenham, a short distance from the former place. To avoid the down train, of the approach of which the poor fellow was aware, he got upon the up rails. It so happened that a train from Bath was passing at the same time, which gave the proper signal by whistle, but it appears to have been unobserved – indeed, it is not unlikely that the noise of the one drowned that of the other; the engine of the up train went over the man and, as may be supposed, death was almost instantaneous.

> On Tuesday night [7 September 1841] a serious accident happened to the up mail train from Bridgwater to London, when about seven miles beyond Chippenham. The engine got off the line, tearing up a considerable quantity of the embankment in its progress, which must be replaced before the traffic can be resumed on both lines. Two of the carriages were very much fractured, and we hear on good authority that, in addition to the fright and shaking experienced by most of the passengers, two of the guards were very much injured, and that one person had his leg literally turned round at his hip joint.

* *The first section of the Bristol & Exeter Railway, from Bristol to Bridgwater, along with the branch to Weston Super Mare, opened on 14 June 1841. When the final section of the Great Western opened two weeks later, several trains from London to Bristol continued to Bridgwater.*

On the arrival at the Bridgwater terminus, on Saturday last [11 September 1841], of the four o'clock afternoon train from Bristol, the engine which brought down the train was employed after the passengers had left the carriages in removing the train from the down line to the other. To effect this transfer it is necessary to remove the carriages from the station to a point of the line about 150 yards distant, where proper means are provided for transferring carriages from one line of rails to the other. Between that point and the station is a crossing for coaches over the rails; the engine had already transferred some carriages from the down to the up line, and was returning for others, with its tender in front, when, on arriving at the crossing, the *Exquisite* stagecoach, with passengers for Exeter, was in the act of passing over the rails. The tender struck the fore part of the coach, which it shivered to pieces. The hind wheels, with a part of the body of the coach, were forced off the line by the violence of the shock, and fell over, while the passengers were scattered about in every direction. The horses, from the complete smash of the coach, were liberated, and escaped with but little injury. Six persons are more or less injured. Mr Burford, of Bristol, one of the passengers, was removed to the Clarence Hotel, where he is suffering under a concussion of the brain and other internal injuries. His head was so far jammed under one of the wheels of the tender that he could not be extricated until the engine was backed; another inch and his skull would have been crushed to atoms. Jones, the driver of the *Exquisite*, and Hatchwell, the respectable and well-known coachman to the sheriff at our assizes, are both seriously hurt.

On Monday afternoon [1 November 1841], one of the trains from Bristol ran off the line in the Brislington tunnel, but fortunately no further inconvenience was sustained than the alarm and the delay.

An atrocious attempt was made on the night of yesterday week [29 December 1841] to cause an … accident on the Great Western Railway. The mail train was on its way from London, and when within about three miles of Bath, the signal was given by the engine driver that something was wrong, and the train was stopped with all possible dispatch. On investigation it appears that some monster had placed two large stones (one on each rail) with the view of sending the engine off the line, but which providentially did not take place. One of the stones was crushed into a thousand atoms; the other stone was forced on one side by the sword or guard, which is placed before the wheels ... The stone that was turned off the road by the guard, and which was brought to Bristol by the driver, was about 40lbs in weight.

It is with feelings of deep regret that we have to record one of the most lamentable railway accidents that, we believe, has ever occurred in this country, and which took place this morning on the part of the Great Western line called the gullet, the deepest part of the Sonning Hill Cutting, rather more than two miles from Reading. It appears that, during the interim that elapsed between the passing down of the goods train about midnight and the arrival of a similar train at half past six this morning [30 December 1841], the embankment on the south side of the gullet, about 100 yards east of the wooden bridge, gave way, completely covering about 40 yards of the south or down line of rails. This unfortunate occurrence being unobserved by the policeman at this district, no intimation of it could possibly be conveyed to the driver of the approaching train. Consequently, on the arrival of the luggage train, at about half past six o'clock, a most terrific scene occurred. The train, which was progressing at its accustomed pace, and consisted of 12 or 14 wagons, two trucks and the engine and tender, was suddenly thrown off the rails, and partially shattered to atoms. The engine, which was called the *Hecla*, ran into the mass of earth, in which it was more than half buried, while the tender and passenger trucks were turned over, and jammed against the wagons immediately behind. The consternation at this moment, amid the expiring yells of some of the passengers, and the shrieks of others less injured, may be more easily conceived than detailed. One of the most distressing features, perhaps, of this awful scene, was the lamentable cries of an aged father, who saw his son, who had accompanied him in this unhappy journey, literally crushed between the tender and the truck, and instantaneously killed. Another of the sufferers, apparently an aged man, was so shockingly mutilated that his countenance was entirely indiscernible. Information of this dreadful catastrophe was conveyed to Reading as speedily as possible, and several medical gentlemen were shortly on the spot. There were about 30 passengers, including some females, nearly the whole of whom were more or less injured; about 20 were brought on to Reading, in a carriage sent up for that purpose, and their appearance, on their arrival at the station, was of the most depressing character.

EIGHTEEN

Excursions and Acts of God

In April 1843, several hundred Bathonians fell victim to a bizarre practical joke:

> On Saturday night the walls of Bath were placarded with notices (having attached to them the names of London printers) stating that, at the request of Mr Roebuck, the "Aerial Steam Coach" ... would commence its proceedings on Monday, by making a trip from London to this city, and that it would alight at Beechen Cliff at 9.30 "Bath time" after a journey of twenty minutes. Experience having shown us that there are no promises, however monstrous, which will not find those who are credulous enough to take them for sober seriousness, we were not surprised to see the crest and sides of Beechen Cliff crowded, at the hour mentioned in the aforesaid bills, by some hundreds of persons, all agape for the appearance of the flying visitor from town. Large numbers stood their ground long after the appointed hour, under the conviction that the delay in the arrival of the machine was more probably caused by some little mishap, incident to its first journey, and that it would certainly arrive in the course of the afternoon. The housetops in the lower part of the city also displayed numerous groups of anxious spectators. All this has given great delight to the author of this hoax – who, however, is, after all, much more foolish than the too credulous people who fell into his trap.

It is unlikely that this wheeze would have been so successful at any other time in Bath's history. People were still reeling from the implications of Brunel's conquest of time. He had achieved what, just a few years earlier, would have seemed impossible. And where he had blazed a trail, why shouldn't others follow?

The railway was the first mode of transport available to just about anyone. In the early days of the Great Western, there were three classes of travel – first (very expensive, very luxurious); second (fairly basic, initially with open sides; later with closed sides but no windows); and third class. You didn't want to travel third class. All you got was a plank of wood stretched across an open wagon, with no protection from the weather. The only concession to comfort was a series of holes drilled in the floor, so that rain could drain away in wet weather. It might have been tolerable on a warm, sunny day – although even then the smoke, smuts and lumps of burning coal from the engine would not have been much fun – but in the depths of a winter's night, hurtling along in the teeth of a blizzard, it would have been all but unbearable. Brunel, who had travelled thousands of miles on the top of stagecoaches, clearly saw no problem in providing a similar standard of accommodation for rail passengers on limited incomes. He failed to take into account that what might be acceptable at twelve miles an hour would not be at speeds of 60 or more. At least one passenger froze to death. One morning in March 1845, John Jonathan, aged around 50, arrived at Bath on the ten o'clock train. On arrival, he was unable to leave the carriage and had to be assisted by one of the porters, who helped him into the street, where he collapsed. He was carried into Bright's chemist's, where, despite receiving medical attention, he died. His widow had left Bristol on foot after seeing her husband off on the train, as the couple had insufficient money for two tickets.

"I left Bristol soon after the deceased," she told the coroner's court, "and walked the distance. It was about three o'clock when I arrived in Bath and I then found my husband was dead ... He had on two pairs of trousers, two waistcoats and a warm woollen handkerchief round his neck, besides two body coats."

The jury returned a verdict "that the deceased died by the visitation of God, but that his death was accelerated by the inclemency of the weather to which he was exposed in a third-class carriage of the Great Western Railway Company." The coroner recommended that "the promise to provide closed carriages be put into effect as speedily as possible."

The single fare to London from Bath was twenty-four shillings and sixpence, first class, and seventeen shillings, second class, with a premium payable for travelling by express. The third class fare was eight shillings and tenpence. If passengers wished to take their private carriages with them, they had to turn up ten minutes before the train was due to leave so that the necessary arrangements could be made. To convey a two-wheel carriage from Bath to London, the charge was forty-eight shillings; a four-wheel carriage cost fifty-eight shillings. The fare for a horse was fifty-three shillings; a pair cost seventy-three shillings. Passengers travelling with their carriages had the choice of staying in the carriage or using a first-class compartment; in either case, they had to take a first-class ticket. Return tickets, costing less than two singles, were only available until 1848, when they were discontinued. Day return tickets were reinstated the following year, but it was several years before period returns were reintroduced.

A popular destination for daytrippers from Bath in the early days was Corsham. On 5 August 1841, the *Bath Chronicle* reported that

> the railway station at the village of Corsham, which is reached from this city in about twenty minutes, and the absence of Lord Methuen from his splendid mansion, have lately attracted throngs of visitors to inspect his lordship's superb collection of paintings, which are now to be seen every day, instead of on Mondays only, when the family are at home.

Many working class people's first experience of rail travel was on excursion trains. Now an almost forgotten aspect of the railway scene, excursions were the forerunners of today's package holidays. Thomas Cook sowed the seeds of a multi-million pound business when he organised an railway excursion for temperance campaigners from Leicester to Loughborough in 1841. The first excursion train from Bath ran to London on 29 September 1842. It left at 7am and returned at 5pm the following day. Tickets cost a pound. The *Chronicle* was of the opinion that "this cheap opportunity of seeing the great metropolis will be embraced by large numbers of persons who have never been there before; and that the train, as in similar cases on other lines, will be a curiosity for its length and freight of passengers." However, take up was disappointing; only 85 people travelled from Bath, along with 173 from Bristol and 14 from Chippenham.

GREAT WESTERN RAILWAY.

CHEAP EXCURSION TO and FROM LONDON.

MICHAELMAS HOLIDAYS.

THE Directors having consented to afford the opportunity of a CHEAP EXCURSION, beg to announce that TICKETS may now be had at the BRISTOL, BATH, and CHIPPENHAM STATIONS, for a Limited Number wishing to VISIT LONDON for TWO DAYS.

The Train will leave Bristol at 7 o'clock on the Morning of MICHAELMAS DAY, the 29th Sept.; and return from London at 5 o'clock on the Evening of the Next Day, FRIDAY, the 30th Sept.

FARES:—

Bristol to London and back	....	21s. each.
Bath to London ,, ,,	....	20s. ,,
Chippenham to London ,,	....	19s. ,,

Children under Ten Years of Age, Half Price.

No Luggage allowed for any Passengers exceeding 14 lbs., and all Merchandize, Packages, or excess Luggage will be Charged at the usual Rates.

N.B. No Tickets for this Train will be issued after 12 o'clock on the 28th September. (26

The first excursion train from Bath: September 1842.

By 1850, the excursion craze was well established. On Sunday 15 September, the Great Western once again risked the wrath of the Lord's Day Observance Society by running three excursion trains from London to Bath. Over three thousand people arrived in Bath between ten thirty and eleven o'clock that Sunday morning. The *Bath Chronicle* reported that

> a vast concourse of people was, in consequence, attracted to the vicinity of the station, and on the departure of the trains in the

> evening the throng was still more considerable. During the interval of arrival and departure, the streets and thoroughfares in all directions necessarily presented scenes very different from the quiet aspect which Bath has heretofore worn on Sundays.

A few days later, a meeting at the Assembly Rooms called on the directors of the Great Western Railway to stop running excursion trains on Sundays, declaring that they were "productive of the most enormous public and private evils."

Just before midnight on Friday 20 September 1841, two excursion trains were returning from London to Bath when the second of them smashed into a horse box which had been blown out of a siding at Wootton Bassett and onto the main line by strong winds:

> The engine and the first four coaches were precipitated down the embankment into a field of mangold-worzel. The first carriage was turned on its side. Its roof had to be broken with a sledgehammer to get its occupants out. The screams of the female passengers was heart-rending.

There were no serious injuries. The down mail, following closely behind the excursion train, managed to stop in time; Brunel was among the passengers and helped in the rescue operation. When William White, the signalman, was arrested, he said he had been told, when coming on duty, that the horsebox had been secured by wooden wedges under its wheels, although he had not checked to see if it was secure. He pointed out that a footpath crossed the line near the siding, and that someone could easily have removed the wedges, but was nevertheless found guilty of negligence and sentenced to two months' imprisonment.

The 1851 Great Exhibition saw excursion traffic rise to record levels. On 7 July, 1,040 people, in 20 carriages, set off from Bath to London on an excursion organised by the Exhibition Travelling Club. On 4 August, a 28-coach train took 1,400 people to the Exhibition, each of whom paid eight shillings and eightpence for the privilege. A few days later, on 10 August, disaster hit an excursion train between Bath and Bristol:

A fearful collision, attended with considerable personal injury, and damage to sundry carriages, occurred on the above line at a quarter before four o'clock on Sunday morning last, a return excursion train which left London for Bristol on Saturday evening having been run into at Fox's Wood, just at the entrance to the No 3 (long) Tunnel, at Brislington, by one of the smaller engines, combining engine and tender on one carriage, in use on this line as pilot engines and for assisting heavy trains up the incline. Several return excursion trains had that evening left Paddington; the first at seven o'clock, containing passengers for Bath, Bristol, and the stations on the Westbury branch; another was started at half-past seven, for Gloucester and Cheltenham; and, at a quarter past eight, a second left for Bath and Bristol, which was the one to which the accident occurred. It consisted of 26 carriages; and its progress is described by the passengers as very slow, besides being interrupted by frequent stoppages. The rumour was spread amongst them that there was something wrong about the engine, but however this might have been it was deemed necessary by the conductors to run the train into a siding at Swindon, where it did not arrive until nearly twelve o'clock, until the mail train passed, to avoid being run into by it, as well as to prevent delay to the mail should it happen to overtake them on a part of the line where there was no siding. After this delay, which is said by the passengers to have occupied nearly two hours, the train was again put in motion, and proceeded at the same slow pace as before, besides stopping at intervals from causes which they could not ascertain, but which had the effect of calling forth loud complaints. At Chippenham, the passengers were surprised to find such as those who had left by the first train and who were going on the Westbury branch, waiting their arrival, in order that any others, with a similar destination, might go with them. The detention here was very lengthened, and the confusion indescribable, consequent upon the change of carriages, passengers and luggage. The train ultimately arrived at the Bath station a few minutes before three o'clock on Sunday morning, and, having taken in water, left again exactly at three. Two minutes afterward, the pilot engine, which caused the accident, arrived at the Bath station. It had left Bristol at one o'clock with a heavy goods train to assist it through the Box Tunnel, and up the incline, and having done so, was again on its return to Bristol. The excursion train, however, having left but two minutes before, the pilot engine was very properly detained for twenty minutes, when it was allowed to proceed, this time being considered sufficient to secure the arrival of the excursion train in Bristol before the former could overtake it. Unfortunately, this turned out not to be the case for, whatever might have been the cause of the previous delays, there was now evidently something wrong about the engine. Three-quarters of an hour had been occupied in getting from Bath to Brislington, the scene of the accident, where the steam was again shut off for another stoppage. The progress was pretty good as far as Twerton, when the engine exhibited unmistakeable symptoms of distress, and just dragged its slow length along. The driver said he could not get the pumps to act, to replenish the boiler with water, and consequently, to prevent an explosion, which was likely to occur if he had proceeded on to Bristol, with so small a quantity of water as was then in the boiler, he stopped his engine to put the matter to rights previously to entering the tunnel, it being a particular injunction to the drivers in the company's service never to stop a train in a tunnel. Here some of the passengers, who were residents of Keynsham, got out, in order to walk home. It was now just a quarter to four o'clock, and, before the train was brought to a standstill, the pilot engine, which was driven by Thomas Coltman, with John Wright as fireman, ran into the last carriage, producing a fearful collision, throwing the passengers in the hinder carriages with great violence from their seats against each other, and filling them with the greatest consternation and alarm. Upwards of twenty persons were more or less bruised and cut about the legs and head ... None of the passengers, however, was so seriously injured but that, when they arrived at Bristol, and had been attended by Mr Keddle, surgeon, by direction of the officers of the company, they were able to be conveyed to their own residences. The engineer and fireman of the pilot engine were uninjured, and the last carriage of the train, which was a strong second-class one on an iron frame, likewise escaped injury; though some of the other carriages were much damaged. The collision was not more serious only because the train was not entirely stopped, and the pilot engine had received a slight check from the attempt of the driver to stop it ... The time of the collision as stated above was a quarter before four o'clock, and the

> time of sunrise being about half past four, daylight had scarcely dawned.
>
> The prime cause of this accident appearing to be the carelessness of the driver and fireman of the pilot engine in not observing the train ahead of them; they were taken into custody, and, on Monday, brought before Mayor James and HE Mynors, Esq., two magistrates of the county, at the Lamb Inn, Keynsham, where they were charged, under the 7th section of the Company's Act – for that they, being servants of the Great Western Railway Company, negligently omitted to stop an engine of which they had the charge, whereby the lives and limbs of divers persons were placed in jeopardy or injured.

At the trial, it was stated that the driver of the pilot engine had continued, "notwithstanding the signals that were exhibited of a train being in advance. These signals were three red lights at the end of the train, a red hand light held up by [the guard], who had got out of the train immediately on its stopping, and another carried by the policeman stationed at the point, who actually proceeded up the line with it to caution any other train or engine from approaching, so that there were no less than five red lights exhibited, either or all of which could have been seen if they had been keeping a proper look out." The driver said that he had seen the lights too late to stop, and that they were obscured by fog or steam. He was fined £5, his fireman £3.

Accidents happened with frightening regularity in the early days of rail travel; despite speeds of 60 miles an hour or more being customary, however, few of them resulted in serious injury. Derailments were the most common cause of accidents. Four-wheeled luggage vans were a particular problem; after a spate of incidents involving them, it was decided in 1845 that they would no longer be attached to passenger trains "because they come off the rails." Landslips were another danger. In the early afternoon of 16 February 1846, 36 labourers were sent in a truck attached to the up mail to deal with a landslip just beyond Corsham. At the entrance to Middle Hill Tunnel, a wheel of the truck gave way and threw it off the rails. Some men were thrown out, some jumped out, while some decided it was best to hang on. They shouted "as loud as they could, but the engine driver, mistaking the noise for singing, kept on till an intimation of the accident reached him." One of the men who was thrown or jumped from the truck died from a dislocated neck; most of the others had "severe contusions" and had to be treated at the United Hospital. In May 1846, after a wall south of Bathwick Tunnel, at "Mr Pike's garden," gave way, a man placed there to watch in case of further slippage was killed by a train.

Given Brunel's fondness for cigars, it is surprising that smoking was initially banned not only in carriages but on stations as well. As Brunel usually travelled on the footplate rather than on the cushions, it was a rule he could conveniently ignore. Not so two first-class passengers who decided to light up on the platform at Bath while waiting for a train to Bristol in September 1840. A railway policeman asked them to desist and showed them a copy of the bye-laws. Despite this, one of them was later caught smoking on the train and given a forty shilling fine.

Two men with a novel approach to rail travel also paid dearly for their presumption. On Saturday 14 August 1847, the 2.50pm down train was heading past Twerton when the driver saw a man waving a red flag near the entrance to Twerton Tunnel. After he had pulled up, the guard ran back to find out what the matter was. The man with the flag explained that he and his companion wanted to go to Bristol but had no money. The guard invited them into his carriage, where they sat in lordly splendour, congratulating themselves on their audacity, until they arrived at Bristol, where they were handed over to the police. They were each fined forty shillings with costs.

Not all infringements of the law were so benign. From the start, the station at Bath was a magnet for criminal activity. Particularly notorious was a gang known as the "swell mob," well-dressed, smooth-talking confidence tricksters who waylaid unsuspecting passengers. In April 1843, the *Bristol Mirror* reported the case of a young lady who

> went to Bath by the railway, and, on leaving the platform, and not being certain of the direction she should take to reach the place she was going to, ... enquired of a genteelly-dressed man, accompanied by two females fashionably attired, who said he would show her the way as he was going in that direction himself. He then led her into a narrow lane, where his companions left him, and soon afterwards he asked to carry some music books that the young lady had with her, which she declined. He then snatched at her reticule, and, with

> a knife which he had in the other hand, cut the strings and immediately ran off with it. Fortunately it contained no item of value. The fellow was tall, with dark hair and moustache; he was dressed in black, with white kid gloves.

In January 1851, a "young man of respectable appearance" called James Simpson, was sentenced to ten years' transportation for "plundering ladies travelling in first-class carriages." At his trial, he was described as the "head of a gang of thieves who have long infested that portion of the Great Western Railway which lies between Bath and Bristol."

Not all the criminals who haunted the station made a pretence of respectability. In September 1852,

> Charles Dodd was charged with being drunk and assaulting PC 14 in the execution of his duty. The prisoner is one of a band of lazy vagabonds who lie about the railway station pretending to gain a livelihood by carrying luggage, but who are an intolerable nuisance to all persons who come near them; so much has this been felt that a policeman, we believe, is now regularly ordered to patrol the neighbourhood with the view of abating the nuisance. Between twelve and one o'clock last night, the prisoner, who was drunk, was creating a disturbance near the station, when PC 14 ordered him away; but instead of going he struck the officer in the face and attempted to throw him down. The prisoner was taken into custody, upon which several of his companions commenced pelting the officers with stones. He was fined 20/- with costs, or in default to be committed for 21 days.

Seventeen years later, in August 1869, the problem was as bad as ever:

> Charles Griffiths was charged with being drunk, using obscene language and assaulting Detective Cox. The prisoner is one of a gang of young men who loaf about the Great Western station under the pretence of carrying parcels for passengers, and on Thursday afternoon he was drunk and annoying passengers. Cox took him into custody, and he was so violent that the detective put the slip on him. He then went quietly until half way up the road, when he

> began to swear and refused to go any further. He struck Cox and then threw him down, and he had to get assistance to take the prisoner to the police station. Adams, a porter at the Great Western station, assisted Cox, and he informed the court that the prisoner and his companions were a great nuisance, not only to the company's servants, but also to the general public. The prisoner said Cox pushed and struck him without any provocation before he did anything, and then he admitted he struck the detective in return. He called Charles Burgess, one of his companions, but he appeared in court drunk, and as he was insolent the superintendent had him taken into custody. It appeared that the prisoner had only come out of gaol on Tuesday, and he was fined two guineas and costs, or in default of payment six weeks' hard labour.

Arguments over seats sometimes flared into violence as well, as this report from May 1849 indicates:

> A young man who gave his name as William Gaylord and said he was a groom out of place was … charged with assaulting Catherine Seymour, wife of a railway labourer. It appeared from the evidence that the complainant and her husband were booked at the Bath station … by the 1.55pm down train, and, as the complainant was subject to a bad leg, she took a corner seat in a carriage for the purpose of avoiding contact with persons having to pass in taking their places. The defendant, who had come by the train, and had got out for a short time, on returning, demanded the complainant's place as previously occupied by him, and on her being unwilling to resign it, he laid hold of her in a violent manner, thrust her out of the carriage, and after she was on the platform, kicked her. The complainant and her husband again got into the carriage, and proceeded to Bristol when [the police's] attention was called to the gross assault by several respectable persons, and the defendant was taken into custody and brought to Bath.
>
> The defendant admitted the assault, but alleged that the complainant, on his asking her to give up her seat for him, slapped him in the face first, and that her husband also struck him. This was contradicted by a witness, though the complainant admitted she struck him in the face after he assaulted her.

Gaylord was fined fifty shillings, with costs.

Violent affray was not just a working-class phenomenon. In October 1852, Sir James Rivers, Bart., of Beacon Hill Cottage, was summoned for assaulting Isaac Crew, a porter in the employ of the Great Western Railway Company:

> The complainant stated that on Saturday evening, about seven o'clock, Sir James was waiting with a carriage and pair at the back of the station, in the place where the omnibuses draw up to receive the down train passengers. According to instructions received from the Superintendent, he requested him to move to a spot which he pointed out, as a place for private carriages, but he would not go. Complainant then took hold of the horses to move them, when Sir James struck him with his whip across the hand. The omnibuses could not pass their places while the defendant's carriage was there ... Charles Carey, driver of the White Lion omnibus, stated that his vehicle had been obstructed by Sir James's carriage. He corroborated the complainant's evidence regarding the assault. This witness gave his evidence very reluctantly ...
>
> Mr Williams [representing Rivers] submitted that Sir James had been justified by the provocation he had received, and said he should call his servant to show this. He also observed that the company ought to place a notice-board to inform the public, if they had set apart a place for private carriages, otherwise the presumption was that any one waiting for a train had a right to draw up with a carriage on the place.
>
> George Fisher, servant of Sir James, stated that he saw the porter put his hand on the carriage, as well as on the horse; but he could not hear what he said. He heard his master say, "take your hands off the carriage," but did not hear what the porter said in reply. Fisher was standing on the ground at the time.
>
> This closed the case, but the Magistrates determined to reserve their decision until another summons, connected with the same affair, had been heard.
>
> Samuel Holmes, a policeman of the company, who looked very pale, and had two of his fingers bound up, stated that after Crew had requested the defendant to remove, he also did so, and pointed where the carriage should go. Defendant having refused, complainant laid

One of the last broad gauge expresses passing through Sydney Gardens.

> hold of both horses by the bits. The defendant then used his whip with all his might, as if to drive on the horses; the animals reared, and, as complainant still held them, the defendant struck him eight or nine times with the thong of his whip on the head and back. Defendant then leaned over the splash board as far as he could, and, turning the whip in his hand, aimed a blow at complainant's face with the butt end, which complainant parried with his hands, and had his finger and thumb struck by it. Complainant went to his post, when the defendant got off the box, and, coming towards complainant, struck him in the stomach such a severe blow that he had been ill ever since, and, on Sunday, discharged blood from his throat from internal injury.

Rivers was convicted on both counts, and was fined fifty shillings for the first assault and five pounds for the second. The mayor, in summing up, said that "such conduct in a gentleman of this rank was discreditable," and that, if repeated, could lead to two years' hard labour.

One perennial problem was that of missiles thrown at trains. In October 1850, John Straghn was charged with throwing a stone at a train in Sydney Gardens and denting the dome of the engine. He got off on a technicality, claiming that the missile in question was a chestnut. Two years later, Mr Davis from the Pulteney Hotel was fined two shillings and sixpence for assaulting youths he suspected of throwing stones at trains.

NINETEEN

Riotous Assemblies and the Arrival of Albert

Among the benefits conferred by the railway was the ability to mobilise troops far more readily than had hitherto been the case. When the Chartists had risen in Monmouthshire in 1839, reinforcements took so long to arrive that, had the rioters been better organised, it is probable they would have overwhelmed the small garrison defending Newport. Three years later, it was a different story.

On 22 September 1842, the *Bath Chronicle* announced that,

> the railway trains that usually leave Paddington at six o'clock in the morning did not arrive in this city on Wednesday and Thursday last week until nearly an hour after their usual time. This delay was occasioned by the transit on each of the above days of a portion of the 73rd Foot, with their baggage, en route for Newport, Monmouthshire.

In February 1855, the realities of war in the Crimea were brought home to Bathonians by the arrival of a contingent of wounded soldiers. "Their arrival," reported the *Bath and Cheltenham Gazette*,

> was the occasion of the most enthusiastic and gratifying demonstration. The whole distance from the Guildhall to the railway station was crammed with an immense crowd, intent on giving to their sick and wounded countrymen hearty welcome. His worship the mayor and a large number of leading citizens were on the railway station platform to receive them, and the windows of the houses were also crowded with ladies enthusiastically waving handkerchiefs. The band of the North Somerset Yeomanry Cavalry were drawn up in front of the railway station, and gave an éclat to

> the occasion by their performance; whilst a number of troopers from the same regiment … acted as pioneers to the carriage which conveyed the sick and wounded men.
>
> The detachment arrived at three o'clock by the express train from Plymouth, where the men have been in hospital since the twelfth of last month, the *Talavera*, in which they were brought to England, having been driven into that port by stress of weather … All were conveyed from the station … in omnibuses and flies; and as the vehicles emerged from the railway station they were greeted with cheers, which were repeated throughout the route. In the market place it required all the efforts of the police and the cavalry to make way for the carriages to the hall, and the cheers of the populace rose again and again in unison with the Abbey bells, which pealed forth joyously as the disabled soldiers found a temporary home in the Guildhall.

In July 1843, the first of a string of distinguished visitors stopped off at Bath station on their way through the city. Prince Albert was on his way to Bristol to launch Brunel's *Great Britain*. As soon as it was known that he would be passing through Bath, a requisition, signed by a large number of "respectable citizens" was presented to the mayor, asking him to invite the prince to Bath. This he did, and Albert agreed to stop at the station to receive an address from the mayor. Brunel and Charles Saunders came down to Bath to make the necessary arrangements, and "it was settled that the centre of the down platform should be fitted up as a drawing room." The job was given to Messrs English & Sons,

> and was executed by them in a most excellent manner. The floor of the portion of the station … set aside for the reception of the prince was covered with crimson cloth. Against the wall was a raised platform or dais, also covered with crimson cloth, and over it was a canopy of crimson and blue, the cornice being studded with tasteful gilt ornaments. Under this canopy was an elegant sofa, covered with crimson silk damask. On the drapery behind the sofa were splendidly emblazoned the Queen's Arms, with two stars, and the initials VR in the centre of wreaths. Rich velvet carpeting stretched across the floor to the foot of the platform, on either side of which

were handsome marble pillars bearing vases of beautiful flowers, which, with numerous lovely plants by which the platform was ornamented, were kindly sent for the occasion by our fellow citizen, Mr G Shaw. A handsome oak seat stood on either side of the dais. On the platform there was also an elegant circular table, with richly ornamented velvet covering, on which stood a glass of cut flowers, sent by W Beckford, Esq. …

In order that the company on both sides of the station might have as good a view of the proceedings as possible, it was arranged that when the special train, with the prince and his suite, should arrive, the carriages should be backed out of the station, and that the engine should go forward so as to be clear of the building, by which means an uninterrupted view across, and from all parts of the station, might be obtained. On the side appropriated to the railway company's visitors, platforms, ornamented by pink hangings, were constructed, to allow those who were present in that part of the building to see over each other's heads.

On Monday and Tuesday the greatest anxiety was manifested to obtain tickets for the station, and large numbers of those who applied were unavoidably disappointed … Soon after 7am [on the day of the visit] the neighbourhood of the station exhibited unequivocal signs that something more than ordinary was about to take place. The bustle rapidly increased as the time drew on, and the booking offices of the station were thickly besieged by those who had obtained tickets to witness the presentation of the address, or by persons anxious to get over to Bristol for the purpose of being in time for the earliest proceedings there. There was a tremendous crush to get at the early trains, and the station was consequently the scene of much animation and excitement.

The exterior of the station, and the line for some extent both ways, were gaily decorated with flags. Merry peals were rung on the bells of the Bath churches, colours were displayed on the towers, cannon were discharged and other demonstrations of rejoicing took place. The situations affording a view of the line were occupied by multitudes of spectators anxious to obtain a glimpse of the royal train in its rapid transit.

The mayor, town council and deputation arrived at the station about nine o'clock. Owing to some mistake as to the proper mode of access to that part of the building appointed for the presentation of the address, there was some confusion, the corporation and deputation having got mingled with the persons waiting to go off by the train. Order, however, was at length restored. The station was cleared of all but those immediately concerned in, or who attended to witness, the presentation of the address, and all waited, with high anticipation, the arrival of the royal visitor ... It was expected that the train would reach Bath at about half past nine. As that time approached, therefore, the most intense anxiety prevailed among the spectators in the station. The buzz of impatient anticipation grew louder as the minutes fled by, and every bosom was thrilled by the shrill shriek of the steam whistle which announced the approach of the special train, containing the illustrious party, which entered the station precisely at twenty minutes to ten, having performed the journey from Paddington to Bath in two hours and twenty minutes ... The train consisted of four carriages, the royal carriage being the last; it was drawn by that fine engine, the *Damon*, which was decorated with flags and driven by Mr Brunel.

As soon as the train appeared in sight, the band of the North Somerset Yeomanry, which was stationed on the exterior of the eastern end of the station, played *God Save the Queen*, and when the train entered the station, the assembled company greeted the prince with enthusiastic cheering. The royal carriage having been drawn up opposite to the spot appointed for the presentation of the address, the door was immediately opened, and, after several members of the prince's suite had alighted and arranged themselves on each side of the carriage door, his royal highness stepped out, and bowing gracefully to the company around him, proceeded to the raised platform ... on the steps of which he remained while the mayor read the address ... His royal highness then shook hands with the mayor, and while the carriage was being brought back to receive him, remarked on the punctuality with which the train had brought him down, adding that he ... was very much pleased with the buildings of Bath, as far as he had been able to see them. The prince and the members of his suite then re-entered the carriage, which immediately left the station amid the most hearty cheering.

Thirteen years later, in August 1856, Prince Albert passed through Bath again, accompanied by Queen Victoria. This time, however, the train did not stop:

> The fact that the royal family would pass through this city was made known officially to Mr Starr, superintendent at the Bath station, late on Thursday evening; but it was accompanied by the intimation that the train would not stop. In order to prevent the overcrowding of the station, the matter was kept as secret as possible, until ten o'clock on Friday morning, when it was imparted to the mayor. His worship at once decided on making some demonstration of loyalty; and, having assembled as many of the town council as he could, donned his official costume, and proceeded, at about one o'clock, with the corporation mace bearers, to the railway station, where the Hanoverian band had already arrived. The royal standard was hoisted on the tower of the Abbey; flags were displayed from other churches; and the Abbey bells sent forth merry peals. These preparations could not be made without some bustle and excitement, and those of our fellow citizens who ascertained the cause of it speedily made their way to the railway station, both platforms of which were filled with spectators anxious to obtain a sight of her Gracious Majesty. The outside of the station was densely crowded. After waiting more than half an hour with intense anxiety, Mr Starr acquainted the mayor that a telegraphic message had been received announcing that the royal train had left Bristol some nine minutes previously. In a few moments the ringing of a bell signalled that the train was in sight, on which the Hanoverian band struck up the National Anthem. The train, which consisted of two first-class carriages, two royal saloons, and a second-class carriage, passed through the station exactly at half past one o'clock, nearly at express speed, so that scarcely a single individual succeeding in obtaining a glance at the Queen. A cheer was raised as the train sped on its way, and the spectators returned into the city, somewhat disappointed at the small opportunity afforded them of obtaining a sight of their august sovereign. In short, it might be said, not metaphorically but literally, that the royal party had no sooner arrived than it was gone – a momentary glimpse of the train being all that we have to record.

Those disappointed by their failure to see the Queen must have been mortified when it transpired, four years later, that another member of the royal family had deigned to stop at Bath, only to find no one there to greet him. The Prince of Wales, who had been on a two-month tour of Canada, landed at Plymouth on 14 November 1860 after a gruelling voyage:

> His royal highness landed at the Royal Victualling Yard, where he was received by the Plymouth Volunteers and a guard of honour of the 12th Regiment. At the platform of the South Devon Railway his royal highness received congratulatory addresses from the corporations of Plymouth and Devonport. A special train was placed at the disposal of his royal highness and suite, who left Plymouth at noon ...
>
> At Bristol the Artillery and Rifle Volunteer Corps were drawn up on the express platform of the Bristol and Exeter Railway, and as soon as the special train conveying the prince and his suite arrived at the station, they presented arms, and the bands of both corps played the National Anthem. The Mayor of Bristol ... and some of the members of the council entered the royal carriage, and his worship, on behalf of the citizens, expressed to the prince the great gratification they felt at his safe return, especially as some anxiety had actually been felt at the delay he had encountered. His royal highness repeatedly bowed his acknowledgements, and, after two or three persons had been presented to him, the train proceeded on its journey, amidst the cheers of the thousands who had assembled in the neighbourhood of the station.
>
> At Bath the train also stopped for two or three minutes, but beyond a few persons who had been informed of the prince's arrival, there was no one on the platform except the railway officials. It was not expected that the train would stop at Bath, and, therefore, there was no demonstration on the part of the authorities. The contrast between the excitement at Bristol and the absence of anything of the kind at Bath was most striking, and was, it is said, the subject of remark by one of the royal suite.

It was a very different story four years later, when Bath got its first taste of celebrity fever. Garibaldi, the liberator of Italy, was the greatest hero of the age, and when he passed through Bath on the midday express on 25 April 1864, en route to visit Colonel John Peard in Cornwall, pandemonium broke loose. Despite an attempt to keep the platform clear of "rude intruders," and prevent the "scenes of irregularity enacted elsewhere," by issuing a limited number of permits to the station, the frenzy of the crowd proved irresistible. The *Bath Chronicle* describes what happened:

> Outside the Guildhall and outside the station, a notice was posted to the effect that the mayor would endeavour to prevail upon Garibaldi to leave his carriage for a minute or two, and appear on the bridge which spans the road from the station to the George Hotel.* This intimation, it was doubtless hoped, would induce the people to wait patiently in the streets and road within sight of the bridge, but it made the intelligence more widely known, and brought out hundreds more people, determined upon getting inside the station by hook or by crook. Shortly after eleven o'clock the corporation assembled at the Guildhall, and at half past eleven, headed by the mayor … walked in procession to the station, where there had already congregated on the platform about 200 ladies and gentlemen. His worship the mayor, the mayoress, the aldermen and councillors, the municipal officers, and some of the leading residents and citizens, took up their station on the platform outside the building, at the upper end, and there proposed to wait the coming of the train in which the general was to be. If the train had come in at once all might have been well. As it was, the crowd increased every minute – the flurried porters admitted people without tickets, persevering folk swarmed in on all sides, and around the municipal body the pressure became unendurable. Boards were laid across the rails, over which it was hoped the General would walk to the hotel bridge, but as the multitude augmented and all prospect of their orderly behaviour vanished, as the time for the appearance of the express came nearer, the idea of bringing the invalid soldier out among such an excited mob of worshippers had to be abandoned. Detained by the overflowing attentions of his admirers at other stations, the General's train was 20 minutes late, and this 20 minutes

* *The Royal. The confusion surrounding its name was because it was known as George's Royal Hotel, after the owner, John George.*

was fatal to the arrangements made for greeting him. A few minutes after twelve the mayor and his party found that they could no longer keep their footing, the crowd behind being all anxious to come to the front, and a change to the other end of the platform was decided upon. Mr Hughes, the chief superintendent, and 50 constables, were powerless against the crush. Across the platform and to the lower end the mayor and those surrounding him went, but the efforts of the police to prevent the crowd following were useless. Through the barriers interposed by the gentlemen in blue, the well-dressed people forcibly pushed, and the crowding became as inconvenient as before. Both platforms were filled by the people, dense crowds had assembled along the line at all points, and the railway officials had much to do to persuade the anxious concourse to remain clear of the rails. The house windows in the neighbourhood were filled with spectators, and in the streets from which a view of the George Hotel bridge could be gained a dense multitude had packed themselves ...

When the train at last steamed into the station, the crushing and the rushing were worse than ever, and thundering hurrahs were uttered as a greeting. Fog signals placed on the rails exploded like a salvo of miniature artillery, and cannon fired from Beechen Cliff added to the general tumult. It was surprising that no one was thrust beneath the carriage wheels in the universal eagerness to get close to the General. The saloon carriage in which was the object of all this enthusiasm was drawn up alongside the mayor and corporation, and as soon as it stopped the Liberator was seen at the door, his head uncovered. A cheering shout was raised, and then everybody seemed smitten with a mania for laying hold of him ... Respect for authority there was none, respect for ladies there was none; the strongest shoved themselves to the front, and in the press parasols were crushed, dresses torn, and discreditable was the confusion which the General and his friends had to behold. An officer of the Metropolitan Police, who was travelling with the General's party, tried to clear a space round the carriage door in vain. Twice the General himself opened the door and essayed to step out, but the eager throng prevented him, and he acted wisely in complying with the entreaties of his friends in the carriage not to venture amongst the excited concourse. If he had trusted himself to their mercies, he would undoubtedly have been injured, for the desire to seize some part of him, and to shake and hug him, had become general, and had deprived the struggling concourse of all sense of decorum, and all notion of what was due to their own dignity, and the dignity and comfort of the invalided veteran they were so roughly honouring. An address from the working men was held out, and was taken by a member of the General's suite. The mayoress, whose position in front of the crowd was really dangerous, handed Garibaldi a bouquet as soon as she could obtain an opportunity, and was rewarded with a kind smile for thanks. When she had done this, the occupants of the carriage considerately invited her within, for safety's sake, and the mayor a few moments afterwards was similarly favoured. The General waved his hand to the people with the simple dignity of which we have lately heard so much, and tried to repress the pressure of the crowd with kindly warnings ... Upon the roof of the carriages excited men clambered, and thrust their hands towards the hero to be touched. After the mayor had entered the carriage, the General proceeded to the other window, to pay his respects to the throng on the other side of the station. This mark of attention delighted the spectators immensely, and they rushed across the rails to the carriage in large numbers, each one anxious to shake the General's hand, or to touch him. He playfully declined the extended palms of the men, but shook hands with as many of the fair sex as possible. Timid women, emboldened by the excitement of the moment, placed themselves in positions of great danger, actually getting between the carriages of the train ... Several times had the engine whistle to be sounded before the train could securely proceed. After it was in motion the mayor had to step from the carriage. The people pressed against him so forcibly that he was in danger of falling between the train and the platform. The door was closed by the pressure, and had to be reopened to let out the mayoress, whose exit was even more dangerous, and but for the assistance of the City Architect, she would hardly have escaped serious injuries. The train proceeded a short distance, when the people again clustered around it. As it moved along the embankment skirting Dorchester Street, the General waved his hat to the multitude congregated there, and in passing over the bridge at the bottom of Southgate Street he returned the greeting of a multitude assembled on the Old Bridge and on the Quay in a similar way ...

> The display proved the hearty regard of the people for the champion of Italian independence, and proved at the same time that in Bath, as elsewhere, English crowds are rude and unmanageable. When the mayor and corporation marched back to the Guildhall, they must have felt that the figure they had cut in the presence of Garibaldi was not a dignified one, but they had the consolation of knowing that they had done the best they could under the circumstances.

Forty-three years after her breakneck passage through the city, in November 1899, Bath got another chance to glimpse Queen Victoria. This time, the royal train "went through the station at the rate of about ten miles an hour, and as she passed Her Majesty stood up and looked northward over the city." The *Chronicle* reporter added that, "there is no doubt, from the fact of the Queen standing in her carriage while passing through, that she had not forgotten that day in the Victoria Park so many years ago." So much for the legend of her pulling the blinds down as she passed through the city – although her failure to stop may well have been because she did not want to hear any remarks about ankles.

One royal visitor, the Princess Helena, arrived in Bath by a somewhat novel method. Instead of alighting at the station, she used a specially-built platform in Sydney Gardens. The *Bath Chronicle* of 13 June 1889 described her arrival:

> To facilitate the alighting of the visitors the entire parapet bordering on the railway, between the iron bridge and the stone arch spanning the road above Sydney Place, had been removed level with the parallel path, which latter was nicely carpeted the entire length … The "special" conveying the faculty steamed through at 12.40, hasty greetings being exchanged between the passengers and friends in the gardens. In about five minutes the train, backed on the up line, returned from the Bath station and the travellers speedily alighted.

It is a cornerstone of Bath folklore that the train failed to stop the first time either because the driver was not privy to the special arrangements or because he forgot. Like the story about Queen Victoria pulling the blinds down, it does not stand up to scrutiny. The platform had to be constructed on the up line because of the high wall on the other side of the line. As Princess Helena was coming from London, her train was on the down line. It therefore had to continue on to Bath station, where an engine was attached to the rear of the train to draw it back towards Sydney Gardens on the up line. So – not a breakdown of communication, but the result of operational necessity.

The reason for the special platform was the dire state of Bath station. As early as 1864, letters such as the following had appeared in local papers:

> Sir, I wish to draw attention to the present state of our railway station. It is without exception, I think, the most disgustingly dirty station I have ever seen. Owing to the use of coal instead of coke in the locomotives, the entire roof and sides are as black as soot can make them; no stranger could ever believe it was ever a lighter colour. I am jealous for the credit of our beautiful city, and as it usually takes a long time to get the authorities to do anything that is not absolutely necessary, it is well to begin speaking . . . etc., etc.

The problem was that the station was not only at first-floor level; it was built on a curve and wedged into a restrictive site, with no room to expand. The stairs to the platforms were narrow, as were the platforms. The pillars supporting the roof were only three feet two inches from the platform edge; when a carriage door was opened next to them, it was impossible to get past. The station was more suited to a prosperous London suburb than a major city.

In 1870, however, Bath did finally get a station worthy of its size and status. The trouble with the station at Green Park, opened by the Midland Railway as the terminus of a branch from Mangotsfield, was that it faced the wrong way. It catered for passengers to and from the Midlands and the North, who were far outnumbered by those to and from London. When the railways were rationalised after nationalisation, it was a foregone conclusion which station would be closed. Plans were drawn up to divert trains from the Midland line into the Great Western station, but these were dropped when it was decided to close the Midland line instead.

The Midland Railway only came to Bath because of a colossal miscalculation, fuelled by high-handed arrogance, by the directors of

Two views of the overall roof at Bath station.

the Great Western. They would probably have got away with it had not a couple of strangers bumped into each other in a railway carriage.

Four years after the Great Western Railway opened from London to Bristol, another line opened from Bristol to Gloucester. Like the Great Western Railway, it was built by Brunel; like the Great Western Railway, it was broad gauge. The directors of the Great Western Railway had every reason to suppose it would, in due course, form part of their empire.

In the meantime, the Bristol & Gloucester merged with the Birmingham & Gloucester, a standard gauge line. The break of gauge at Gloucester soon became a *cause célèbre*, with passengers and goods between Bristol and Birmingham having to be transhipped. Despite these operating difficulties, the directors of the Great Western were confident that both companies would soon fall into their laps, and that, having taken them over, they would extend the broad gauge north to Birmingham. When negotiations started, they did what powerful companies always do when they think the cards are stacked in their favour. They offered them less than they wanted – £60 a share instead of £65 – and sat back to wait for them to come running. Which they did. Unfortunately, the train they chose to come running by happened to be carrying the deputy chairman of the Midland Railway, John Ellis. By chance, they happened to get into the same carriage.

It was an historic journey. By the time they reached London, the Bristol & Gloucester and the Birmingham & Gloucester had been delivered into the hands of a railway which, until then, had been hardly a cloud on the horizon of the Great Western. What John Ellis had done, without reference to his board or any of his fellow directors, was agree to pay the asking price for the shares. The Midland now had a clear run – except for the change of gauge at Gloucester – from their headquarters at Derby right into the heart of Great Western territory. The inevitable conversion of the Bristol & Gloucester to standard gauge followed in 1854.

Had the Midland not taken over the Bristol & Gloucester Railway, had it indeed fallen into the lap of the Great Western, the railway map of Gloucestershire and Somerset would have been very different. There would have been no branch from Mangotsfield to Bath, no station at Queen Square, no northern extension of the Somerset & Dorset Railway, no inter-company rivalry in the Somerset coalfield. Less railways, certainly, but – with only one company in the frame – almost certainly a more rational network. And who knows – perhaps one that one would have survived the Beeching Axe in the 1960s somewhat better.

If Bathonians imagined that the opening of the Midland station would spur the Great Western into upgrading their facilities, they were wrong. Even when the railway inspectorate notified the directors in 1875 that the station's facilities were inadequate for both passengers and goods, all they did was build a new goods station at Westmoreland Road. By 1889, the year of Princess Helena's visit, the situation was becoming desperate. The mayor sent a petition with 1,100 signatures to the directors, making the following points:

> That the passenger station of the Great Western Railway in the City of Bath was erected nearly 50 years ago when the line was first opened and that except for lengthening of the platforms remains as it was originally built.
>
> That the traffic has enormously increased since the erection of the station which is in consequence totally inadequate for present requirements.
>
> That the construction of the station is faulty and the presence of pillars on the platforms so near to the edge thereof highly objectionable and productive of accidents.
>
> That the want of a carriage approach on the level of the platforms is a serious drawback, and that the staircases are narrow, exceedingly steep and otherwise inconvenient.
>
> That the defects lastly mentioned, which would in any case be objectionable, are in the case of Bath intolerable; because the city is the resort of invalids who are yearly flocking thither in greater number and to whom the means of easy access to the platforms is a matter of absolute necessity.
>
> That the City of Bath is the most important place and the most lucrative to the company between Bristol and London, and yet the station accommodation is almost the worst in the whole distance.
>
> That the station, quite apart from the special circumstances of the city, is antiquated and unsuited for modern requirements and contrasts most unfavourably with the station of the Midland Railway Company in Bath.
>
> That it is understood that plans were prepared many years ago for extensive improvements, the carrying out of which was delayed for financial reasons.
>
> That the time has now arrived, when having regard to the financial position of the company and the increasing importance of the city which results in a very largely augmented revenue to the company, these improvements ought not to be any longer delayed.

> That if the company should (as it is submitted they ought to do) undertake improvement works at the Bath station it is desirable that the provision of refreshment rooms should form part of the scheme.

Two years later, having achieved absolutely nothing, the council sent a deputation to the directors. A few days later, the Chairman of the Board wrote back, with breathtaking arrogance,

> I'm afraid the expenditure at Bath wouldn't be remunerative. It would improve the accommodation for traffic, but wouldn't bring us in a penny directly.

In 1895, however, there was a change of heart, and it was announced that £15,000 would be spent on improving facilities at the station. The broad gauge had been abolished three years earlier, and, as the standard-gauge tracks took up less room, they were slewed so that the width of the platforms could be increased. Two years later, the overall roof was removed, the platforms were extended, and a bay platform was added at the east end of the up platform.

Plans to build a new station after the Second World War came to nothing, and, over a century later, the station still looks much as it did after the 1897 revamp. Letters still appear in the *Bath Chronicle*, just as they did over a century ago, complaining about the station's lack of facilities. "The station is a disgrace," runs a fairly typical one from 2002, "and needs something done about it. It certainly doesn't give the right sort of welcome to the tourists who, we are told, are so vital to the city." Plans have now been drawn up, however, to redevelop the station as part of the Southgate Project, and to improve its facilities. Although some Brunellian features, such as the ramp to the original goods station and the remnant of a row of detached offices at the back of the station, will be lost, the new station will, we are told, be one that Bath can be proud of.

TWENTY

The Narrowing of the Line

The abolition of the broad gauge marked the failure of one of Brunel's most audacious, visionary, and, some would say, quixotic, enterprises. The superiority of the broad gauge has never been seriously challenged; but the jury on Brunel's wisdom – or lack of it – in advocating a non-standard gauge is still out. There can be little doubt that, in 1835, he believed that the broad gauge would last as long as his railway. He was overtaken by two events – the rapid, uncoordinated expansion of the rail network, and the extent to which it supplanted coastal shipping. The national rail network Brunel envisaged was one with a handful of main lines – the London & Southampton, the Great Western, the London & Birmingham, and the Eastern Counties Railway – fanning out from the capital, and branches radiating from them. Each set of lines would be relatively self-contained, with coastal shipping continuing to handle the lion's share of commerce between major provincial ports. Given such a scenario, the difference in gauge between the Great Western and other trunk lines was not a major issue.

But the growth of the railway network did not conform to this pattern. Planned, organic growth gave way to mania, a new South Sea Bubble of get-rich-quick schemes in which sharp operators like George Hudson, the "Railway King" clawed their way to the top of the heap. In 1838 there were 500 miles of railway in England; in 1848 there were 5,000. At the height of the railway boom, in 1845, parliament sanctioned 2,700 miles of new line. As far as Brunel was concerned, it had all gone terribly wrong. "The whole world is railway mad," he wrote in 1844,

> *I am really sick of hearing proposals made. I wish it were at an end ... I wish I could suggest a plan that would greatly diminish the number of projects; it would suit my interests and*

An up express approaches Bathampton in the closing days of the broad gauge.

> *those of my clients perfectly if all railways were stopped for several years to come.*

His words were echoed, a few years later, by Thomas Carlyle, in a review of the career of George Hudson:

> For all manner of reasons, how much could one have wished that the making of our British railways had gone on with deliberation; that these great works had made themselves not in five years but in fifty and five!

In such a context the broad gauge could not survive. Its fate was sealed in 1845, when the gauge commissioners appointed by the government decided that four feet eight and half inches should be adopted as standard. As almost 90% of lines had already been built to this gauge, their decision seems to have been a foregone conclusion. The broad gauge managed to hang on for another 47 years, however, before the Great Western Railway bowed to the inevitable.

A standard gauge train on mixed gauge tracks at Keynsham.

The broad gauge held sway at Bath until June 1874, when the line from Bathampton to Westbury and onward to Salisbury and Weymouth, along with other branches in Wiltshire and Somerset, was converted from broad to standard gauge. However, as the lines west of Exeter would remain broad gauge for the foreseeable future, it was necessary to convert the main line from Paddington to mixed gauge, so that both broad and narrow gauge trains could use it. It was only in this way that through services from Paddington to Plymouth and Penzance could be maintained.

The work of conversion took place over a single weekend, with about 2,000 men being employed on the project. Each of them received one shilling and threepence per day for rations, while the company provided them with "oatmeal and good water for making a wholesome and strengthening beverage." Sheds were erected where sleeping accommodation was scanty, and the navvies worked 17 or 18 hours out of 24.

The mixed gauge tracks through Bath lasted until 1892, when the decision was taken to abolish the broad gauge in its last enclave, west of Exeter. By then, only a handful of the trains passing through Bath were broad gauge. The conversion of the remaining broad gauge lines took place over the weekend of 20-23 May 1892. The last broad

Gauge conversion.

gauge express left Paddington at a quarter past ten on the morning of Friday 20 May, calling at Bath at half past twelve. For several days, a motley collection of broad-gauge engines, carriages and wagons had been passing through en route from Devon and Cornwall to Swindon where they would be scrapped or, in a few cases, converted for standard gauge use. By Friday evening, all broad gauge stock – unless it was to be broken up on site – had to be on its way to Swindon, ready for the conversion of the entire system west of Exeter. The last up broad-gauge train – of empty carriages – left Penzance at ten past nine of the evening of 20 May. As it cleared each section eastward, gangs of navvies moved in behind it to slew the tracks into their new position, ready to carry standard gauge trains. It passed through Bath, unheralded and unmourned, just after eight thirty the next morning. Just over an hour later, it rolled into the yard at Swindon. Brunel's dream was over, and, despite the pleas of a few early enthusiasts, no carriages or main line engines were preserved to remind future generations of its glory.*

The final gauge conversion had one bizarre consequence, ushering in a brief mailcoach revival. The complete closure of the Great

* *One diminutive engine, appropriately named Tiny, did survive, and is now on display at Buckfastleigh on the Dart Valley Railway. A replica of the broad-gauge locomotive Firefly can be seen at the Great Western Railway Centre, Didcot.*

Western west of Exeter could not be allowed to interfere with the passage of Her Majesty's mails, and so, having been diverted over the rails of the London & South Western Railway, which by now had its own line to Plymouth, they were loaded onto a steamer, which took them on to Fowey and Falmouth. From there they were sent forward by a network of horse-drawn coaches, accompanied by uniformed guards who announced their arrival at each staging post by the blowing of post horns.

The ultimate failure of the broad gauge, like that of the attempt to run trains using atmospheric pressure west of Exeter, has to be seen within the context of Brunel's overall achievement. Everything Brunel did pushed the technological and engineering resources of his time to the limit, and frequently beyond it, disdaining trivial issues such as the problems attendant on gauge incompatibility. He was convinced, not only of his own genius, but that everything he did was a force for the betterment of mankind, sweeping away the old, and ushering in a golden age of unlimited progress.

TWENTY ONE

Decline and Fall

The railways could not have been built without the engineering expertise gained building canals. Once the railways arrived, however, the canals never recovered. The Kennet & Avon Canal saw its receipts fall from £51,174 in 1840-41 to £39,936 in 1841-42. In 1845, the canal company discussed the possibility of converting the canal to a railway. This was done successfully elsewhere – the Andover Canal, for example, became the Andover & Redbridge Railway – but the number of locks on the Kennet & Avon – in particular the flight at Devizes – was an insuperable obstacle. The directors decided instead to offer the canal to the Great Western Railway, and the transfer was effected in 1852.

At Twerton, Charles Wilkins' hopes that the railway might reverse the fortunes of his weaving mills proved groundless. Nothing could stop the industry's headlong decline in the West Country; the railway could only accelerate it. In September 1841, Hobhouse's Bank in Bath failed due to the bankruptcy of two large mills in Bradford on Avon. A month later, Charles Wilkins sold "all the mills and adjoining premises in Twerton, the Manor or Lordship of Twerton, and all relating lands not sold to the Great Western Railway" to his bankers for £7,000. Eight years later, the *Bath Postal Directory* noted that Twerton "was formerly noted for its extensive manufacture of superfine woollen cloth. As late as 1838, two mills gave regular employment to upwards of 700 persons; at present there is only one mill, the productions from which are very limited." The coal mines at Twerton owned by Charles Wilkins also closed after the railway arrived. A newspaper clipping from May 1845 records that the circular steam boiler from "Newton Coal Work" had stuck fast under the railway arch at Claverton Street while en route to Dunkerton Colliery, and the flue had to be taken off before it could be moved.

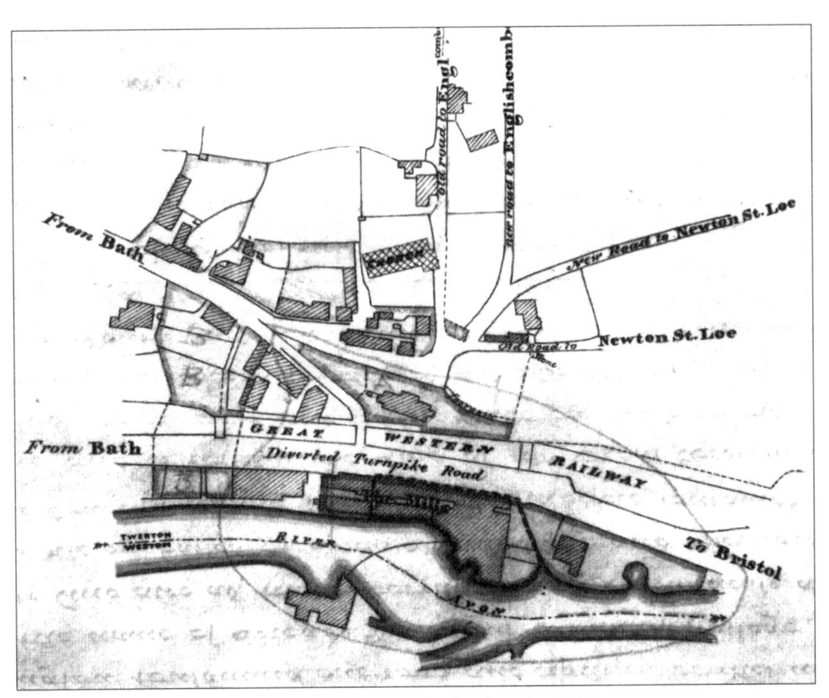

A plan of the land sold by Charles Wilkins to his bankers in 1841.

The impact of the railway on Bath's development – or lack of it – in the latter half of the nineteenth century is more difficult to assess. The city had been in decline for some time. The future George IV had made his preference for Brighton plain ever since his first visit to the resort in 1783. Far from being Europe's top pleasure resort, as it had been in the days of Beau Nash, Bath was decidedly old-fashioned by the time the railway arrived. The uncoordinated way in which the city had grown in the eighteenth century had created a breeding ground for social unrest, which had first become apparent with the Gordon Riots in 1780. Chartist demonstrations and drunken elections continued the tradition, giving Bath an unsavoury reputation which the corporation struggled, with varying degrees of success, to hush up.

Bath's glory was not only faded when the railway arrived; it was soot-black. The buildings whose stone Jane Austen had found too dazzling at the beginning of the century, were black before it was half over. In 1835, when it was being debated whether North Parade

North Parade Bridge as originally built. Stone cladding was added in the 1930s.

Bridge should be built of iron or stone, iron was chosen on the grounds that "the dark shade, speedily acquired by the Bath stone, in and near the city, will give the structure a heavy and sombre appearance in a few years." Brunel's trains only speeded up the blackening process. Things got no better in the following century. When the Great Western Railway published a guidebook to Somerset in 1928, it describe the city as "very grey."

In 1840, a leading authority on Britain's spas predicted that those "who have not yet seen the English 'Spa of Spas' (as I trust it will soon again become) will proceed thither in numbers as soon as Sir Isambard the magician shall, with his Great Western wand, have brought Bath within three hours of the metropolis." Any hopes for a revival of Bath's fortunes proved short-lived, however. Railways made the Highlands of Scotland, popularised by Sir Walter Scott and given the royal seal of approval by Queen Victoria, more accessible than Bath had been just a few years earlier. Places that had previously been off limits to all but the most intrepid travellers were suddenly within reach. Those who wanted spas could travel to newly-fashionable towns such as Llandrindod Wells or to watering holes on the continent; those in search of pleasure had their pick of burgeoning resorts such as Bournemouth or Weston Super Mare. Bath, with its blackened buildings and social problems, living on past glories, began to look very frayed at the edges.

Invalids – a high proportion of them elderly – continued to visit the city, and an increasing number elected to stay. The city which, a century earlier, had been synonymous with dice, dancing, and dangerous liaisons, began to resemble a retirement home. When Charles Dickens returned to give a reading at the Assembly Rooms, he said that it had been "built by a cemetery-full of old people, who, making a successful rise against death, have carried the place by assault and, bringing their gravestones with them, have contrived to build the city, in which they are trying to look alive. But it's a miserable failure."

It was not just the upper and middle classes who stopped coming to Bath. The new breed of working-class excursionists wanted to go to the seaside. The idea of traipsing around Bath admiring its heritage was not one that would have appealed to them. Charles Saunders' conviction that Bath would double in size once the railway arrived was wide of the mark. Bath stagnated, just like the towns and villages on the Bath Road, such as Hounslow, Longford, Colnbrook, Theale, Thatcham, Marlborough and Beckhampton, that had relied on its coaching trade.

Bath was not alone in its problems. It is sometimes said that towns by-passed by the railway declined, while towns served by it prospered. The reality is far more complex. Thomas Carlyle saw this in 1850, when he declared that

> Railways are shifting all towns of Britain into new places; no town will stand where it did, and nobody can tell for a long while yet where it will stand. This is an unexpected, and indeed most disastrous result. I perceive, the railways have set all the towns of Britain a-dancing. Reading is coming up to London, Basingstoke is going down to Gosport or Southampton, Dumfries to Liverpool and Glasgow; while at Crewe, and other points, I see new ganglions of human population establishing themselves, and the prophecy of metallurgic cities which were not heard of before. Reading, Basingstoke and the rest, the unfortunate towns, subscribed money to get railways; and it proves to be for cutting their own throats. Their business has gone elsewhither ...

Not only did the railway fail to arrest Bath's decline as a tourist destination; it failed to encourage the establishment of new industry in the city. Since the early eighteenth century, Bath had had the advantage of the Avon Navigation; goods produced in Bath could be sent to Bristol, from whence they could be forwarded to ports around the country. Transporting goods by water was far cheaper and easier than sending them by land. This not only helped industrialists in Bath to export their products; it also facilitated the import of goods into the city. The biggest industry in Bath in the late eighteenth and early nineteenth century was brewing; more beer was brewed in Bath than in Bristol. By the time the railway arrived, Bath had the biggest brewery in the West Country – the Northgate Brewery, on the site now occupied by the Podium. The brewing industry had grown because Bath was a port, and distribution of beer over a wide area, at a competitive rate, was thus possible. When the railway arrived, Bath lost its competitive edge: when every town had a station, every town had exactly the same opportunity for distributing its products. With the arrival of the railway, competition from breweries previously too far away to be a serious threat increased dramatically. People started trying different beers, and very quickly started to develop a taste for lighter beers, such as those brewed with the gypsum-rich waters of Burton on Trent, instead of the Old Ale on which the reputation of the Northgate Brewery was founded. Burton's breweries boomed when the railway arrived; Bath's started to decline. James Grant Smith of the Anchor Brewery in Southgate Street, who had been such an implacable opponent of the railway, went bankrupt in 1842: his brewery became a cabinet works. The Northgate Brewery closed in 1868 and became a furniture warehouse.

One company that did expand after the railway arrived was Stothert's. In 1855 it became Stothert & Pitt's, and two years later it relocated from Newark Street to larger premises on the Lower Bristol Road, where a series of further expansions followed. Measom, in his *Official Guide to the Great Western Railway*, tells us that, "under the superintendence of the late lamented Mr Brunel, a number of works of almost national interest were either wholly or in part conducted at these works. Amongst others we may mention the machinery for the excavation of the Box Tunnel, through the first three-quarters of a mile in solid stone." The railway undoubtedly encouraged the

The eastern portal of Box Tunnel, with the entrance to the stone quarries on the right.

expansion of Stothert's, although the company was well established before the railway arrived. Although it would be an exaggeration to say that the railway was incidental to its development, it was Bath's status as a port that was the crucial factor in its initial success. Stothert & Pitt's later reputation as a world leader in the manufacture of cranes was due to the business acumen of the company's directors rather than any special advantage bestowed by the railway. It is also significant that, although small, specialised companies such as Horstmann's did later operate successfully in Bath, no other major companies were established in Bath after the arrival of the railway.

Another local industry that was given a major boost by the opening of the railway was the quarrying of Bath Stone. The excavation of Box Tunnel not only revealed the extent of the deposits under Box Hill, but also trained up an army of men to excavate them. Once the railway was open, it offered unprecedented opportunities for shipping stone all over the country. The goods yard at Corsham became a major transhipment point for Bath Stone, linked to underground quarries by a tunnel next to the east portal of Box Tunnel. The great step forward in the history of the Bath Stone industry, however, had occurred over a century earlier, when Ralph Allen introduced new working practices and built a tramway and river navigation to transport the stone, transforming a small-scale operation into one of national importance. The expansion at Box and Corsham after the railway opened was not a new departure, but the development of an already well-established industry.

It is worth recalling that, from the outset, Bath had been lukewarm towards the railway. Perhaps Bathonians knew instinctively it held little for them. Perhaps they simply assumed it would come because Bristol wanted a link to London and the only way to London lay through Bath.

The Great Western Railway did arrest the decline in Bristol's fortunes, although not in the way that Brunel and the promoters of the line anticipated. Brunel's dream that Bristol would once again be Britain's major transatlantic port was never to be realized. The hotel he built for passengers transferring from his railway to his steamships soon became a white elephant. The city's docks were simply too small, too inaccessible. Even Avonmouth, despite all the money spent on it, was never to wrest more than a small share of the traffic handled by Liverpool or Southampton. But, within a few years – and despite the legacy of the two gauges – Bristol became what Brunel had never envisaged, one of the country's major rail junctions. It was on that that much of its future prosperity was to rest.

The railway changed England and English life more profoundly than any other invention. But, although the railway came to Bath early, with better services and faster trains than many places two or three times its size, it had less real impact on the city than on almost anywhere else in the country.

For Brunel, the Great Western Railway was more than an engineering challenge. For him, it had a quasi-mystical significance. Brunel the artist saw Bath as a backdrop for one of the greatest works of all time. Bath's faded pleasure gardens became a stage set through which his steam hauled expresses clattered and roared, linking Britain to the New World. He believed that the railway would usher in a new age: the country would shrink to a sixth of its former size; international travel would become an everyday reality. The railway would not only be the means by which it would be achieved: it would be the defining symbol of the new age. Brunel chose architecture that recalled a glorious semi-mythical past, grounding his vision in values he sought to resurrect and embody in the coming age. The future would not be ruled by the dead hand of those who had resisted reform – the same ones who had resisted railway development – nor would it succumb to mob rule, rioters, or Chartists. It would be guided and transformed by men of vision, the knights of a new industrial age. Brunel's position as one of those knights had been earned, not by virtue of birth, nor by engaging in the art of political intrigue, but by the strength of his vision, and by the force with which he imposed it on the land whose destiny was never far from his thoughts.

Over one hundred and fifty years on, however, Brunel's railway is vital to Bath's prosperity. A frequent, high-speed service between Bath and London is essential to the city's economy. The vision of the Great Western Railway that Brunel embodied in his bridges, viaducts and tunnels can still inspire us today. But his legacy goes deeper than that. The modern world relies on fast communication – faster and more various than anything Brunel could have imagined. Steam trains today are objects of nostalgia. But they were the first means by which the old world, where nothing travelled faster than the fastest horse, was conquered. The pre-industrial age was, despite all the poets' dreams of pastoral bliss, a place where rumour, superstition, poverty, hunger, and ignorance held sway to a terrifying extent. Brunel saw, more clearly and more single-mindedly than anyone else, that the key to the future lay in the conquest of time and space. With that dual conquest the modern world was born.

The Story Of Box Tunnel

Brunel did not have to build a tunnel under Box Hill. He could have followed, as many suggested, the course of the Kennet & Avon Canal. If set on going north of the Marlborough Downs, he could have followed the valley of the Avon from Chippenham, through Melksham and Bradford, to Bath, adding at most six miles to the journey. Most engineers would have taken one of these options.

Today, nobody gives much thought to railway tunnels. You might notice a rush of air as your train enters one, or be dazzled by the light at the other end. You will certainly be aware of them if you are on a mobile phone. At night, you probably won't notice them at all. As phobias go, fear of tunnels is well down the list. But that was not always the case.

There had been tunnels before, but only in mines or on canals. They were not open to the general public, nor were they threaded by steam engines travelling at 60 miles an hour or more. Such tunnels as had been built for public use did not have a good track record. In 1812, the spectacular collapse of the Highgate Road Tunnel had been celebrated in a melodrama called *the Highgate Tunnel, or the Secret Arch*. The tunnel was abandoned and Archway Road was built instead. In 1827 and 1828, there had been the two disastrous floodings of the Thames Tunnel, the second of which had nearly claimed Brunel's life, and caused work to be suspended indefinitely.

The early Victorians had an ambivalent attitude to tunnels, however. Their perceived danger made them immensely attractive to those in pursuit of the sublime. The abandoned workings under the Thames were one of London's top tourist attractions. They inspired one of the top artists of the time, John Martin, when he produced a series of illustrations for Milton's *Paradise Lost*. Martin was a friend of Brunel, and travelled on the footplate of an engine driven by Brunel through Box Tunnel, which Brunel allegedly notched up to speeds approaching 90 miles an hour.

The East Gate at Blenheim, a triumphal arch celebrating one of England's greatest military leaders.

John Martin's vision was essentially an apocalyptic one, and this, in an age which seems to have been obsessed by apocalyptic themes, ensured that he was one of the country's most celebrated artists. The sense that society was on the brink of momentous changes inspired this preoccupation with apocalyptic imagery. In 1816, Lord Byron published a poem called *Darkness*, in which humanity and freedom are

Even today, trains are dwarfed by the monumental arch of Box Tunnel.

defeated, God is replaced by the Fiend of Famine, and the earth is transformed into "a lump of death." The poem's influence can be seen in works such as Mary Shelley's *The Last Man* (1823), Bulwer Lytton's *Last Days of Pompeii* (1834) and Thomas Carlyle's *French Revolution* (1837). Martin's canvases, vast perspectives of the lost cities of the ancient world at the apocalyptic hour of their destruction, were not the only paintings to take up this theme. Francis Danby's *The Opening of the Sixth Seal* was one of William Beckford's most prized possessions when Brunel visited him in 1830; Turner's apocalyptic fantasies included *Shade and Darkness: The Evening of the Deluge* (1843) and *The Angel Standing in the Sun* (1846).

If Brunel influenced Martin, it is also possible that he was influenced by him in turn, basing the design for the western portal of Box Tunnel on Martin's Egyptian style architectural fantasies. There is, however, another possible source for the portal. Christian Barman has shown how Vanbrugh's design for Seaton Delaval Hall almost certainly inspired George Stephenson when he designed Euston station. The east gate of another of Vanbrugh's great houses, Blenheim, has a striking similarity to the western portal at Box. This gate – looking more like the entrance to a citadel than a stately home – was not only a monumental arch and a national war memorial, but a clever piece of civil engineering, for a water tower above the arch supplied the palace with water. This blend of architectural magnificence and utility would undoubtedly have appealed to Brunel.

The east gate at Blenheim was the entrance to the greatest of English country houses, built for one of the greatest Englishmen. The Duke of Marlborough had elevated the nation's fortunes by defeating its enemies; Brunel's conquest – of space and time – had not been by force of arms but by force of technology. The western portal at Box was the gateway not simply to a tunnel but to a new age. It was appropriate that it should recall one of the most monumental tributes to a national hero. Brunel's vision was no less apocalyptic than John Martin's. The difference was that, whereas Martin was obsessed by destruction, Brunel saw his railway as an apocalyptic force by which society would be transformed and led forward to a golden age:

> The voice of him that crieth in the wilderness: Prepare ye the way of the Lord, make straight in the desert a highway for our God. Every valley shall be exalted, and every mountain and hill shall be made low: and the crooked shall be made straight, and the rough places plain: And the glory of the Lord shall be revealed, and all flesh shall see it together.

Christian Barman has described the mixture of hostility and fascination that characterised attitudes to tunnels:

> When the railways were built, it was the tunnels above all other works that caught the popular imagination. They represented the most adventurous aspects of engineering, the side that connected it with the wildness and the mystery of nature at its most untameable. Already the delicious thrills of caves and caverns and mines had stimulated the public appetite for the horrific. Poets had told of their wanderings about the coal mines of Whitehaven and elsewhere … Their readers had followed eagerly, admiring the subterranean scenery of the many caves in the Matlock neighbourhood and eating picnic meals in the Northwich salt mines, three feet below ground. But these were mild excitements compared to a railway journey through the bowels of the earth, drawn by a fiery monster belching smoke and steam. Lord Broughton, describing in his diary his first railway journey, … confesses that "the effect was overpowering … I

> was more affected by this display of power than by any other work of art, the Simplon Road or Menai Bridge not excepted. There was something awful, bordering on the terrific, in our moving through the … tunnel, but all portions of the work seemed performed with such accuracy as to diminish much the sense of danger." The experience, it is true, was too much for some travellers. "What," says one of the early railway guides, "are the evils with which tunnels are charged? They are, the excitation of an injurious feeling of dread in persons not accustomed to pass through them – a density of atmosphere, its dampness, its admixture with carbonic-acid gas – the sudden transition from darkness to light, and the consequent effect on the eyes." The author, Arthur Freeling, advises passengers to shut their eyes as soon as they begin to see daylight, and to open them very slowly after coming out.

Eminent doctors advised against travelling through tunnels, which "would expose healthy people to colds and consumption" or bring on apoplexy through "the deafening peal of thunder, the sudden immersion in gloom, and the clash or reverberated sounds in a confined space."

Not all the hostility to tunnels came from ill-informed laymen. In April 1836, the editor of the *Railway Magazine* declared that,

> it is not merely on account of the great cost of their construction … but the excessive nuisances which it is morally impossible to prevent, and the danger to delicate constitutions of travelling through such holes of impurity … It is to be hoped … that the legislature will consider the objections there ever must be to tunnels, the nuisances they will be to the public, the extravagant expense of their construction, the certainty of such lines being ultimately superseded by other lines without tunnels; and that they will really prove themselves the guardians of the subscribers and friends to the public, by setting their faces against any bill in which tunnels are proposed.

One civil engineer went further, claiming that

> the inevitable, if not the necessary consequence of constructing such a tunnel would be occasionally the wholesale destruction of human

> life, and that no care, no foresight, no means that had been ever applied up to that time could prevent it.

Many objections were raised at the committee stage of the Bill authorising construction of the line. "No person would desire to be shut out from the daylight with a consciousness that he had a superincumbent weight of earth sufficient to crush him in case of accident," claimed one witness, while another believed that the noise of two trains passing each other in the tunnel would be so great that no human being would be able to stand it.

One of the expert witnesses who appeared before the committee was the infamous Dr Lardner. He objected to the tunnel because the line through it would be on a gradient of 1 in 100, requiring all but the lightest up trains to be banked by an extra engine. Down trains would encounter a far more serious problem, however. Dr Lardner produced elaborate calculations to prove that, if the brakes of a down train were to fail as a train entered the tunnel, it would shoot out at the other end at a speed of 120 miles an hour. He had, however, left friction and air resistance out of his equations. Brunel did the sums again and showed that the speed of a runaway train would be no greater than 56 miles an hour.

The committee was still not convinced, and so Brunel constructed a model of the cutting at the mouth of Box Tunnel, with the rails on an incline of 1 in 90.

"Now, my Lords," said Brunel, "kindly point out whether this dreadful gradient is an ascending or a descending one."

Brunel, it seems, had constructed his model so that the rails appeared to be drop down towards the tunnel mouth, even though they actually dropped away from it. When the committee all came up with the wrong answer, Brunel took a miniature wagon, loaded with chalk, and it placed on the rails at the mouth of the tunnel, at which it rolled down the gradient in the opposite direction to which the committee had predicted and tipped the chalk all over the table.

* * *

The section west of Chippenham was a difficult one to build. Leaving the town over a monumental viaduct, the line continued past Patterdown on a two-mile embankment, before entering a cutting, nearly three miles long and between 40 and 70 feet in depth, through solid stone, as far as Corsham.

Then came the most monumental engineering feat of all – Box Tunnel, nearly two miles long, and, at the time of its construction, the longest in the world. Over 400,000 cubic yards of earth was chiselled and blasted out by candlelight and drawn to the surface by horses. Over three million bricks were used to line it. It would be an astonishing achievement today; in 1835 it was, literally, at the cutting edge of technology.

Work started on it early in 1836, when Messrs Paxton and Orton were awarded the contract to dig exploratory shafts. Miners who had worked on the Thames Tunnel were brought in to help with the work. On 18 June 1836, Brunel wrote to the Great Western directors:

> *Beyond Bath the Box Tunnel is the most important work and that which, in conjunction with the cutting and embankment to the east of it, will determine the time of completion of the whole line. Active steps are consequently being taken to put this part of the work in a train for proceeding. Five temporary shafts have been sunk in the line of the tunnel to various depths varying from 40 to 90 feet to determine the position of the strata of the oolite through which all of them have been carried – a sixth has been found necessary at the west end before I can determine with sufficient certainty the exact position of the clay or Fuller's Earth which lies under the oolite and the proportionate lengths of which the tunnel will pass through must govern the relative distance of the permanent shafts. This remaining shaft will be worked at day and night and as soon as the required information is obtained, which I hope will be in a fortnight, we shall be able to prepare and to let the contracts for the construction of these permanent shafts which I propose to do separately from the tunnel in order that the materials through which each portion of the latter is to be carried may be ascertained and worked by the parties most accustomed to the particular description of material and not contracted for blindly as a mere speculation.*

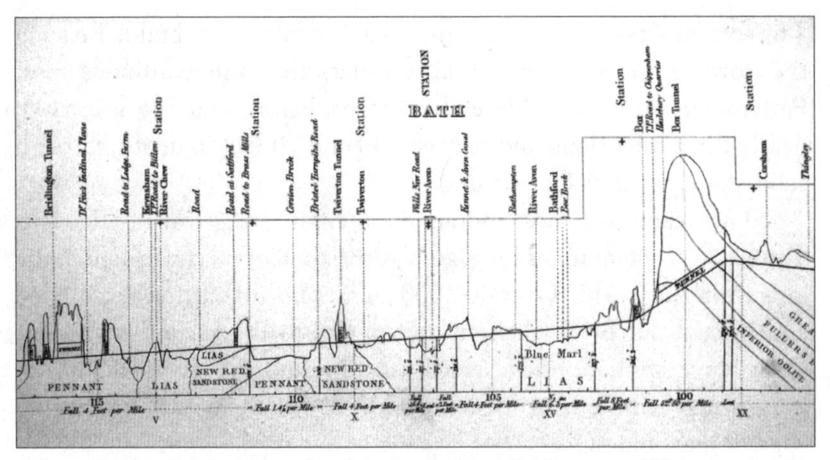

The gradient and geological profile of the line between Brislington and Thingley, showing the 1 in 100 climb through Box Tunnel.

In June 1836, Brunel interviewed candidates for the post of assistant engineer to the project. A couple of days later, he wrote to William Glennie, offering him the position. Misconstruing Brunel's words, Glennie wrote back, accepting the post of resident engineer. Brunel wasted no time in putting him straight:

> *You have entirely misunderstood me … I think I explained that this position of resident engineer was attainable by you – not promised by me … All I can offer you is the post of assistant engineer … What I offer must not be a certain or permanent position. My responsibility is too great to allow of my retaining … anyone who may appear to me to be inefficient … It is an understood thing that all under me are subject to immediate dismissal at my pleasure … It is for you to decide if you are likely to proceed satisfactorily and whether the chance is sufficient inducement.*

Glennie accepted Brunel's terms, and was later appointed resident engineer, on a salary of £150 a year, after winning Brunel's confidence.

Work was already well behind schedule when, in November, the workings were flooded by a massive influx of water. In some shafts it rose to a depth of over 50 feet. Work came to a standstill, while steam pumps, supplied by Stothert's, were brought in. These were hardly up to the job, and for much of the time, they did little more than stop the waters rising any higher. An added complication was the lack of water supply for the engines on top of the hill; this all had to be carted up the hill by horses. By February, rumours that the directors were contemplating abandonment of the project provoked a strongly-worded denial:

> Unfounded reports were circulated industriously during the first application to parliament respecting imaginary difficulties to be encountered in the tunnel through the Box Hill to the east of Bath, and it may be a satisfaction to the proprietors to know that trial shafts have been sunk and the strata, through which it passes, fully ascertained; the result of which not only proves the incorrectness of such reports but gives full assurance of the work being free from all unexpected or unusual difficulties.

This official line seems to have held, for as late as 20 April the *Bath Chronicle* reported that

> the seven permanent shafts of this stupendous undertaking are now more than half completed. Two of the shallow shafts are nearly finished towards the Chippenham end of the line, and the remainder are sunk 150 feet. The construction of these works, being of greater magnitude than any similar undertaking in this or any other country, will be viewed by geologists and others with much interest. The shafts describe a circle of 30 feet diameter, and the tunnel will be 30 feet by 40. The machinery for lifting the soil is worked by horse-power of good contrivance, the application of steam being impractical, from the want of water at the summit of the hill to feed an engine. There is no doubt that the work will be completed before the time allowed to Mr Orton, the contractor.

Eight days before this report appeared, however, Messrs Paxton and Orton appealed to Brunel to bail them out, as the additional expenditure they had incurred meant they were running out of money and could not afford to continue with the project. When Brunel passed their request onto the directors, it was met by a firm refusal.

This left them with no option but to tender their resignation, at which point confidence in the project – and in the Great Western generally – took a sharp knock. For a time it seemed as though Brunel may indeed have taken a step too far, as though the unhappy saga of the Thames Tunnel would be repeated in Wiltshire.

Fortunately, Brunel was able to find two men willing to take over the job – Stothert from Bath and Brewer from Box. Stothert later passed the contract onto Thomas Lewis, a surveyor and builder on Wells Road in Bath. Working with around 300 men, the preparatory work was completed in the autumn of 1837. Brunel decided to award two contracts for the tunnel. Lewis and Brewer were given the job of digging 880 yards from the Corsham end, through great oolite, otherwise known as Bath Stone. Brunel had more trouble finding anyone prepared to take on the remaining 2,332 yard-stretch, through a mixture of clay, blue marl and lesser oolite. Eventually, in February 1838, George Burge from Herne Bay agreed to take the contract, and to complete it within 30 months.

Although the eastern section was more the more difficult one, Lewis and Brewer both had experience of working with Bath Stone. They started from opposite ends, blasting their way through, and building the tunnel in the shape of a Gothic arch. The influx of water was a constant problem, but, because of the perceived stability of the strata, it was not considered necessary to line the tunnel with brick. Much of the western section could be excavated by pick and shovel, gunpowder only being needed to blast a way through some of the lesser oolite. There was, however, a much greater risk of the tunnel falling in, and lining with brick was essential.

Thomas Gale, a foreman working for George Burge who later became office porter at the station in Bath, has left this record of his time at Box:

> The tunnel commenced in June 1838 … Mr George Burge [had] a hundred and odd horses working night and day drawing the earth up out of the tunnel to the surface, and otherwise engaged at the different works of the tunnel; and as many at least as 40 boys to drive the horses, and as many as eleven or twelve hundred men continually working night and day while the tunnel was in progress … The bricks used in the construction of the tunnel were made on this side

of Chippenham in the meadows by Mr Hunt, who had a hundred horses and carts at work bringing bricks to the tunnel for three years, and hauliers he engaged besides. For the use of the bricklayers and miners we had a great quantity of timber from Bath; and from Tanner's Lime Kiln we had three wagon loads of ash three or four times a week, and five or six cart loads of lime daily when the weather would permit. During the time the tunnel was making, a very large quantity of sand was dug out of the earth about two miles from the works, and mixed with other things, and used as mortar. There was a lime kiln on the tunnel continually burning lime from the stones that were dug out of the deepest parts of the tunnel, which made very good lime, we also had a large house for keeping our cement in, of which we always had several hundred casks on hand. Now all those different articles were delivered to me, or my men, and put down at the different parts where they were wanted for the use of the bricklayers and miners. The number of horses engaged at the different works and the tunnel could not be less than 300 until the tunnel was finished.

I, being foreman for the great contractor, Mr G Burge, and sub-contractor over all the day work on the top, and to see to the repairing of the gin rings where the horses travel round for bringing stuff up out of the tunnel, I was continually over Mr G Burge's works daily. From the bridge and tunnel mouth I had a very good opportunity of seeing how the works were carried on, which I will try to explain as well as I possibly can.

Box Tunnel is 9,680 feet long; it contains five shaft holes for ventilation and light; there were twelve or thirteen, but the rest were arched over and filled in when the work was finished. The depth of the deepest shaft hole would be about 306 feet, the others were not quite so deep. There was supposed to be about 414,000 cubic yards of earth and rock taken from the tunnel and over thirty millions of bricks were used to brick up the tunnel. It took nearly one year to sink the trial shaft, and nearly two years to make the shafts, which are now open for light and ventilation, so that it took nearly six years to complete that great undertaking; and every week one ton of gunpowder, and one ton of candles were consumed during the time the tunnel was making. From commencement to finish just one hundred men were killed in different parts of the works and in different ways; and quite as many were injured, some for life, but most of them being strangers to the neighbourhood they went to their respective homes – Cornwall, Wales and other parts of England – and no doubt a great many of them died. Drunkenness and fighting were carried on to an alarming extent; no teetotalism was known in those days with that class of men. We had 26 inspectors on the works, and a portion of them were sent to different villages to keep the peace on Sundays, as well as they could, there being no county police in those days.

Thomas Gale's claim that 100 men died during the building of Box Tunnel has been challenged by some writers, due to the lack of corroborative evidence. Until such time as a detailed examination of coroner's reports is conducted, however, all we have to rely on are the somewhat hit and miss reports contained in local newspapers, which by their very nature are unlikely to comprise a complete record. One thing beyond question is that the accident rate was appalling. In 1846, when Brunel appeared before a parliamentary committee, he was shown a list of 136 navvies admitted to the United Hospital in Bath between 1839 and 1841, most of them after accidents at Box Tunnel. Asked if he did not consider the figure unduly high, he replied that, on the contrary, "I think it is a small list considering the very heavy works and the immense amount of powder used."

The first recorded death occurred on 10 May 1838:

A fatal accident happened at one of the shafts on Box Hill on Thursday last about half past seven o'clock in the evening, to Giles Long, of Hullavington, near Chippenham, one of the workmen; who, while in the act of going down into the pit, accidentally slipped and fell to the bottom (a distance of about 60 feet), and, as might be expected, was killed instantaneously. Several men were at work in the pit at the same time, on the head of one of whom he nearly fell. The sense of the narrow escape this man had from the jaws of death, joined to the melancholy sight of the dreadful end of his fellow workman, is said to have produced such a powerful effect on his mind as to produce frequent fits since the accident.

The line east of the tunnel, with its heavy earthworks, also had a high fatality rate. On 24 May 1838, the *Bath Chronicle* reported two accidents to men working on this stretch of line:

> An accident of a serious nature occurred [near Corsham] on Tuesday morning the 15th inst to a labourer on the Great Western Railway, named John Bancroft, a native of Bradford, Wilts, whilst working in the open cutting. A fall of earth took place unexpectedly at the spot under which he was engaged, and although he saw it moving, his escape was prevented by a tram wagon. About three tons of earth fell on his legs, fracturing both in a shocking manner. He was attended immediately after the accident by Mr Little, surgeon to the works, and fears were for some days entertained that amputation of one leg would be necessary, but we are happy to state that the man is now doing well.
>
> Another accident occurred in a manner similar to the above, on the Thursday following, which has terminated fatally. The deceased, John Howel, an aged man, was overwhelmed by a fall of earth, the weight of which came full upon his body, producing great internal injury, which terminated his existence on the Sunday after. Deceased was an old pensioner, and a native of Kington St Michael in this neighbourhood. It is worthy of remark that the accidents which have occurred here have always happened to persons residing in the neighbourhood, and are comparatively unaccustomed to the work. The old tramps or navigators never even dream of anything of the kind happening to them. Thirteen men have now lost their lives on the works in this vicinity.

On 7 June, the *Bath Chronicle* reported that

> the Box tunnel work … is progressing as fast as the nature of it will admit. The miners and bricklayers are actively engaged upon the eastern and western faces of shafts nos 2, 3, 4, and 5; the most laborious and difficult portions of this great work. At shafts nos 7 and 8 the contractors are proceeding with the headings with considerable perseverance, although they have to contend with great disadvantages in consequence of a continual influx of immense volumes of water from the surrounding springs; indeed,

> notwithstanding that hundreds of hogsheads have for several months been daily drawn off from no 7 by the means of a steam engine working there both day and night without any cessation, yet more than 20 feet of water is still remaining in that shaft. This is now, however, since the dry weather has commenced, rapidly decreasing: so that there is every probability of that section of the work being completed to the entire satisfaction of the company.

On 30 June, a workman who had come up to the top of shaft no 5 "to take refreshment," lost his footing, slipped down the shaft and was killed. On 4 August an inquest was held at the Box Tunnel Inn

> on the body of Charles Davy, aged 20, a bricklayer's labourer. It appears that the deceased was engaged on Friday evening on a swinging scaffold, about fifty feet from the bottom of shaft no 3, on the tunnel, with two others, repairing the brickwork, when an empty skip descending touched the scaffold, and tilting it, Davy was precipitated to the bottom, whilst the others clung to the ropes until the scaffold had righted itself. When picked up, he was found perfectly insensible, having received a dreadful fracture of the skull. Mr Little, surgeon, attended from Corsham immediately, and Mr Goldstone from Box, shortly after. They tried every means which the case required, but to no purpose; the unfortunate young man lingered about twelve hours, when death put a period to his sufferings.

On the same day,

> a young man, known amongst his companions by the name of Clockline, received a severe blow on the side of this face, which fractured his jaw, and exposed it in a dreadful manner. He was endeavouring to stop an empty wagon which was coming down the inclined plane on the ballast heap at Thingley, by sprigging or throwing a piece of wood into the wheel, but not doing it very skillfully the stick was carried round, and struck him in the face with desperate force. He was attended immediately after the accident by Mr Little, surgeon to the works, and he is now fast recovering.

On 16 August, the *Bath Chronicle* reported two accidents at Thingley, midway between Corsham and Chippenham, both caused by the inappropriate use of gunpowder. The first was to a boy called Isaac Horne,

> who was amusing himself by blowing in imitation of the process used by the men employed on the railway, when the powder exploded, burning his face very severely, the small stones cutting into the flesh to a considerable depth; he is, however, doing well. Another awkward accident happened to a man called Sailor Jack who had just prepared a shot for firing, and imprudently used powder instead of touch paper to start it. The explosion took place before he had time to leave the spot, and he was hoisted about 15 feet into the air, and, strange to say, was comparatively unhurt, only bruising his ankle in the fall. Every person who witnessed his ascent expected to see him fall dead, or nearly so, but the spectators were agreeably surprised to see him start on his legs and run away from so dangerous a neighbourhood.

On 22 September,

> a fatal accident occurred to a boy named Daniel Thomas, who unfortunately fell into the shaft no 6 of the Box Tunnel, a depth of upward of 100 feet. He was immediately removed from his perilous situation, and as he had fallen into a considerable quantity of water, it was hoped that his life might be saved; but the injuries he received were of so serious a nature that he expired on Sunday afternoon.

The winter of 1838-39 brought problems similar of those of the previous year. On 27 December, the *Bath Chronicle* reported that

> the excavations of the Box Tunnel has almost ceased in some parts. In the shafts nos 6, 7 and 8 there are but few men enabled to work, the shafts contain such a quantity of water. The contractors are, however, erecting at no 7 an additional steam engine of 50 horse power, whose work will be entirely to pump the water from that shaft. We hear that at no 6 also a steam engine will be immediately erected for the same purpose. A powerful locomotive engine is daily

> running in the open cutting from Thingley ... to Patterdown, drawing a long train of tram wagons after it; this has caused the work to proceed with much greater rapidity.

Despite efforts to overcome these problems, the Great Western directors grew increasingly concerned about the delay, and on 5 January 1839 served a notice on George Burge instructing him to "proceed more expeditiously." Two weeks later, Brunel contacted them with the news that work on the tunnel had been partially resumed.

February 1839 saw two more fatalities added to the tally. On 21 February, Charles Higgins was killed during blasting operations. Five days later, Charles Griffin, a miner at no 5 shaft, was passing under scaffolding erected for the bricklayers when it fell and killed him.

On 1 March, the directors were informed that 531 yards of the tunnel had been excavated, against the 1,071 yards required by the contracts. At the eastern end, Lewis and Brewer were 230 yards behind schedule; George Burge was 310 yards in arrears.

In early April,

> a number of men were at work in shaft no 5 and, in the operation of blasting some rock, the explosion loosened the scaffolding, which had been erected for the use of the bricklayers, which caused a large portion to fall, and with it a quantity of stone and rubbish by which one man was killed on the spot, two had their legs broken (both of which are since dead), two others had a leg broken, and a sixth had his shoulder dreadfully crushed.

With the coming of spring, the stoppages of the winter were forgotten, as the contractors worked flat out to make up for lost time. On 23 May, the *Bath Chronicle* announced that

> about half of the great tunnel at Box is now completed, and not the slightest difficulty exists in keeping the works clear of water. Where the excavation is carried through the oolite or freestone, the work proceeds with a rapidity greater than that required by the contract.

On 25 May, £2,000 was advanced to George Burge "in consideration of measures for expediting the work (now 298 yards in arrears on his contract)."

There was no let up in the casualty rate, however. On 11 July, the *Chronicle* reported that

> a poor fellow employed on the works of the Great Western Railway at Box was brought to the United Hospital in this city on Friday afternoon, with both his thighs broken.
>
> On Saturday last, a shocking accident happened at the shaft no 4, Box Tunnel, to a man named Falkin, who was blasting the rock. It appears that the poor fellow, not being aware that the match was lighted, advanced too near, when suddenly the mine exploded, and the stone cut his head dreadfully. He is now lying in a shocking state, and little or no hope is entertained of him.

On 17 October two more accidents were reported to the east of the tunnel:

> A serious accident occurred on the line of the Great Western Railway near Chippenham on Tuesday morning week. A boy named William Olive (son of a labourer at Lacock) was thrown down in front of the tram waggon, and his foot severed at the instep. He was almost immediately removed to the Chippenham workhouse, where amputation was resorted to. He is, we hear, doing well.
>
> Another fatal accident occurred at Pound Pill, on the previous Friday. The high road under which the railway is in course of excavation is unprotected on either side, where the depth is at least 20 feet, and in parts even more. At present it is covered with water, and, to some depth, with a mass of mud. The keeper of a beerhouse had, it seems, on the evening alluded to, turned out a workman somewhat in liquor, who going towards Corsham fell over the side of the road into the excavation; he is supposed to have laid groaning and nearly suffocated for at least an hour, when his moans attracted the attention of a passer-by, who sought assistance and rescued him. He was found greatly bruised, and from lying in the water much chilled; and although removed to a public house in Corsham, where his case received every possible attention, he expired the next evening.

On 17 November, a workman wheeling a barrow over a shaft missed his footing and fell to his death. On 22 November, a subcontractor called David Lee descended a shaft to inspect some work and was killed by falling timbers.

On 17 December, despite efforts to catch up, it was reported that excavation of the tunnel was 573 yards in arrears. The *Bath Chronicle* of 9 January 1840 was more sanguine:

> Considerably more than half of the excavation of this stupendous work has been executed, and as new shafts have been sunk by the contractor to regain the arrears at certain points, no doubt is entertained that the tunnel may be completed within the present year.

Despite the *Chronicle's* confidence, the workings had once again flooded, and by early March, the tunnel was 639 yards in arrears, with a total of 1,910 yards having been excavated. Powerful steam engines were once again brought in to pump out the workings, with mixed results. On 2 April, Brunel wrote to Burge:

> *Sir,*
> *While you are wasting so much valuable time at Shaft no 6 in a bungling attempt to make the present machinery do that for which it is totally unfit, you are neglecting to drive the heading between Shafts 5 and 6 which would have shown some intention of providing against similar difficulties next winter. While such a lack of management continues I shall not recommend to the directors any further payment.*

By 19 April, however, the *Chronicle* could report that

> the contractors of the shafts Nos 5, 6 and 7 of the Box Tunnel, have at length succeeded, by means of powerful engines, in getting the vast body of water out of the above shafts; and the workmen will now proceed with the excavation with great rapidity.

On 20 February, there was another fatal accident at shaft no 5, when Robert Price, a workman from Bradford on Avon, "was following his occupation when he unfortunately advanced too near the mouth of the pit, and fell a depth of 296 feet, and was literally smashed to pieces." On 14 May, the *Chronicle* reported

> a shocking accident to a boy on the works of the Great Western Railway near Wootton Bassett on Wednesday week. He was employed at the wagons to run at the tip, and unfortunately missing his footing he fell, the wagon, which was laden, passing over him and nearly severing his thigh from the body. The poor boy had the prompt and skilful attendance of Mr George Hooper; but this gentleman gives no hope of his recovery. We understand that the unfortunate sufferer is an orphan who made his escape from Banbury Workhouse a short time since with another boy, and obtained employment on the railway, by which we fear there is too much reason to suppose he has lost his life.

In early June, there was another serious accident east of Corsham:

> A man named William Gough, in attempting to stop a tram wagon, fell across the rails, when it passed over his foot, dreadfully crushing it. He was removed to the Chippenham workhouse, where amputation was found to be necessary.

It was at Box, though, that the worst accidents continued to occur. On 22 July,

> a fatal accident took place … at no 5 shaft, Box Tunnel. As seven men were at work sinking the shaft, the sides of the pit fell in, killing one man on the spot; another in the course of the day; two more are not expected to recover; and the other three are very much injured.

Just over a month later, on 27 August, a labourer died when he was buried by falling earth at Middle Hill. On 5 November, the *Chronicle* reported that, "within the last fortnight three men have lost their lives at the works of the Box Tunnel, and two others have had their limbs dreadfully mangled." Some accidents, however, were the result not of dangerous working practices but of over-indulgence. On 23 July, for instance,

> a dreadful accident occurred at the engine house of the shaft no 7, of the Box Tunnel, to a young man named Sheppard, a native of Atworth. The deceased (who, it is feared, was in a state of intoxication) had gone into the engine house to lie down. There he fell asleep; and during his slumbers he rolled himself under the sway beam, which, in its action, came down violently on his head, and crushed it to pieces.

In early 1841, Brunel persuaded Burge to go for broke to get the tunnel finished. "The last six months before the tunnel was opened," Thomas Gale later recalled,

> there could not be less than 4,000 men working to hurry on the completion so as to get it finished by opening day. Now the question might be asked, where did those men live and sleep? In the neighbouring villages of Box and Corsham, and being on day or night duty, as soon as one lot turned out another lot turned in, so that their beds were never empty.

In February 1841, Brunel wrote to the directors:

> *The small tunnel in Middle Hill and the adjoining cuttings are nearly finished.*
> *The works between Chippenham and the Box Tunnel, which have generally been considered as likely to be the latest, are now in such a state that by proper exertion, their completion within the time required may be ensured; this exertion shall not be wanting on my part.*
> *The Box Tunnel itself will be completed and open throughout from the western face to the Shaft no 8, which has always been considered as the eastern extremity, during the next month; and if the whole tunnel cannot then be said to be finished, it is only because the eastern end, which is entirely in rock and belonging more properly to the contract last referred to, has been extended a few yards in order to diminish the quantity of excavation required in the open cutting. The permanent way in the tunnel will shortly be commenced.*

On 25 February, the *Railway Magazine*, which had been so hostile to the ideas of tunnels five years earlier, declared that

> this stupendous work, by far the greatest of its kind in this or any other country, is fast approaching completion – less than 50 yards in length now remaining to be excavated, and there is every probability that the entire work will be finished within a month or six weeks. The length of the tunnel is 3,128 yards, or 48 yards more than one and three-quarter miles. The width is 30 feet and the height from the line of rails to the crown of the arch, according to the nature of the ground excavated, from 25 to nearly 40 feet. The total amount excavated cannot be less than 450,000 cubic yards. The work being unavoidable in this locality, we cordially congratulate the company on its successful progress and near approach to completion.

On 10 April, a labourer called Stafford, "of steady and industrious habits," was at work in the cutting to the east of Box tunnel when a stone dislodged by blasting struck him on the head and killed him. Four days later, it was announced that George Burge had nearly completed the western end of the tunnel, with only 16 yards of brickwork left to finish. Four days later, the directors were informed that the excavation of the tunnel was complete. On 2 June, they were informed that the masonry was complete, and the permanent way – except for a 380-yard stretch between shafts 6 and 7 – could be laid. Thomas Gale takes up the story:

> The work now being finished, the opening day was the last day of June 1841; the engine ran through from London to Bristol. The advent was celebrated by a day's rejoicing in Box, and upwards of a hundred flags decorated the tunnel mouth, banks and bridge. Close by was a band of music playing, and three hogsheads of beer were given away by me on behalf of the contractors. On the same day several thousands of people came from all parts to witness the scene. In the evening we had an entertainment at the Queen's Head for the principal men of the tunnel.

The portal of the tunnel, with daylight visible at the far end.

At first there was only one line through Box Tunnel, and Daniel Gooch, the Great Western's locomotive superintendent, was instructed to be on hand to act as pilotman, travelling with every train through the tunnel. Unfortunately, this seemingly foolproof system was the victim of human error, as he later recalled:

> At about eleven o'clock on the second night we had a very narrow escape from a fearful accident. I was going up the tunnel with the last up train when I fancied I saw some green lights in front.* A second's reflection convinced me it was the Mail coming down. I lost no time in reversing the engine I was on and running back to Box station with my train as quickly as I could, when the Mail came down behind me. The policeman at the top of the tunnel had made some blunder and sent the Mail on when it arrived there. Had the tunnel not been pretty clear of steam, we must have met in full career and the smash would have been fearful, cutting short my career also.

* *Engines carried green headlights at this time.*

Inside the tunnel, with a signalman giving the all clear.

But, as though mishaps never come alone, when I was taking my train up again, from some cause or other the engine got off the rails in the tunnel, and I was detained there all night before I got straight again. I need not say I was not sorry to get home and to bed at Paddington, after two days and nights pretty hard work ... Box

> Tunnel had a very pretty effect for the couple of days it was worked as a single line, from the number of candles used by the men working on the unfinished line. It was a perfect illumination extending through the whole tunnel nearly two miles long.

Gooch also recalled that Brunel, who was staying in Bath, sent him "plenty of good food, etc., to keep my steam up."

Derailments in the tunnel seem to have been a common occurrence in the early days. On the evening of 8 July, just over a week after the line opened,

> two of the evening down trains on the Great Western Railway were detained several hours in the deep cutting near the east entrance to the Box Tunnel ... in consequence of an engine of one of the up trains getting off the rails in the tunnel. This unfortunate affair is said to have happened through the carelessness of the workmen, who had taken up the rails during the interval of the passing up [sic] of the trains, to raise them where they were a little sunk, and they were not screwed down again in proper time. The passengers who were in the train which was detained in the tunnel were "boxed up" in the carriage during the whole of the time, to their very great annoyance and terror. Various reports about "lives lost" were circulated in our city, but fright was the most serious consequence of the occurrence ... From the fact of there being only one line of rails through the tunnel some little delay takes place in the passage of trains and great caution is used by the engine drivers in this part. The second line will be completed in a few days, and all causes of delay removed.

It is hardly surprising that an enterprising coach proprietor saw the tunnel's safety record as a business opportunity. "Persons fearful of Box Tunnel," ran a series of advertisements in local papers, "may go to Chippenham by coach and proceed on the line of railway by the eleven o'clock train." One of the problems was lack of illumination. A correspondent in the *Railway Magazine* suggested that the tunnel should be lit by gas, and this was considered for a time, only to be rejected on grounds of expense. There were also ingenious proposals to use reflectors to beam daylight down the ventilation shafts. Apparently an attempt was made to light at least part of the tunnel by reflector lamps, but this proved unsuccessful, as Brunel had predicted it would. "I am afraid," he declared, "there are no means of remedying the evil of darkness in tunnels (the extent of evil, however, is this, that the tunnel is during 24 hours as dark as the rest of the line frequently is during the night, but is otherwise exposed to fewer casualties), unless by a general and brilliant illumination, which would, of course, be very costly."

The evil was eventually removed by the introduction of oil, and later gas, lights in carriages. This took many years to become universal, however. As late as 1870, when Rev Francis Kilvert travelled through Box Tunnel, passengers were still being plunged into darkness:

> Wednesday 18 May 1870
> Went down to the Bath Flower Show in Sydney College Gardens. Found the first train going down was an excursion train and took a ticket for it. The carriage was nearly full. In the Box Tunnel as there was no lamp, the people began to strike foul brimstone matches and hand them to each other all down the carriage. All the time we were in the tunnel these lighted matches were travelling from hand to hand in the darkness. Each match lasted the length of the carriage and the red ember was thrown out of the opposite window, by which time another lighted match was seen travelling down the carriage. The carriage was chock full of brimstone fumes, the windows both nearly shut, and by the time we got out of the tunnel I was nearly suffocated. Then a gentleman tore a lady's pocket handkerchief in two, seized one fragment, blew his nose with it, and put the rag in his pocket. She then seized his hat from his head, while another lady said that the dogs of Wootton Bassett were much more sociable than the people.

On 17 September 1841, after a couple of narrow escapes, the tunnel claimed its first victim since the opening of the line:

> A gang of men been employed during the whole of the last week in removing the ballast from the transoms and supplying its place with faggots, etc. Being thus employed (to the number of between 30 and 40 men) on Friday morning, an up and a down train met in the

> tunnel, and came upon them so suddenly that two out of the number, being unable to get out of the way in time, were knocked down by the trains. One of them, John Burns, received such severe injuries that he died in an hour afterwards, and the other had his feet and hands dreadfully lacerated.

One of the men who gave evidence at the inquest was Eli Sainsbury, a labourer who had been working on Box Tunnel for about eighteen months. "On Friday morning, about half past eleven o'clock," he began, "I was, together with the deceased, John Burns, and several other men, at work in the tunnel. We were employed in picking out the ballast from the transoms. The deceased was about eleven or twelve feet from me. There were four men working near him, but only two saw the occurrence. The accident was caused by two trains, one up and the other down, meeting in the tunnel. One was going up and the other going down. We were much alarmed, and did not know what to do to get out of the way. None of us heard any whistle given by the coming down train, and did not know that it was coming till we heard the watchman near us give the signal, by saying 'Clear the road.' On hearing him say this we were looking out to see which way we could move with safety. We were all afraid of being killed, and did not know what to do. We heard the signal given by the watchman, 'Clear the road,' but we did not know at first that there were two trains coming. We tried to get out of the way as best we could. When the signal was given we were upon the south road. I got out of the way, and so did the man who was with me. I got between the roads, and saw the deceased get near the wall on the south side. The two trains did not pass me exactly at the same moment; they were about eleven or twelve feet apart. The up train passed me first, and then I jumped on the north road, and the down train passed me immediately. The deceased was standing by the south wall, and by the light from the fire of the engine I saw him fall as soon as the down carriages reached him. I don't know the distance there is between the rail and the wall of the tunnel. On my going to work in the tunnel I received directions that when we heard the watchman we were to take care of ourselves and get out of the way as soon as possible. In some places I don't think there is sufficient room for a man to stand between the train and the wall."

"Then," a juror asked, "if a man were to stand between the train and the wall in some parts of the tunnel he must be killed?"

"Yes," replied Sainsbury, "I believe that he must. Our instructions were that in getting out of the way we were not to be down under the trains. We have been told that when we heard the signal we were to clear one line, but not two. When a train is coming the watchman generally cries clear the North or South road, according to which road the train is on. When they cry out, 'Clear North road,' we generally get on the South road. We were never told that we ought not to get on either road. I have known before that two trains have been in the tunnel at the one time, but never to meet close opposite each other where the men are working. There are niches in the wall for the watchmen to get into, but none where we were working. After the trains were gone we called for a light, and having placed the deceased on a shutter carried him to the Bath Hospital. We were sober."

Mr Napp, the solicitor representing the Great Western Railway, told the court that there was another man present who could explain the accident more clearly. John Wilkins was then called to give evidence.

"I am a miner," he said. "I also keep the Box Tunnel Inn, a beerhouse. I was standing in the tunnel at the time of the accident, about eleven feet from the deceased. At about half past eleven o'clock I heard the up train coming, and a signal given by the watchman, 'Clear the North Road.' We then got off the North road, and almost immediately heard an alarm given, 'Clear the South road.' We hardly knew what to do, for we thought both trains would meet, but after a moment's consideration, I got against the south wall. The deceased Burns and the other man were also standing against the south wall. I do not know how he was knocked down for after the train passed we were left in complete darkness. There was plenty of room for the train to pass me, and also where the deceased stood. I should think three feet six inches from the rail to the wall. I cannot say how much from the steps of the carriages to the wall. I do not know any part of the tunnel where there is not room. I heard the up-train whistle, but not that of the down train. There was a great deal of confusion, and we were calling out to each other. The engines do not generally whistle after entering the tunnel."

James Sherriff was also called to give evidence. "I am an assistant engineer under Mr Brunel," he told the court. "I live at Box and am well acquainted with the road under the Box Tunnel. There is quite sufficient room for a person to stand out of the way all through the tunnel. There are 18 inches between the steps of the carriages and the wall, and six feet between the two lines, leaving two feet between the steps in the centre. In several parts the distance from the steps of the carriages to the wall is two or three inches more; and I am certain it is not more than two or three inches less in any part. I should not like myself to try the experiment of standing in the centre between two passing trains. I never knew any man to do so. There has not been any order given by us for the men not to lie down, and many do lie down. Indeed, it is the way I direct the men employed by the Company; but the deceased and these men were employed by the contractor."

When the coroner asked if the jury required any further evidence, one of them stood up to criticise the lack of safety procedures on the railway: "I cannot help thinking," he said, "that there is great negligence shown by the company on many parts of the line between Bath and Bristol. I have myself seen at Twerton, men, women and children standing on the line and a train only 50 or 60 yards from them, without any person troubling themselves to warn them or order them off. I feel satisfied that unless something is done we shall have very many such accidents as the present one."

"These remarks," the coroner pointed out, "do not apply to the present accident, which is the only one we can interfere with."

"But I must say," the juror continued, "the Company ought to adopt some means of preventing accidents."

"The Company have no fewer than 30 constables between Bath and Bristol," said Mr Napp, rising to the Great Western's defence. "They do all they can to prevent accidents, and if they could be satisfied that they ought to increase even this number, they would readily do so. There are twelve watchmen in the tunnel alone, and one would think that such a number was certainly sufficient."

The Coroner then summed up the evidence. He did not see that there was any blame attributable to the Company; but that the death was an accidental one arising from the confusion of the men, in consequence of the two trains meeting.

An express for Bath is given the all clear by the signalman at the mouth of the tunnel.

The jury returned a verdict of accidental death, with a deodand of one shilling on the engine.

On Saturday 26 March 1842, another inquest was held, in the Bear Inn at Box, on the body of Henry Couzens, aged 25, a watchman on the Great Western Railway. From the evidence of Jacob Marchant, the landlord of a beerhouse near shaft no 7, it appeared the deceased had spent Friday evening on his premises, and left about ten o'clock, "without the least appearance of intoxication." This statement was confirmed by James Wooten, who parted with Couzens near the east entrance to Box Tunnel.

John Heppell, driver of the banking engine, *Ariel*, deposed that, about a quarter past eleven o'clock on the same night, he assisted with his bank engine the up luggage train through Box Tunnel, when, on returning on the down line, he saw a man lying across the up line. He got down and found him dead, being nearly severed in two. There was congealed blood on his forehead and on the ground, and his clothes were soiled with dirt. The head of the deceased was on the middle of the north rail, and his legs towards the bank.

James Sherriff, the assistant engineer, stated that, at about one o'clock on Friday afternoon, he had examined the rock at the entrance to the tunnel, a few yards from where the deceased was found, which was upward of thirty feet high, when he discovered footmarks, as if someone had fallen over the rock; and there were also marks in three different places on the side of the rock, which seemed to have been rubbed by something falling over. There was a rope suspended close to the spot to assist the men in getting up and down, from which he inferred the deceased had fallen whilst endeavouring to descend into the open cutting of the line.

The deceased was buried at Box, the funeral being attended by the resident sub-engineers and officers of the company, along with "many other persons." A great number of members of the Lodge of Oddfellows also attended the funeral, to testify their respect for the deceased.

Eighteen months later, one of the banking engine's drivers found himself in the dock, along with his fireman, on a charge of being asleep on duty. Incredibly, this was not while they were awaiting a turn of duty, but while the engine was running down the incline so fast that it smashed into the goods train in front of it and damaged several trucks. Both men were dismissed.

In March 1845, the banking engine was returning down the incline when there was a heavy rock fall just in front of it, derailing both engine and tender. It was later discovered that a large block of stone, weighing almost a ton, had missed the locomotive by only a few feet. During clearance and stabilisation work, which took over six

Smoke lingers around the portal of Box Tunnel, with evidence of recent internal maintenance work lying around on the right.

hours, there were two more roof falls. The year after the tunnel opened, Brunel had responded to fears that the roof of the unlined section of the tunnel was liable to falls by stating his conviction that there was no possibility of this happening. Despite this, Major General Pasley, the Inspector General of Railways, decided to inspect the tunnel. He too found no evidence to suggest that roof falls were likely. Unfortunately, they continued to recur at intervals over the ensuing years, and parts of the eastern section of the tunnel were eventually lined. In 1909, serious structural faults were found throughout the tunnel, and it was closed for an extended period to allow repairs to be carried out. Trains were diverted via Bradford on Avon and Melksham, adding around ten minutes to the journey.

When it was built, Box Tunnel was the longest in the world by far. Since then, it has slipped to 13th place in this country alone – 14th if the Channel Tunnel is included. But in terms of the myths it has generated, no other tunnel comes close. Even better, the two most abiding myths are rooted in fact.

The first myth is the improbable-sounding claim that the sun shines through the tunnel on 9 April, Brunel's birthday. The first reference to this phenomenon, according to Muriel Searle, appeared in a "now unidentifiable local journal" in 1842:

> On Saturday, the Box Tunnel presented a most splendid though singular appearance, caused by the shining of the sun straight through it, and giving the walls a brilliancy, to use the expression of an eye witness, "as though the whole tunnel had been made gilt."

Thomas Gale, who worked on the tunnel, also claimed that "two days in the year the sun could be seen shining through the tunnel, providing it was clear from smoke." Neither of these early observers made any connection with Brunel's birthday. It was not until 12 April 1859 that the *Daily Telegraph* informed its readers that

> it is a remarkable fact that annually on the morning of 9 April the sun's rays penetrate through the great Box Tunnel of the Great Western Railway, and on no other day of the year.

Since when the legend has taken on a life of its own, generating almost as much astronomical speculation as Stonehenge or Avebury. The general consensus these days is that the sun does indeed shine though the tunnel on one or two days a year, but not on Brunel's birthday. It misses this auspicious anniversary by only a few days, however, appearing either on 6 or 7 April. It is one theory, however, that devotees of astronomical arcana are recommended not to put to the test.

The sunrise myth pales in insignificance beside the cluster of myths that can be loosely grouped together under the heading "unexplained goings on." Wiltshire has more than its fair share of mysterious sites – Cley Hill, Stonehenge, Silbury Hill, Avebury – but none is more mysterious, according to some, than JSU Corsham (formerly RAF Rudloe Manor) on Box Hill. This, they allege, is home to the UK's UFO Monitoring Centre, and – the more knowledgeable will inform you, with a conspiratorial lowering of the voice – much, much more. The sunrise theory cannot be put to the test because it involves standing in the middle of a high-speed railway line; the UFO theory cannot be put to the test because it would involve penetrating a high-security military base.

Many more myths and legends surround the tunnel. One of the most persistent is that, midway through, a siding branches off the main line, leading to … what? A secret military bunker, a centre for research into the paranormal – there are as many theories as there are conspiracists capable of putting a website together. Box being Box, there is also a rail buff's version of the Holy Grail, known as the Strategic Reserve. This concerns a motley collection of steam locomotives, withdrawn in the 1960s when steam power was being phased out, which – allegedly – disappeared under mysterious circumstances. It soon became "common knowledge" among those "in the know," that these engines were destined not for the scrap heap, but to form the basis of a strategic reserve. The theory was that, if supplies of oil were cut off, the engines in the strategic reserve would be fired up to take over from the grounded diesels. The location of this strategic reserve was a closely-guarded secret, except, of course, among the people who believed this story. They always knew precisely where it was – although few could agree on the location. One site that came up more often than most, however, was Box Tunnel, where the siding midway through the tunnel led into a vast underground Valhalla of steam.

Such ideas can be dangerous. In 2004, three teenagers set off in search for the secret military bunker they believed to be in Box Tunnel. Eventually, a train driver spotted one of them cowering in a niche and raised the alarm. Train services were suspended for six hours, with widespread disruption to the network.

So much for the myths. The truth, as it happens, is more remarkable still. The excavation of the eastern end of Box Tunnel revealed hitherto unrealised deposits of high quality Bath Stone. Much of the stone quarried during the building of the tunnel was used by the Great Western Railway for railway buildings elsewhere on the network – at Chippenham and Swindon for example. In September 1844, a narrow tunnel was built next to the eastern portal of Box Tunnel to give access to these deposits. This was served by a mineral line leading to Corsham station. Later, the tunnel was enlarged so that standard-gauge wagons could use the tunnel, and stone could be loaded straight onto them at an underground loading bay. Over the next few years, vast caverns, linked by a network of tunnels, honeycombed the hillside, as stone from the quarries was shipped to the farthest corners of the empire.

By the 1930s, most of the quarries had been worked out or abandoned. Come the Second World War, the quarries were ideal not

The eastern portal of the tunnel, with the entrance to the stone quarries locked and shuttered.

only for storing priceless works of art from London's galleries and museums, safe from Hitler's bombs, but as secure ammunition stores and factories. At Ashley, west of Box Tunnel, rows of sidings, once linked to Monkton Farleigh quarries by a tramway, were extended, and a new tunnel, over a mile long, took ammunition to and from a vast ammunition dump on a conveyor belt. The tunnel next to Box's eastern portal was enlarged and a vast underground station built inside the complex, to handle not stone but bombs and shells.

With victory over Germany came the Cold War, and, very soon, the threat of nuclear annihilation. It was decided to use one of the quarries deep under Box Hill, codenamed Burlington, and used as an aircraft factory in the Second World War, as the seat of government in the event of nuclear war. It was all, needless to say, top secret. Built in 1961, the 35-acre radiation-proof site was a replica of Whitehall, with a "main road" running through it. If the ultimatums had finally run out and the final countdown begun, the royal family, the Prime Minister, the cabinet, top civil servants and military commanders, would have scuttled into tunnels under Box Hill "to act as the ultimate source of authority during the period of survival and reconstruction after nuclear war." As well as government offices and military command centres, there was a medical centre, a dentist's, a bakery, a laundry and a pub – the Rose & Crown. An underground lake and treatment plant would provide drinking water, while the Prime Minister would address the nation – or what was left of it – from a specially-equipped BBC studio. The bulk of the network's broadcasts would have consisted of pre-recorded public information films, kept in the studio and regularly updated until the mid-1980s.

As the threat of nuclear war receded, it was eventually decommissioned, although the government refused to acknowledge its existence until 2004, when top secret documents were released. It is not surprising that the secrecy surrounding the site should have generated so much speculation. As to what Brunel would have made of it all, who can say? That Box should still, 165 years after it opened, be one of the most celebrated, not to say notorious, tunnels in the country, would no doubt, however, be a source of great satisfaction to him.

A Brunel Trail From Keynsham To Box

This trail should, of course, start where the Great Western did, in Bristol, under the hammerbeam roof of Brunel's original train shed at Temple Meads. But the line out of Bristol has been so overlaid by later accretions, and is so difficult of access, that Keynsham has to be our starting point. Keynsham station also has the advantage of a regular train service from Bath and Bristol.

Box, where the trail ends, is no longer served by train, but it does have a half-hourly bus service to and from Bath. The distance by rail from Keynsham to Box is 13 miles. The distance via the trail is 21 miles. It could be done in a day, but it has been devised not as a challenge, but as a way of looking at the rural and urban landscapes of Bath, North East Somerset and West Wiltshire in a different way, and of gaining a deeper appreciation of Brunel's achievement. It has therefore been divided into a series of manageable sections, ranging from 1. 5 to 4 miles. Although the sections are, by definition, linear, most can be adapted to form circular walks; alternative routes back to the starting points have been suggested wherever possible.

Another option is for two or more sections to be combined, with a return to the starting point by public transport. There are regular trains between Keynsham, Oldfield Park and Bath, and regular buses between Bath, Bathford and Box.

The walks were devised in the winter of 2005-2006 and all rights of way were open and unobstructed at this time. All (except for a minor rerouting in Section One) correspond to the footpaths shown on the latest editions of Ordnance Survey Explorer Maps 155 (covering Keynsham to Bathford) and 156 (covering Box). Use of these maps is strongly recommended, as is the use of walking boots, except on the sections through Bath, which should be mud-free. Every effort has been made to check directions, but no responsibility can be taken for errors, still less for any future changes or footpath diversions. All distances are approximate.

Feedback on the walks or suggestions for future amendments are welcome:

email: *info@akemanpress.com*

or write to: Akeman Press, 58 Minster Way, Bath BA2 6RL.

The line between Bristol and Box is, due to its familiarity and the speed with which trains travel along it, one of the most underrated scenic rail routes in the country. This is largely due to Brunel's success in building a high-speed route through difficult terrain. There are none of the sharp curves or steep inclines that generally characterise scenic rail routes. Today's inter-city trains swoop down the Avon valley and up the valley of the By Brook so smoothly and so fast, that it is easy to overlook the landscapes rocketing past outside the window.

It is a pity that we cannot return, if only briefly, to the days when passengers were exposed not only to wind and steam, but also to Brunel's awe-inspiring tunnels, bridges and viaducts. Today's passengers, walled in behind toughened glass, have to concentrate in order to appreciate the journey. One trip is not enough; it is a journey that has to be taken again and again, each time spotting some new feature, another part of the jigsaw falling into place. And there is no better way of deepening our understanding and appreciation of the line than by following it, as closely as we can, on foot, and seeing it, like Brunel did, as part of the landscape.

Except for the first two miles out of Bristol, Brunel would have no difficulty recognising the line today. The first tunnel out of Temple Meads, whose Norman portico formed the frontispiece to Bourne's engravings of the Great Western, disappeared when the line was widened in the 1880s and a deep cutting took its place. Once the train plunges into the 154-yard tunnel at St Anne's, however, Brunel would be on familiar territory. A brief glimpse of the river at Conham, followed by the 1017-yard tunnel under Broomhill, and the run alongside the river opposite Hanham, makes this one of the most dramatic sections of the line. It is, however, virtually impossible to get close to the line here, although the Avon Walkway, on the other side of the river does give us an opportunity to appreciate Brunel's achievement, albeit at a distance. It is at Keynsham, however, that we can first get close to the line, and it is at Keynsham that the trail starts.

SECTION 1:

Keynsham Station To Saltford Brass Mills:

4 miles (7. 5 miles as a circular walk)

Although much of what we will see on this walk was either built by Brunel or was there when he built the line, it starts somewhat inauspiciously. Keynsham station dates from the opening of the line from Bath to Bristol on 31 August 1840, but the Tudor-style buildings designed by Brunel were demolished in 1970. However, the station is still open, and provides an ideal way of getting to the starting point.

Arriving at Keynsham from Bristol, turn right out of the station; arriving at Keynsham from Bath, cross the line and turn right.

Cross the road and walk down the hill. The gateway on your left, guarded by a massive pair of pillars, dates from the 1920s, when a siding was built to serve Fry's Chocolate Factory, which had relocated from Broadmead in Bristol to Somerdale after the First World War. The siding branched off the main line east of Keynsham station, crossed the road and continued through the gate. Beyond were over two and half miles of track serving the factory. The siding survived until 1980.

At the bottom of the hill, turn right into Avon Mill Road. Passing the old brass mills, with their black bricks manufactured from brass slag, turn right and go under the railway. This is Mortimer's Bridge, built of local stone, with a Tudor-style arch characteristic of most of the bridges on the line between Bristol and Bath, and echoing the design of the hammer-beam roof in the original Temple Meads station. It is a style rarely seen on railways elsewhere, probably because pointed arches are weaker than rounded ones. It is likely that Brunel chose it for this section of the line in homage to the rich late medieval and Tudor architectural of Bristol, which is also characterised by flattened arches.

The River Chew bridge at Keynsham.

Once through the bridge, turn right into the park and walk down to the footbridge. High up above you is another bridge – with one of the few rounded arches between Bristol and Bath – carrying the railway across the River Chew. Cross the river, turn left, go under the dual carriageway, and, just past the water wheel and fish pass, cross back over the river.

Bridge west of Saltford.

Go through the gate, cross the road, and turn right. At the main road, turn left and carry straight on up Bath Hill. At the roundabout at the top of the hill, turn left along Bath Road.

After a quarter of a mile, turn left down Unity Road, go through the subway, and, just before the railway bridge, turn right. At the end of the road, turn left under the railway and then right. This, it has to be said, is one of the least inspiring parts of the walk, with disused sidings on the right, and scrubby fields and abandoned orchards on the left. To add to its unique charm, there's even an abandoned caravan.

After half a mile of this, the road swings to the right, but you carry on down the track leading to Avon Valley Country Park. Continue on (ignoring the left turning into the country park) until you reach a cluster of buildings with dire warnings of what will happen if you go any further. The footpath has recently been diverted, so you need to cross the stile in the hedgerow on the right, carry straight on down the field for 100 yards, turn left through a gap in the hedge and head for the far hedgerow. When you reach it, turn right and head for the corner of the field. Turn right again and follow the hedgerow out of

The Railroad Arms at Saltford.

the field. (If this all sounds complicated, it might help to remember that all you actually want to do is get from one side of the field to the other).

You've now rejoined the railway, beside one of the most attractive bridges on this section of the trail. You don't want to cross it, however, but turn left and walk alongside the railway to Saltford. As you approach the village, look out for the 176-yard tunnel, with Tunnel House sitting on top of it.

Saltford station.

When you reach the road, turn left to take a closer look at Tunnel House. In December 1838, while building the tunnel, navvies cut through a spring supplying much of Saltford with water. The company was given 21 days to put the matter right, but this proved easier said than done, and water carts had to be used to supply houses in the village for several years.

Carry on past Saltford House down the High Street. No 18, on the right, was, for a brief period, the Railroad Arms Beerhouse. Its attic was converted to a dormitory for 20 navvies. Take the alley (or drungway) to the right of the old beerhouse to rejoin the railway line.

After 300 yards you reach a bridge, which gives a good view back to the tunnel entrance. Notice the measures that have been taken to prevent the sides of the cutting slipping. The lias here is notoriously unstable, and several trains have been derailed by landslips over the years. Below you in the other direction is the site of the old station, closed in 1970, and now a maintenance yard. The original wooden station, opened in December 1840, burnt down in 1872, when a burning piece of coal from a passing engine landed on it. It was rebuilt, but closed less than a century later, on 5 January 1970, a victim of the anti-rail policies then current.

Towpath bridge with the railway embankment in the background.

Our route takes us, not across the bridge, but down the footpath to the left of the line. A little way along, steps lead down to the road. Here are more brass mills; inside – not unfortunately open to the public – one of the stones bears the legend "Begun Digging the Rail Road June 11 1836."

To return to Keynsham station, turn left and follow the road along to the Bird in Hand pub. The pub car park has access to the Bristol & Bath Railway Path. This follows the railway line built by the Midland Railway in the 1860s, when navvies once more descended on Saltford. It closed in the 1960s. Turn left along the path, and half a mile further on, after crossing the river, drop down to the river bank on your left and take a leisurely stroll back to Keynsham. Upon reaching the main road, a left turn will take you back to the station.

SECTION 2:

Saltford Brass Mills To Oldfield Park Station

(4 miles; 3. 5 miles as a circular walk)
To get to the starting point by road – as you approach Saltford from Bath, take the first turning on the right, signposted The Shallows. If coming from Bristol, the turning to The Shallows is on the left just before leaving Saltford. Go under the railway bridge, and the Brass Mills are 200 yards ahead on the right.

A few yards east of the Brass Mills, take the footpath leading along the river bank. The riverside footpath, which is very easy to follow, runs alongside the railway embankment for much of the way to Newbridge. Apart from some splendid scenery, and the trains rushing past on the embankment, look out for some attractive Tudor-arched bridges under the line. The footpath was once a towpath, built when the river was canalised in the 1720s. Barges were usually towed by teams of men rather than horses. About a mile and a half along the towpath, there is a bridge over a small brook. Nearby, some early graffiti, added only a few months after the railway opened, can be found carved under one of the bridges.

Shortly after this, the river, and the towpath, curve away from the Great Western line to go under the Bristol & Bath Railway Path.

If you are returning to Saltford, climb up to the railway path and turn left. After a mile and a half (just after crossing the river for the second time), turn off the railway path into the car park of the Bird in Hand pub. Go to the front of the pub, turn left and walk along the road to the Brass Mills.

To carry on, turn right along the railway path. After half a mile, you go under a bridge. Walk up the wooden steps on the left, turn left at the top and walk along a very narrow pavement as far as the traffic lights.

Early graffiti.

For those of an adventurous disposition, there is a short diversion here, which involves negotiating a busy road. Cross the road at the lights – with extreme care – and walk up the lane opposite. The overbridge 200 yards up the lane gives an excellent view of the castellated portal to Twerton Long Tunnel. Looking back towards Bristol, the road bridge across the line marks the approximate site of the Roman Villa discovered – and largely destroyed – when the line was built. This area was once the heart of the Twerton coalfield. There was a mine at the bottom of the lane you have just walked up, and another on the far side of the dual carriageway. Owned by Charles Wilkins, they were still operating when the railway opened, but closed shortly afterwards.

Retrace your steps down the lane, cross the road and turn right and head along the Lower Bristol Road towards Bath.

For those wishing to forego the diversion, turn left along the Lower Bristol Road towards Bath. The Great Western line is on the right, obscured by trees, although you should catch glimpses of Twerton's two castellated tunnels – Long Tunnel (264 yards) and

The west portal of Twerton Long Tunnel.

Short Tunnel (45 yards), referred to by Brunel in an early sketch, as Wilkins' Covered Way. The design of these tunnels, which can also be seen at Fox's Wood near Bristol, echoes the castellated style used at the entrance to Temple Meads and in the Claverton Street viaduct in Bath. It was adopted by other tunnel builders – George Stephenson at Grosmont (1836) on the Whitby & Pickering Railway, Thomas Grainger at Bramhope (1845-49) on the Leeds & Thirsk Railway, and Robert Stephenson at Shugborough (1847) on the Trent Valley Railway – but nowhere to better effect than between Bristol and Bath.

After three-quarters of mile, the 638-yard viaduct carrying the line through Twerton comes into view. The numbered doorways in the viaduct now lead into industrial units; originally they led into a row of two-roomed houses, replacing those pulled down to build the railway. The houses were fitted with fireplaces; their flues ran at ceiling height to the back of the viaduct, where the chimneys were disguised as buttresses. The only light came from small windows fronting the road. There were no windows – or doors – in the back

The bridge over Twerton High Street.

rooms of the houses. Even by nineteenth-century standards, they must have been pretty grim.

This section of the Lower Bristol Road was built by Brunel when the railway cut off access to the old turnpike road through Twerton. A hundred yards beyond the old houses, cross the road, turn right under the second road bridge, and walk up Mill Lane to Twerton High Street, the old turnpike road.

Turn left, cross the road, continue along the High Street and go under an impressive skew bridge. The buildings of Twerton station, in the Jacobethan style, are on your left. Before the line opened, Twerton was also known as Twiverton. The opening of Twerton station seems to have fixed the spelling for good. However, the renaming of the station as Twerton on Avon in 1899 did not catch on in the same way. The station closed in 1917 as a temporary wartime economy measure. Passenger numbers had been so badly hit by the introduction of electric trams between Twerton and Bath, however, that it was not considered worth reopening after the war.

Turn right and walk along the Lower Bristol Road. As you pass the bottom of Jew's Lane, notice the low bridge on the right.

Take the next right up Burnham Road and turn left into Inverness Road. At the top of the road, cross the Linear Park (built on the trackbed of the Somerset & Dorset Railway) and turn right, crossing the bridge over the Great Western. The disused bridge on the right carried the Somerset & Dorset uphill on a gradient of 1 in 50.

To the left there is a view of the Great Western line, with yet another Tudor-style bridge. Just beyond it is Oldfield Park station, opened in 1929. Carry on and turn left down Lyndhurst Road. Follow the road as it swings round to the left. Another left turn will bring you to Oldfield Park station.

SECTION 3:

Oldfield Park To Bath Station

(1. 5 miles)

Starting at the bridge spanning the tracks at the west end of Oldfield Park station, take the footpath alongside the platform on the left. At the end of the footpath, cross the road and look over the bridge parapet. This bridge originally had a Tudor arch, but it was rebuilt when an extra line was added. Looking towards Bath, the sidings on the right, which originally served a stone yard, are now used to ship out Bath's sole remaining railborne cargo – rubbish. Fifty thousand tonnes of the stuff leaves here every year, bound for a landfill site at Calvert in Buckinghamshire.

Walk down the hill to the bottom of Brougham Hayes, and turn right along the Lower Bristol Road. Take the second right up Westmoreland Street and go through the foot tunnel under the railway. As you leave the tunnel, turn left. At the end of the road, turn left again and go under the bridge. At the bottom of the road, turn right at the Green Park Tavern and walk along the Lower Bristol Road.

Just before Pickford's depot, the old stone-built railway goods shed – now home to the Cramer Technology Centre – can be seen up by the line. The building on the other side of the Lower Bristol Road is the old Stothert & Pitt factory, dating from 1857.

Take the next right up Oak Street to see how the railway sliced through this part of Bath. Just before the bridge, turn left into Wood Street. Here you can see how, when the line was widened, different material was used to extend the arches.

Follow the road as it curves back to the Lower Bristol Road and turn right. Just past the sole surviving building on Angel Place, cross the road at the pelican crossing and carry on towards Churchill Road Bridge. Cross Churchill Bridge and then cross the road at the zebra crossings. From here there is a good view of Skew Bridge and the

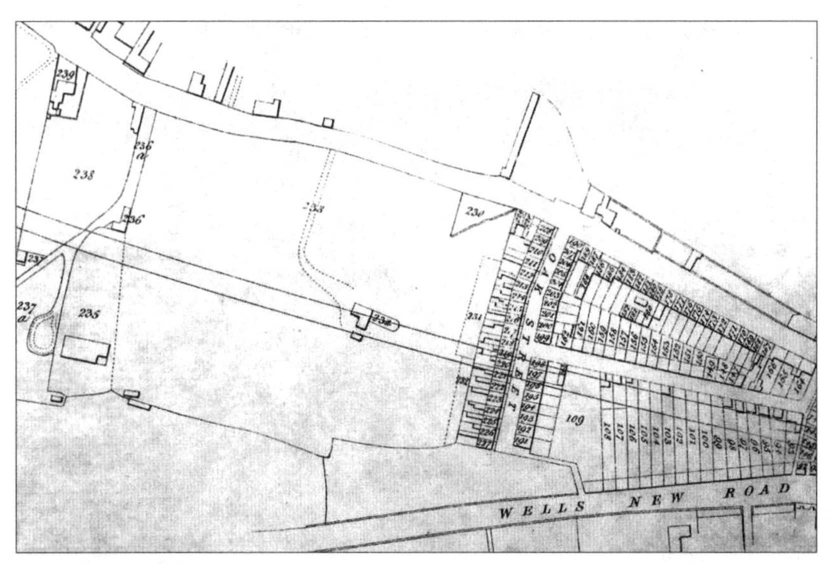

Brunel's plan for Oak Street.

castellated viaduct. The two road bridges (one now disused) originally had Tudor-style arches. These disappeared in 1911 when they were rebuilt to carry heavier locomotives. The smaller arches have seen a variety of uses – a police station, a greengrocer's, even a mortuary for bodies dragged from the river.

It is not known why Brunel chose such an elaborate design for this section of the viaduct. True, it could be seen from Southgate Street, and would have appeared, standing as it did on the far side of the Old Bridge, like a medieval city gate. Even so, it seems an extravagant gesture. Possibly, it was intended to mollify the inhabitants of Widcombe, who had risen en masse to object to the proposed tunnelisation of Claverton Street (not to mention the nasty things he said about them at the parliamentary enquiry). Although the planned demolition of buildings went ahead, Brunel had to abandon the tunnel scheme, and rerouted Claverton Street through the viaduct in an inverted S shape. Although the castellated viaduct he subsequently built provided a grand entrance to the street, however, its south face was far less imposing, even before the inferior Bath stone he used for it was replaced by brick.

The Skew Bridge on the left, originally built of wood, crosses the river at such an oblique angle that, although the river is only 80 feet wide, the bridge is 164 feet long. Not everyone was in favour of the

An early photograph of Bath Station from the west, with the goods shed on the left.

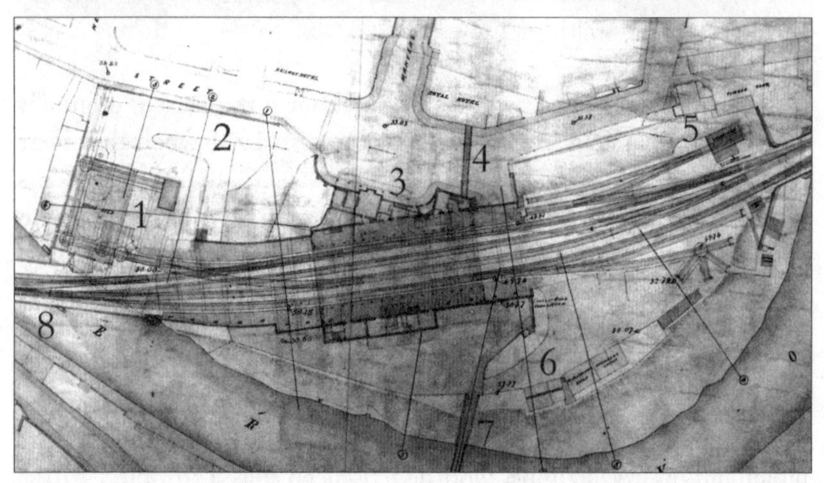

Bath station in 1867. 1 The goods shed (removed c 1891); 2 The ramp to the goods shed; 3 The station frontage, at an angle of about 25 degrees to the line; 4 The footbridge to the Royal Hotel (removed 1936); 5 The engine shed (closed 1880); 6 Engineer's Office; 7 Halfpenny Bridge; 8 Skew Bridge.

bridges Brunel built at Bath. In a Guide to Bath published in 1864, Rev GN Wright declared that "the railway bridges at Bath display great but unnecessary ingenuity, and show how a simple and inexpensive object has been effected by means both complicated and costly."

A 200-yard walk along Dorchester Street brings you to Bath station.

SECTION 3a:

Bath Station

Bath station deserves a section to itself, but two things need to be borne in mind. First, it is scheduled for redevelopment as part of the scheme for the new Southgate, so any observations are likely to be overtaken by events. Second, although there is public access to most of the station, it is Network Rail property and, apart from the route under the station and across the Halfpenny Bridge, there are no automatic rights of way. Access to the platforms is also ticket controlled.

Bath station's most significant drawback – the lack of scope for expansion – has also contributed to its survival. Space restrictions have hampered its development, ensuring that it has changed far less than most major early Victorian stations. However, although redevelopment proposals will preserve the integrity of the main structure, other features dating from the opening of the line are earmarked for removal.

From the outside, the station looks much as it did when Brunel designed it. Inside, however, the wooden roof which covered the tracks and platforms disappeared as long ago as 1897. Another feature which has disappeared is a footbridge which crossed from the station to the Royal Hotel. One unusual feature of the station is that, although the viaduct carrying the lines runs obliquely across the bottom of Manvers Street, the station is at right angles to it. The station frontage is thus at an angle of about 25 degrees to the viaduct.

The platforms were originally much shorter than they are today. At the east end of the station there was an engine shed and sidings to the north of the line; south of the line were more sidings, with a wagon turntable, and small buildings housing engineer's offices and a blacksmith's shop. This cared for horses shunting wagons in the yard as well as those delivering goods in the city. The last shunting horse at Bath station retired in 1959. The engine shed has long gone, as

A railmotor in the down platform at Bath in the early twentieth century. Two long-gone features are the signalbox rising above the canopy and the dip in the nearside platform.

have the sidings, but an engineer's office has survived at the right-hand side of the ramp leading up from Halfpenny Bridge. It is understood that this may be demolished as part of the redevelopment of the area.

The large level area at the west end of the station, on the north side, was originally occupied by a goods shed. Because of space limitations, this was at right angles to the running lines. Wagons were shunted into the southern end of the shed, where turntables gave access to loading bays. No trace remains of the goods shed, which was superseded by a new shed at Westmoreland Road in 1877 and demolished around 1891. The sidings survived and, when the electricity works opened next door in 1895, chutes were installed so that coal could be delivered directly. The sidings were removed in 1960 when the platforms were extended. Now all that remains as a reminder of the original goods yard are the masonry walls which once supported it. A recent structural engineering survey of the site concluded that there had been "virtually no disturbance of the retaining walls or of the viaduct arches," making them "of considerable interest, dating as they do from the original construction. " It is understood that, as part of the Southgate Redevelopment, the ramp leading to the goods yard, which dates from the early days of the railway in Bath, and was probably designed by Brunel, will be demolished. The fate of the goods yard is unclear.

SECTION 4:

Bath Station To The Old Folly

(2 miles; circular walk 3. 5 miles)

Starting outside the main entrance to the station, go through the tunnel on the east side and cross the footbridge over the river. In 1842 a wooden toll bridge was built here, which cost a halfpenny to cross. In 1877, when the Bath & West Show was held on Beechen Cliff, hundreds of people swarmed off an excursion train and onto the bridge, which collapsed beneath their weight, with the loss of ten lives. It was later rebuilt in metal. The accident also provoked demands for the Skew Bridge to be rebuilt on the grounds that wooden bridges were unsafe.

Turn left at the end of the bridge, take the first left and cross the canal. The site of a wharf built by Ralph Allen in the 1720s as the terminus of a tramway carrying stone from Combe Down – Bath's first railway – is about 50 yards along the river bank. Prior Park Road now follows the course of the tramway.

The railway east of Bath did not open for almost a year after the arrival of the first train from Bristol. St James's Bridge, which lies ahead, was one of the last works on the line to be completed. In January 1841, when work was well advanced, a flood swept the structure away, and it had to be started again. Originally in stone, it has been extensively patched with brick, but is still a magnificent structure. The consoles supporting the parapet are particularly fine. As you pass underneath, it can be clearly seen how this bridge, as well as that at the other side of the station, was built on the skew.

Go under the bridge, turn right and walk alongside Dolemeads viaduct. Take the second right under the viaduct along Broadway. Immediately after walking under the viaduct, look to your left. The building marks on the second arch are those of a school, built under the viaduct by HE Goodridge in 1856.

The school built by HE Goodridge against the viaduct at Dolemeads.

In October 1882, the railway viaduct provided an even more vital service to the residents of Dolemeads. Another major flood had forced occupants of nearby houses to move to the upper floors. As the waters continued to rise, rescuers scrambled down long ladders from the parapet of the viaduct onto the roofs of the houses. By removing the tiles and breaking through the ceilings they managed to rescue about 50 imprisoned families.

Carry on to the end of the road, turn left and cross Pulteney Road at the lights. The railway bridge here was once a structure to rival St James's Bridge. It was replaced by the present structure in 1975. Tom Hartigan, one of the men who erected the new bridge, sealed a bottle of Guinness in one of the abutments, together with a note: "When this bottle is found, I'll be long gone. Whoever finds it, say a prayer and have a drink for me."

Go through the gap in the bridge abutment, follow the footpath up to the canal and turn left along the towpath. If you look carefully to your left, you will see the entrance to Bathwick Hill Tunnel through the trees.

The top house of Raby Place, on the right, was pulled down and rebuilt by Brunel when he drove a tunnel underneath it.

The bridge across the canal a little further on is typical of the elegant Bath-stone structures which reach their climax in the great aqueduct at Dundas. It is a style echoed by Brunel's railway bridges east of Bath. Gone are pointed arches of the Bristol-Bath section, gone too the ubiquitous pennant stone. The viaduct west of Bath station, where pointed arches are rendered in Bath stone, marks the transition between the two styles. From St James's Bridge east, there are a succession of classically-proportioned bridges – like those on the Kennet & Avon Canal.

Walk up the steps at the side of the bridge, cross over, walk down the hill and turn right into Raby Place. The railway goes under the house at the top – no 18 – which was pulled down and rebuilt by Brunel. The line can be seen, between two tunnels, over the wall at the back of no 18.

When the diarist, Francis Kilvert, visited his mother at No 13 Raby Place in 1872, she was looking after a sick relative whom, he recorded, "had a bad night, disturbed continually by the passing of the trains under that row of houses."

The building ahead of you, on the corner of Raby Mews, was a pub called the Cleveland Arms, which also sits on top of the railway. It closed as long ago as 1932 but its name can still be seen on the back wall.

The cutting west of Sydney Gardens.

At the white gate beyond the pub, turn left and walk onto the railway bridge. On your left, the line can be seen running through two short tunnels; on your right it runs through a cutting towards Sydney Road Bridge. This stretch of line is reminiscent of the North Midland Railway cutting through Belper in Derbyshire, built by George Stephenson at almost exactly the same time, and now a Grade II listed structure.

At the end of the railway bridge, turn right. Cross over at the end of the road, walk down the hill and go through the gateway into Sydney Gardens. Turn right and head towards the railway. Most other railway engineers would have hidden the railway in a cutting at this point. Not Brunel. He wanted people to see his trains, and Sydney Gardens was the ideal place to show them off to their best advantage. A plaque in memory of him can be seen on the bridge abutment to the right.

Walk under the bridge on your left, carry on under the next bridge and walk up the steps just beyond it. Cross the bridge, walk up the hill, and, just before the bridge over the canal, go through the small gate on the right, and turn left along the towpath. Note the iron

Sydney Gardens: a grandstand for Brunel's trains.

bridges (which probably gave Brunel the idea for the iron bridge over the railway below) and the carving of Father Thames over the tunnel mouth. Just past the tunnel, you come to the section of canal diverted by Brunel to build the railway.

Just before the canal resumes its original course, some steps lead down to a footbridge. So many navvies worked on the line here that four out of the 14 houses in Hampton Row, on the other side of the line, were converted to beerhouses.

Later, there was a station here – Hampton Row Halt. It closed in 1917, and no photographs of it are known to exist.

Instead of crossing the footbridge, take the path to the right. After 200 yards, you will see a stream trickling down the hillside. This was the boundary of the Folly Pleasure Gardens, owned by the Great Western Railway. A brick wall and a flight of steps mark the site of the Folly Public House, hit by a stray bomb in 1942.

There is a choice of two routes back to Bath from here. You could turn left under the railway bridge, cross Grosvenor Footbridge, and head into town along London Road. A more scenic alternative, however, is to turn right, walk up to the canal, and walk back along the towpath to the starting point.

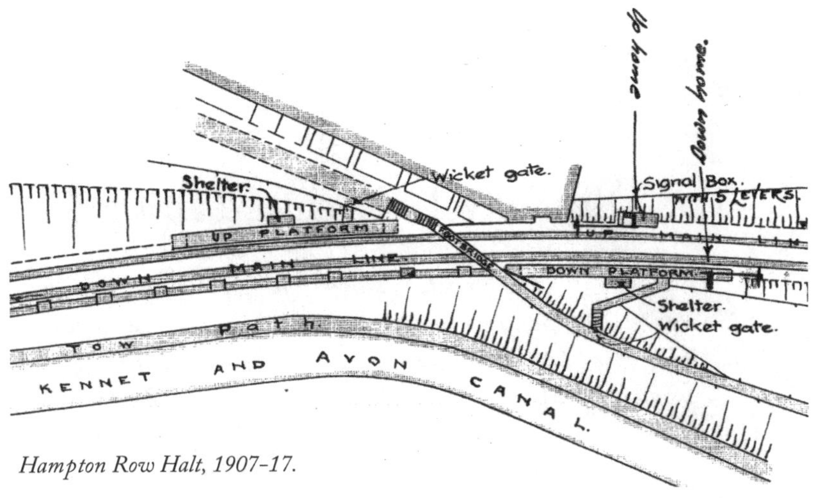

Hampton Row Halt, 1907-17.

A down goods train approaching Hampton Row in the early twentieth century.

SECTION 5:

The Old Folly To Bathford Bridge

(2 miles; circular walk 4. 5 miles)
The starting point of this walk can be reached from the London Road. Coming from Bath, turn right down Grosvenor Bridge Road, three quarters of a mile past Cleveland Bridge.
Coming from the east along the A4, Grosvenor Bridge Road is the first turning left after the A4/A46 roundabout.
Cross the Grosvenor Footbridge, and the starting point is just beyond the railway bridge.

Take the path heading east alongside the railway for half a mile, until you come to a minor road. (The bridge over the railway to your left is worth a quick detour as it gives a good view of the line.) Join the canal towpath on the other side of the road and continue eastward for half a mile to the George Inn at Bathampton. Walk down the steps to the road and continue on, with the church on your right, to the railway bridge. To the right of the bridge was Bathampton station, opened in 1857 and closed in 1966 (this is a busy narrow road, so care is needed when looking over the bridge parapet).

If Brunel had stuck to his original plan, the line would have taken a different route at this point, wedging the George Inn between the railway and the canal and cutting across what is now the southern extension to the graveyard.

Retrace your steps, cut through the churchyard, and, at the crossroads below the canal bridge, turn left along Tyning Road, passing the school. Note, as you do so, the sturdy iron gates at the entrance to Station Road. The station house, halfway down this road, is all that is left of the old station.

At the end of Tyning Road, cross the railway line (with extreme care). On the other side of the line, go down the steps to the right of the gate, and head across the field towards the electricity pylon. Go

The Glory of the Great Western: an express passing Bathampton around 1905.

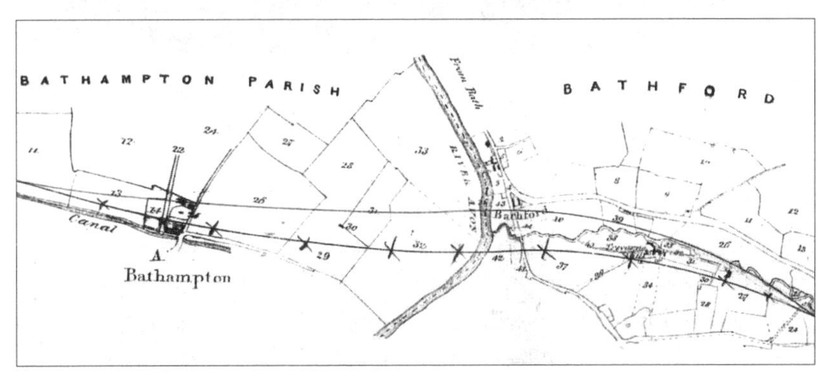

The revised course of the line through Bathampton and Bathford. The original course is marked with crosses.

through the metal kissing gate in the fence just past the pylon and follow the path up towards the railway line. Cross the bridge and walk down towards the road.

Bathford Bridge, which you have just crossed, was described by JC Bourne in 1845 as "one of the most beautiful structures on the line; it is a bridge of one arch, elliptic, of 54 feet span, and 27 feet rise; the arch is flanked by two projecting piers, and meets the embankment with low walls; above the whole is a plain entablature and parapet." To get a good view of Bathford Bridge, take the dead-end path leading off into the woods on the right before you reach the road.

Bathford Road bridge.

The bridge over the road on the left, reminiscent of a triumphal arch, is another architectural gem. The contractor's path leading up to the railway line on the other side of the road once led to Bathford Halt, opened in 1929 and closed in 1965. This is the point at which the railway leaves the valley of the Avon and heads up the valley of the By Brook.

To return to the Folly, turn left under the bridge, carry straight on over the roundabout, and walk through Batheaston (passing the old Poor House, once the navvies' Episcopal Chapel, on the right). After a mile, take the left turning down to the toll bridge. 400 yards beyond the bridge, a footpath on the right will take you back across the meadows to the starting point.

SECTION 6:

Bathford Bridge To Middle Hill

(Shorter version: 4 miles; longer version: 4. 5 miles)

This section of the walk does not have the option of a return to the starting point, save by retracing your steps. It does, however, come in two versions: the shorter version, although liable to be muddy, is relatively straightforward; the longer version, which gets closer to the railway and other interesting industrial features, is less easy to follow in parts and also includes a third of a mile on a narrow footpath alongside a busy road.

Although a pleasant country walk, this is the least satisfying section in terms of railway interest. The short version of the walk, in particular, only crosses the line at one point, and for much of the time is either high above it or on the opposite side of the valley. Unfortunately, the lack of suitable footpaths makes this unavoidable.

One option for anyone set on keeping as close to the line as possible would be to walk along the A4 from Bathford to Middle Hill. The road parallels the line for much of the way, and there is a pavement alongside it. However, the road is very busy and the pavement is narrow, with much overhanging vegetation. The longer version of the walk does follow the pavement for a short distance, but an extended walk along it is recommended only for the most intrepid.

Turn right at Bathford Bridge, and, taking advantage of the new wooden bridge across the By Brook, turn left at the Crown Inn and head up to Bathford village.

SHORTER VERSION

Walk up the hill through the village and take the third left along Ashley Road. The road soon turns to a muddy track which you follow for about a mile.

LONGER VERSION

Walk up the hill through the village and take the second left past Whitehaven (built by John Wood and originally known as Titan Barrow). After 50 yards go through a stile on the left and walk down through a kissing gate and across a field towards Bathford paper mill. Go through another gate, walk past the mill and through a tunnel under the railway. The impressive stonework at the entrance to the tunnel has been somewhat marred by repairs in brick. After leaving the tunnel, cross the main road with care and turn right. The combination of narrow pavement, overhanging branches and busy road mean that extreme care needs to be taken on this stretch. A third of a mile along the road, just past Box Road Gardens and opposite a sign (Farm Shop: 200 yards), another footpath leads down to the railway. Cross the road again and walk down the path, under the line, over the brook, and follow the bridleway straight up the hill. When you reach the fence, turn left, following the hedgerow. Cross a stile and carry on. Cross another stile and turn left, going round the edge of the field. Ignoring the footpath going up the railway embankment, carry on round the field, and, when your way is blocked by an embankment leading down into the field, turn right and carry straight on uphill until you reach a gate. Go through the gate and turn left.

From here, both walks follow the same route. Cross a narrow footbridge over a stream, and shortly afterwards, where the path swings to the right, go through a stile in the hedgerow on the left.

Here you will see a Second World War pillbox ahead of you. Down by the railway line are more abandoned buildings of Second World War vintage. This was the site of Farleigh Down sidings, built in 1882 to serve a stone quarry at Farleigh Down, to which it was linked by a tramway. When quarrying ceased around 1930, the sidings closed, only to be reopened in 1937, when the government took over the quarry as a vast underground arsenal. An underground conveyor belt was built to carry weapons between the sidings and the quarry. The sidings closed for the second and final time in 1950.

After crossing the stile, turn right and follow the hedgerow. When you come to a gateway, walk diagonally across the field, heading to the right of a large barn-like building. Go through into the next field and carry on along the edge of the field until you reach a stile.

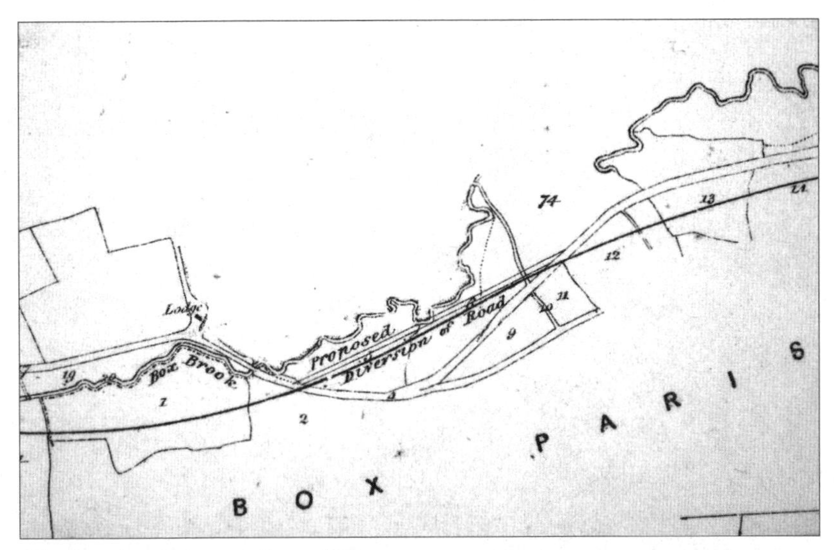

The diversion of the turnpike at Ashley.

Walk across the lane and go over another stile. Take the steps down to the lane and turn right. Go through the gate at the end of the lane and turn right along the road. This was once the turnpike road from Bath to London, which Brunel diverted when he built the railway.

Shortly after passing the entrance to Upper Sheylor's Farm on your right, a footpath on the left takes you down to the railway. The footbridge over the railway was built to replace a level crossing after a tragic accident in 1900. The wife of Lieutenant Colonel Arthur Coney of Sunnyside, Middle Hill, was on her way to see Major General Hunter at Ashley House. After waiting for an up goods train to pass, she stepped onto the crossing and was cut down by a Bristol-bound express. Her identity could only be established by the rings on one of her fingers.

On the far side of the line is the diverted turnpike road. The rerouting of the road was carried out by Hugh Hart, who was awarded the contract in 1839. Crossing it with care, take the lane opposite towards Shockerwick. Shockerwick House, which lies ahead, was built by John Palmer for Walter Wiltshire in the 1780s.

After crossing a bridge over the By Brook, turn right, go over a pair of stiles and follow the footpath through the field. Cross another

The footpath under the line near Middle Hill.

set of stiles and carry on, keeping to the left of a fenced-off pond. At the gate, carry straight on, taking the lower of the two marked footpaths, and aim for the gap in the far hedge. In the next field, head to the left of the small stone building, to come out at a crossroads.

At one time, a right turn here would have taken you up to Box station, which closed in 1965. Very little of it remains and, as the site is very definitely in private ownership, a visit will have to be foregone.

SECTION 7:

Middle Hill To Box

(3. 5 miles; circular walk 4. 5 miles)

This is the grand finale of the Brunel Trail; if you only have time to do one of the sections, this is the one to do. To get to the starting point by road, drive east along the A4 from Batheaston for two miles. Take the second left (signposted Middlehill, Ditteridge and Colerne). The starting point is the crossroads a couple of hundred yards down the lane.

If using public transport, the bus from Bath to Chippenham will set you down at the Northey Arms, just past the turning off the A4.

Starting at the crossroads, head east down the lane marked with a footpath sign, passing a short row of houses, and cross a stile. Head straight on to an archway under the railway. Once through the archway, which the footpath shares with a culverted stream, carry on across the field, noting above you to the left the western entrance to Middle Hill Tunnel. At only 198 yards long, it is less well known than Box, although its two portals are extremely attractive. Their monumental classicism is relieved by a deep bracketed cornice. The arch is divided into segments, with a scroll-pattern keystone. It is flanked by pilasters rising to the parapet, decorated with fasces – an architectural feature derived from the bundle of rods borne before a high-ranking Roman magistrate. If Brunel was aware of the derivation of the motif, he may have been indulging in a sophisticated architectural joke here, decorating the tunnel leading to the great Box Tunnel with the symbol of something carried before a dignitary. The tunnel was built by George Findlater of Brislington.

As the path curves round the hill, you will see, above you, the spoil heap on top of the tunnel, crowned with beech trees. Climb towards

Middle Hill Tunnel.

it, go through the gateway to the left, and, through a break in the fence on the right, you will see the top of the eastern portal of Middle Hill Tunnel.

The view from here, looking towards Box Tunnel, is one of the most splendid railway panoramas in the country, yet, because it is not near a road, it is almost unknown.

Retrace your steps down the hill, rejoin the path and head in the direction of Box Tunnel (ignoring the footpath heading towards the church). Go through a kissing gate and carry straight on. A small diversion to the right here, over a small wooden bridge, will give a good view of another culvert, once again displaying fine stonework, under the railway.

The path comes out in Box village, with a high-arched skew bridge to the left. On the far side of the road was Mill Lane Halt, opened in 1930 and closed in 1965. Turn right and walk up the road. When the pavement gives out, take the footpath to the right. At the main road, turn left and head towards the bridge over the railway line. The steam engine you pass on the right, incidentally, has nothing to do with the railway. Known as a Marshal Portable, it was used to power farm machinery.

One of the most splendid railway panoramas in the country: the view from Middle Hill.

Looking back down the line towards Middle Hill Tunnel from the railway bridge, the area now covered by storage tanks was once occupied by a siding where Bath stone was loaded onto railway

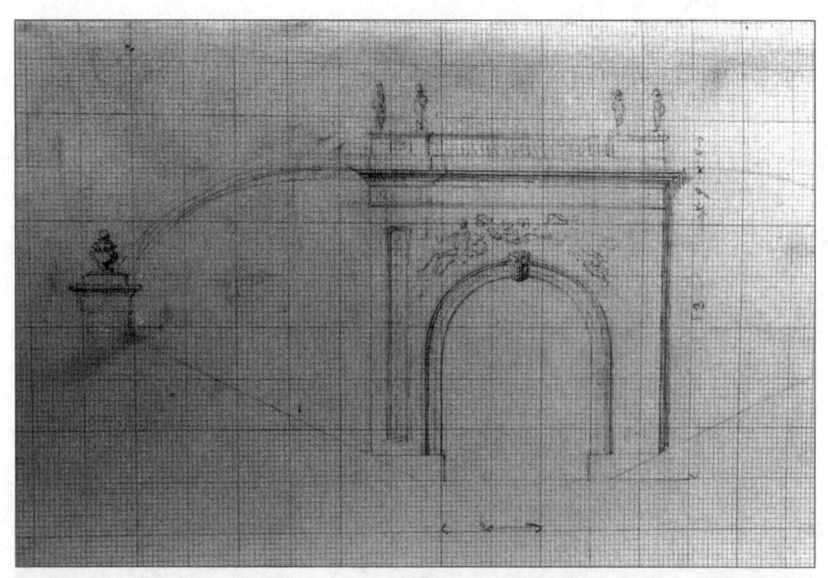

Brunel's original design for Box Tunnel: a sketch from March 1838

wagons. It is still known as the Wharf. The viewing platform looking towards Box Tunnel, on the other side of the road, was added in 1986 with a plaque recording the restoration of the tunnel portal. Unfortunately, vegetation has somewhat obscured the view since then. It is still a magnificent sight, though, like a triumphal arch dwarfing the trains scuttling in and out of it.

If Brunel had kept to his original design, it would have been even more monumental, flanked by urns, with classical figures in bas-relief above the arch, and statues atop the balustrade.

Fifty yards up the road on the right, go through a stile and walk up the field towards the beech-covered spoil heap. At the corner of the field, cross another stile. The next stile is just left of centre in the hedgerow at the top of the field. Once through it, turn left up the road.

At the next road junction, take the right-hand fork. If you look carefully, you will see, behind the houses on the right, a wall round one of the circular shafts up which spoil from the tunnel was hauled, and which were later used for ventilation. To build Box Tunnel, 247,000 tons of oolite and Fuller's earth was dug out by pick and gunpowder and hauled up shafts by horses walking round gins. The shafts and the

Box Tunnel Inn.

tunnel were frequently flooded, and over 100 men died in the course of construction. It took five years to build and when it opened in 1841 it was the longest railway tunnel in the world.

At the next crossroads is the old Box Tunnel Inn, one of many beerhouses opened to serve the navvies building the line. It is a quiet enough spot now, but at one time it was the hub of one of the nineteenth century's most ambitious engineering projects, with as many as 4,000 men working on it.

If the Cold War had spun out of control, and the bombs had fallen, this spot would have been quieter still. Deep below, in a warren of caverns and tunnels hacked out in the nineteenth century, however, 4,000 men and women (it is curious how the figure recurs), would have been going about their business, running what was left of the country.

With that thought in mind, retrace your steps down the road, but, instead of crossing the stile back into the field, carry on down Quarry Hill. Just after passing Barn Piece on your left, you will see an old factory. This is where a ton of candles a week were made for the men

A ton of candles a week came out of the factory at Box.

building the tunnel. Just past the factory, turn left into Townsend – the oldest part of Box – and take the alleyway to the left of Townsend House. At the bottom is the old Chequers, closed for several years, but with an embargo on conversion to housing.

Carry on past the old Box Brewery on the right and the old Steam Mill on the left. At the main road, cross over to the old Manor House and Barn. Turn left and walk up to the Queen's Head, where celebrations were held to mark the opening of the tunnel. There could be no more appropriate place to finish our Brunel Trail.

To get back to the cross roads at Middle Hill, carry on past the Queen's Head, and, just before the Bear Inn, turn right down Church Lane, passing Springfield House (the old Poor House) and the church. At the end of the lane follow the footpath down to the right. Cross the stream at the bottom, and you will see Middle Hill Tunnel ahead of you. All that remains is to retrace your steps across the field, under the railway and back to the crossroads.

BIBLIOGRAPHY

Keynsham and Saltford: Life and Work in Times Past, 1539-1945, Keynsham, 1990

Report on Newark Street Milk Factory, Bath Electricity Works, Stothert & Pitt Newark Street Works and the GWR Goods Yard and Shed of 1841, Structural Perspectives Industrial Archaeology, Halifax, n.d.

Awdry, Christopher, *Brunel's Broad Gauge Railway*, Yeovil, 1992

Balston, Thomas, *John Martin, 1789-1854: His Life and Works*, London, 1947

Barman, Christian, *Early British Railways*, Harmondsworth, 1950

Boumphrey, Geoffrey, *British Roads*, London, 1939

Bourne, JC, *The History and Description of the Great Western Railway*, London, 1846

Brunel, Isambard, *The Life of Isambard Kingdom Brunel, Civil Engineer*, London, 1870

Buchanan, R Angus, "Brunel in Bath," in *Bath History*, Volume X, Bath, 2005

Buchanan, RA & M Williams, *Brunel's Bristol*, Bristol, 1982

Burke, Thoams, *Travel in England*, London, 1942

Chapman, WG, *Track Topics*, London, 1935

Chesney, Kellow, *The Victorian Underworld*, London, 1970

Clinker, CR, *New Light on the Gauge Conversion*, Bristol, 1978

Cooke, RA, *Atlas of the Great Western Railway*, Didcot, 1988

Cooke, RA, *Track Layout Diagrams of the GWR and BR WR: Section 21, Bath and Westbury*, Harwell, 1988

Elliott, Kirsten & David Purchase, *Hidden Paths & Secret Gates: Six all-day Walks around Bath,* Bath 1996

Francis, John, *A History of the English Railway: Its Social Relations and Revelations, 1820-45*, London, 1851

Gale, Thomas, *A Brief Account of the Making and the Working of the Great Box Tunnel*, Bath, 1884

Gloug, John, *Mr Loudon's England*, Newcastle upon Tyne, 1970

Gren, André, *The Foundation of Brunel's Great Western Railway*, Kettering, 2003

Hay, Peter, *Brunel: His Achievements in the Transport Revolution*, London, 1973

Klingender, Francis, *Art and the Industrial Revolution*, London, 1968
Leitch, Russell, *The Railways of Keynsham*, Long Stratton, 1997
Loudon, JC, *Encyclopaedia of Cottage, Farm and Villa Architecture and Furniture*, London, 1833
MacDermot, ET & Rev CR Clinker, *History of the Great Western Railway*, Vol I, London, 1964
Maggs, Colin, *The GWR Bristol to Bath Line*, Stroud, 2001
Maggs, Colin, *The GWR Swindon to Bath Line*, Stroud, 2003
Measom, George, *The Official Illustrated Guide to the Great Western Railway*, London, 1852
Perkin, Harold, *The Age of the Railway*, Newton Abbot, 1971
Phillips, Daphne, *The Great Road to Bath*, Newbury, 1983
Rolt, LTC, *Isambard Kingdom Brunel*, London, 1957
Russell, Ron, *The Batheaston Excavators*, Batheaston, 2005
Searle, Muriel V, *Down the Line to Bristol*, London, 1986
Sims, Percy, *A History of Saltford Village*, Bath, 1976
Stone, SJ, *The Contribution of Brunel to Railway Architecture*, Unpublished Thesis in Bath Central Library, nd.
Swift, Andrew & Kirsten Elliott, *Awash With Ale: 2,000 Years Of Imbibing in Bath*, Bath, 2004
Swift, Andrew & Kirsten Elliott, *The Lost Pubs of Bath*, Bath, 2005
Torrens, Huigh, *The Evolution of a Family Firm: Stothert & Pitt of Bath*, Bath, 1978
Vaughan, Adrian, *Isambard Kingdom Brunel*, London, 1991
Vaughan, Adrian, *A Pictorial Record of Great Western Architecture*, Oxford, 1977

INDEX